D1206835

The Eastern Trail

NED
SMITH

The Eastern Trail

EDITED BY L. JAMES BASHLINE

Illustrated by Ned Smith

FRESHET PRESS

Rockville Centre, New York

Library of Congress catalog card number: 72-81481

Manufactured in the United States of America

Contents

PART III SMALL GAME HUNTING

PART IV FISHING

PART V CAMPING

Preface

Deciding who would write about what was the editor's chief problem when *The Eastern Trail* was first considered. We are fortunate in having in the ranks of the Pennsylvania Outdoor Writers Association, Inc., outdoorsmen who can write with authority about a dozen or more specialties. It would have been possible to play musical chairs with the subject material and the individual authors and still have realized a book of exceptional quality. I have hunted, fished, camped, hiked, and talked with all the contributors to this collection, and I have found that the total amount of outdoor know-how represented by the authors gathered here is more than impressive—it is astounding!

The Eastern Trail is difficult to categorize. It is a how-to volume; it is narrative; it is anecdotal; and, yes, it is even in a sense philosophical. Like some political speeches, it contains something for everyone. Although the material is eastern in flavor, much of the information herein applies across North America, and those readers who enjoy the outdoors will surely find it good reading no matter where the reading chair is parked.

Jim Bashline
The Iron Blue Dun
Bowmansdale, Pa.
July 4, 1971

INTRODUCTION:

The Voices in the Wilderness

WILL JOHNS

Like the prophets of old, today's outdoor writers are a strange breed—a motley group of characters whose message to humanity is often one of nonconformity.

The men and women who write, talk, photograph, or illustrate the news of the world outdoors cannot be stereotyped. More often than not, the outdoor writer will be the man down the street who works each day for a local business or industrial firm. Some are with government agencies, quite often in public-information positions, while others can be found in the high-pressure commercial world of the public relations and advertising agencies. Still others are housewives, retired persons, schoolteachers, shopkeepers, insurance salesmen. Few, and very few, are full-time employees of newspapers, radio or television stations, or book publishers.

In short, the outdoor writer today is more likely a normal wage earner and head of a household than a Thoreau, a John

Muir, or a Nessmuk; he is much more likely a man, or woman, leading a normal sophisticated life than a recluse wandering the lonely wildernesses. But after the office hours are over, the PTA and civic meetings attended, the lawns mowed, and the houses painted, they are different. For once the necessities of their vocations are overcome, these people turn to their compelling avocation of telling others about their first love—the fields and forests, the oceans and brooks, the mountains and lake shores, for it is the world of nature that gives real meaning to their lives and in which they find the true quality of their living.

Aldo Leopold once said, "There are some who can live without wild things, and some who cannot. Like winds and sunsets, wild things were taken for granted until progress began to do away with them. Now we face the question whether a still higher 'standard of living' is worth its cost in things natural, wild and free. For us of the minority, the opportunity to see geese is more important than television, and the chance to find a pasque-flower is a right as inalienable as free speech."

Outdoor writers, then, are among those who cannot live without things "wild and free." They differ, however, in the extent of their desire to share their convictions and enlist support for their concerns. Their one common characteristic is their drive to communicate in some manner—written word, public speech, skilful painting, dramatic photograph—with as many people as possible on this spaceship, earth. And unlike most other reporters, they participate in those things which they write about or depict.

There is no exact count of American outdoor writers; perhaps the best indicator of total numbers is the membership roster of the Outdoor Writer's Association of America, which currently numbers over 1800 active members. Others belong to such state or regional organizations as the Pennsylvania Outdoor Writer's Association, the Mason-Dixon Outdoor Writer's Association, and the Association of Great Lakes Outdoor Writers. Some, of course, belong to more than one such association.

There is no formal training course required before one

becomes an outdoor writer. Some are graduates of schools of journalism, but many do not hold a college degree of any sort. Almost without exception, outdoor writers have developed their skills through trial and error, through hard work and years of experience. In other words, there are no short cuts to becoming an outdoor writer; the best teachers are the rejection slips on the manuscripts that come back unsold from the editorial offices.

Not everyone can join this fraternity, of course. Somehow you make special efforts to acquire the basic skills—writing, public speaking, photography, art. Some tools of the trade are mandatory—a typewriter, a top-quality camera along with a wide range of accessories, especially a telephoto lens, perhaps a portable tape recorder, and certainly reams of paper, a good supply of film, and above all else, a determination to share your creative ability with the public. But far more than this is needed. In no other writing profession is personal knowledge and skill in subject matter more important. A science writer can compose a newspaper column, magazine article, or book without being a scientist; a sports reporter can describe an off-tackle play or a batting style even if he can't carry a football properly or swing a bat well enough to hit the broad side of a barn. But an outdoor writer must be comparatively expert in the skills of the sports about which he writes, and he must have a personal knowledge of the places where these pursuits take place—the fields, forests, mountains, lakes, rivers, and streams that are the settings for his plots and accounts.

This is not to say that every outdoor writer is a champion flycaster or holds a world's record in rifle marksmanship or trapshooting or skeet. Far from it! Very few, if any, outdoor writers have their names recorded in the trophy books or rosters of champions. Nevertheless, all those who are truly effective are experienced in the things they write about. They have personally been there, done those things, and done them well. For example, the men who have contributed to this book are all experts with long years of experience in the kinds of hunting and fishing about which they have written.

Most of all, however, the professional outdoor writer is

always part of that great cavalcade of citizens concerned with the conservation and wise use of the soils, waters, woods, and wildlife that form the basis of every outdoor story. They know far more than most that these natural resources are threatened as never before, that population growth and a technological culture have resulted in a seriously polluted environment. They realize that the hunting and fishing they have enjoyed, and through their writing have led others to enjoy, depend entirely on clean waters, pure air, rich soils, and abundant plantlife. And they have witnessed the slow but steady deterioration of these resources through man's ignorance, indifference, and greed.

And so they are compelled to speak or to write or to illustrate, not just for their own amusement or satisfaction, but more because they realize that the safety and sanity of all men are closely related to the outdoors. You don't often find juvenile delinquents in the ranks of kids on fishing trips; you don't, as a rule, find mentally disturbed adults among the millions of American sportsmen who annually escape the tension and confusion of their high-pressure world by returning to the peace, tranquillity, and beauty of the natural world.

Yes, outdoor writers may be a strange breed. Their stories, films, and speeches seldom become great literature or classics of the written or spoken word. But they lead the way to improved sportsmanship, to a better environment, and to a quality of life all too often missed by those who think success can only be measured in profits and possessions.

Outdoor writers are men and women who are doing their best to make the world a better place. Follow their example and advice, heed their warnings, and listen to their experiences, for their messages show the way to an infinitely better quality of life for all of us.

PART ONE
Big Game Hunting

Big-game hunting in the area covered by The Eastern Trail *means deer and bear. It is the kind of big-game hunting that involves smoky little cabins and a big pot of slumgullion stew that lasts all week. It is cold-weather hunting that tests the mettle of city and country hunter. This is also the type of hunting that sees a shirttail cut off when a case of buck fever causes a miss at a bounding whitetail.*

Al Shimmel and Bill Walsh know this kind of hunting and write about it with a light-hearted reverence that seems to take the reader by the hand and say, "Here it is." If you have a feeling for the chase and also believe, as many do, that the white-tailed deer is the grandest big-game animal in the United States, you'll like their chapters.

CHAPTER 1

White-tailed Deer and Black Bear

AL SHIMMEL

DEER! There's so much magic in the word that blasé indeed must be the one whose pulse does not respond to the thought of deer stealing like phantoms through the laurel thickets or the remembered picture of an antlered buck, his flag held high, clearing the windfall with a graceful bound.

The basic urge to hunt wells from the instincts of the past, when the successful chase was closely bound to the survival of the race. More recently, the pioneer, facing the stern realities of the wilderness, proved equal to the test and made the land his home. In defence of his meager crops, the sturdy woodsman not only became an expert shot but also, of necessity, taught his family the art of marksmanship. In response to the need for a more accurate weapon, the Lancaster rifle was perfected by the Pennsylvania German craftsmen. Buckskin and jerky were staples for home consumption. When hunting was good, the surplus was bartered for necessities that the wilderness did not provide. History fails to record how many volunteers in the War for Independence were sustained by the original "combat ration," parched corn and jerky.

An intellectual of urban background noted with amazement the mass exodus of the participants in the annual big-game hunt. He concluded that a large segment of our population was afflicted with an incurable mania. He puzzled inconclusively over what motives could force otherwise normal people to leave the comforts of suburbia to spend nights in drafty cabins and days wandering through unfamiliar forests, scaling treacherous mountains, risking pneumonia, and sitting in the cold for no greater reward than the chance shot at a deer. After much thought he dismissed the problem with a shrug. To the uninitiated, "hunting fever" is a mysterious affliction.

Those fortunate enough to live in or near deer country begin their "homework" almost as soon as the last hunter has left the woods. When the restlessness of winter becomes unbearable they visit their hunting grounds, check the condition and size of the herds, renew the salt licks, and on occasion (with permission) cut deformed or weed trees to bring browse within easier reach of the deer.

In spring, when fields begin to green before the woodlands feel the quickening touch, the deer come out in early morning or late afternoon to sample the new growth. At this season many families find recreation in cruising the secondary roads "to see the deer." The animals are making the transition between the dull, heavy coat of winter and the orange-brown of summer. Later they will acquire the sleek beauty so pleasing to the observer. If one looks closely, the buck can be distinguished from the smooth-headed doe. Erect hair, pushed aside from the budding antlers, give him a tousled, uncombed appearance.

All through the spring and summer the antlers continue to grow, and by the end of August they are fully developed. For the next few weeks the bucks are busy clearing the velvet from their weapons. Saplings and brush are used as a foil.

NED
SMITH

Branches are broken, bark is shredded, and the raw wood is exposed. "Buck rubs" is the hunter's term for these marks.

The exercise of brush fighting and rubbing is continued as a conditioning process for the rut. When they meet, the bucks spar playfully. As the season advances, the play becomes more and more vigorous until they are fighting to prove which is the fittest buck.

When undisturbed, deer seldom range beyond the area of a square mile. Inside this territory they are familiar with the trails, bedding grounds, food supplies, and hides. The hunter does not belong. Small wonder whitetails are so elusive.

Fall scouting should include hardwood ridges. Good crops of beech and acorn mast attract deer. White and scrub oak produce small, sweet acorns that are preferred as food, but when these are gone other species are not neglected. Often the snow around oaks will be marked where deer have searched for the hidden nuts.

In one of our autumn grouse hunts we found a small area where scrub oak had produced a heavy crop while the other oaks of the ridge had failed to crop because of a late frost. We killed two fine bucks within a half hour of each other on opening day by watching the trails that led into this area.

Deer are fond of mushrooms. One of the finest, the shaggy-mane (*Coprinus comatus*), grows among a scattering of beech trees on a certain hillside. They are prime during late September and early October. I must confess that deer harvest most of the crop. The thought occurs to me that perhaps next season I might use a broadhead and collect a venison steak to go with these mushrooms.

Old orchards and wild crabapple thickets are choice feeding grounds for deer. An archer of my acquaintance scores regularly from a tree stand that overlooks a wild-crab thicket. I dressed out a buck last season that had breakfasted on the hard, green fruit. The nearest source of supply was over a mile from the spot where he was killed.

To my knowledge I have yet to meet a hunter who carried a soil-testing kit as part of his hunting equipment. Should you meet such a one, don't be too quick to mark him as a candidate for the laughing academy. Remember that studies have proved that the heaviest animals and the best trophy antlers are found where the mineral content and soil fertility are in proper balance.

Farm deer are special. Many a rural dweller who watched with envy as his neighbor prepared for a trip to the mountains has gone out during the open season and found a trophy buck eating windfalls in the orchard or hiding in that little patch of brush between the back pasture and the creek. His neighbor, returning from the hunting camp with an animal smaller in both size and rack, pauses to ponder the difference.

Farm deer are adept skulkers. Although they have become accustomed to machinery and routine activities, they are clever at avoiding contact with humans. Often they hide in cover that seems inadequate for even small game. Brush rows, weed patches, and shrub-grown gullies are used for day beds and escape routes. At night they forage freely. With the gunfire that marks the opening of small-game season they become even more furtive or seem to vanish altogether.

One farm buck, well known because of a deformed antler, disappeared from his usual haunts during the open season. A quarter mile from the farm, a small brook flowed through a village. The stream was bordered by thick evergreens, rhododendron thickets, and alder tangles. It formed a long, narrow triangle entirely surrounded by residential streets. Not a spot within the area was more than two hundred yards from an occupied dwelling. In this tangle the buck and four does passed the season unobserved. When the danger was past they returned to their former haunts.

One of the finest racks I have ever observed was standing in a pasture field where beef cattle were fattened for market. It was night, and my light did not frighten him. His antlers spread at least a span beyond his shoulders, and the tines on his twelve-point rack were close to a foot in length. When open season came he left the farm for the rugged woodlands of the steep river slopes that border the farm. He was seen for several years in the area. His end is a mystery.

In deer-camp areas much of the sport is a co-operative effort. Each group has a leader, or leaders, who do the planning and suggest the rules. The comradeship of the deer camp cuts through social barriers with an equality that is truly democratic. For a time, each has laid aside his profession, trade, or pursuit to become another deer hunter.

Camps generally spend the first day of season "trail watching." Most of the better stands are well-known. To avoid favoritism, lots are drawn for assignments. Long before shooting time, flashlights wink as hunters hurry to be in position. Quiet settles, the light strengthens, tension builds, and even the veteran checks his watch repeatedly. Occasionally someone has a fast timepiece.

The magic moment arrives. The season is open! Deer are on the move. Bursts of rifle fire tell of bucks afoot. An hour passes and then another. The beginner grows impatient and is tempted to commit the tyro's cardinal sin, that of leaving his stand. *Don't do it.* Your friends know where you are. Should you leave, almost invariably a buck will come by. Patience, my friend . . . patience.

After the first day the camp generally practices a technique called driving. The crew is divided between watchers and drivers. The watchers are posted where they can command trails along which deer travel. The drivers form a line some distance from the watchers and at a signal move toward them. Sometimes the drivers are silent, but more often they shout, blow whistles, and make as much noise as possible. Those on the stands are instructed not to fire until the game has passed them. Likewise the drivers do not fire at game that breaks back through the line until it is beyond the line. This safety measure is rigidly adhered to by all members of the hunt. Deer become accustomed to the drive. Many stand or crouch in thickets or laurel patches while the drive passes them by. Others slant to the side and so avoid both watchers and drivers. A pair of the best riflemen are often placed to each side and some distance ahead of the drive. These flankers often cash in on animals that would otherwise escape. The truth of the matter is that deer refuse to be driven but are stirred up by the drive and move along escape routes of their own choosing. Another trick sometimes practiced by deer is to circle the drive then fall in behind and move back even while the drive is in progress. It pays to look behind on occasion.

The crew gathered about the fallen buck. It had streaked out of a twenty-acre tract of pulpwood cuttings, dodging the lead thrown in its direction before breaking down the point toward the watchers. Three shots echoed from the lower stand. Two hits in three shots is not a bad average for a veteran, but the girl who stood there, half laughing, half crying, was in her early teens. The buck was a wide spread—eleven points. The girl's father, the target of much good-natured banter, stood at her side. He had been one of the drivers who missed.

"Why don't you give her the rifle?"

"It would be a shame to ruin the tail of that new shirt!"

"How many times did you miss?"

The buck was heavy and fat, the rack was good. A fine pulpwood buck.

I stand near the Crooked Pine, listening and waiting. Before me is a rough triangle of dense laurel that follows the crest of the ridge. I look at the tracks again. It is easy to pick those made by the buck. He drags his toes while the does step daintily, leaving clear-cut prints.

Some three hundred yards ahead my son has a stand in the forks of an oak. He is just high enough to see over the tops of the laurel. We have played this game before. If I can panic the buck, he will leave by one of two trails, both visible from the oak. If I follow too slowly, the animal will skulk within the thicket without giving either of us a shot.

Now! I push ahead, moving as fast as the thicket will permit. I catch a glimpse of their flags as they jump. A split second only and they are gone. I keep moving, listening intently. Suddenly I hear the crash of the rifle. Silence. I move out to the stand. It is unoccupied. I whistle sharply and thrill to the answer.

"I got him!"

We perform the ancient ritual of the hunt. For a few minutes we stand silent, each busy with his own thoughts.

"A few years and Steve will be with us."

Our eyes meet. Steve is almost nine.

A few years? With a start I realize that this is my fiftieth year in the deer woods. A few years? It was only yesterday. . . . Deer hunting is like that!

The hunter tilted his hat to shade his face and squinted through slitted lids. He tugged the lacings of his buckskins until they lay open at the throat. He reached for the long-barreled rifle that lay beside him. The hammer clicked softly as he thumbed it smoothly to half cock. With thumb and forefinger he reset the cap, twisting it slightly to be sure it was firmly seated on the nipple. The hammer was carefully lowered to hold the cap in place. With an appreciative eye he examined the smooth maple stock and the decorative engravings that covered the lock. The rifle had cost rather more than he could afford, but he had no regrets.

It had taken nearly two weeks to make the trip to Lancaster and return to the Moshannon Mountains, but he had seen the fabled Seven Mountains, the Juniata Valley, the Tuscaroras, the Susquehanna Crossing, and the rolling hills of the Dutch settlements. In the shop of a famous Pennsylvania German gunsmith he had taken his time to examine the pieces offered for sale. After a thorough testing he had made his choice. Its accuracy had been proved. Today he hoped to make a trial of its effectiveness against game.

Below the rocky ledge on which he sat lay a mountain bench covered by a growth of huge chestnut trees. Their leafy crowns formed such an effective shade that the undergrowth had been killed, giving the bench the appearance of an open park. A hundred yards to the south, a rocky cove cut into the bench. Down this ravine the overflow of a mountain spring tumbled toward the creek below. Along the edge of the stream was a well-traveled game trail.

The heat of Indian summer loosened the frost-crisped leaves. They drifted down with a whispering that resembled the murmur of summer rain in distant trees. This gentle sound was occasionally punctuated by the sharp noise of a falling chestnut thumping the ground after dropping from a frost-opened burr.

It had been five days since he followed the creek to the sand bar that marked the mouth of the ravine. Bear tracks printed the sand. A casual glance showed that the game trail was in constant use. Only an abundance of food and the urgency to store fat for winter hibernation could curb a bear's inclination to wander widely. The chestnut grove was the attraction. Two years before he had killed a bear as it entered the grove.

The hunter waited patiently. He was aware of a change of weather in the air. Tomorrow it would storm. Confirmation came from a flock of geese, counting cadence as they drifted steadily south. Game would feed early.

A flock of turkey wandered over the edge of the bench from the spring run where they had been gathering gravel. The hunter counted eleven mature birds led by a big tom. The leader's beard was the diameter of a man's thumb and at least a span long. He was tempted to try a shot, but he knew he might frighten larger game. Although the flock was intent on feeding, there were always several heads searching the surroundings. Suddenly they ceased to feed, looked back toward the spring, then turned quickly toward the top of the ridge.

The hunter reached for his rifle. He saw the bear turn into the bench. There was the shine of water on its muzzle. It had stopped to drink at the run. It padded through the fallen leaves, stopping now and then to test the air. Once it bent its head to peer nearsightedly at the fresh earth left where the turkey had raked the leaves aside. Reassured, it moved a few feet forward, dropped its head, and began to pick up the rich nuts from among the fallen leaves.

Soon it was within the 40-yard limit he had set as a fair trial for his new weapon. Although the front sight covered the spot where the shoulder and neck joined, he did not touch the trigger.

From past experience he had learned that a wounded bear invariably dashed straight ahead after being hit. He recalled that one of his friends had accidentally gotten into the path of a wounded bear and had been knocked to the ground as the animal almost ran over him. He smiled, remembering how the story had grown with the telling until his friend had been convinced that the bear had purposely charged him and that his escape had been in the nature of a miracle.

Suddenly the bear raised its head, turned, and looked back in the direction of the ravine. Now! The poised finger touched the set trigger. The hunter was barely aware of the report. A puff of powder smoke partly obscured his vision. Dimly he saw the animal pitch forward. Its hind legs moved convulsively, then were still.

He recharged the rifle, forcing himself to act deliberately. This done, he swung down from the ledge and approached the fallen game from the rear. Twice he prodded it with his rifle barrel. It did not show any sign of life. Satisfied, he parted the hair to examine the shot. The bullet had entered just in front of the shoulder and had broken the animal's neck.

He dressed the carcass, noting with satisfaction that the accumulated fat was already three fingers thick. The pelt was full, prime, and glossy. When it was tanned into a sleigh robe it would find a ready market. The fat he would render into bear oil. This commodity was so highly prized among lumber-camp cooks that his limited supply was never sufficient to meet the demand. The meat, sweet, and prime from the animal's nut diet, would command a premium price. All in all, it had been a satisfactory and profitable afternoon.

John Blair Linn's *History of Centre and Clinton Counties* (Pennsylvania), published in 1883, makes the following terse statement concerning Samuel Askey of the preceding sketch. "In one season he sold two thousand seven hundred pounds of bear meat." Other noted pioneer hunters were Simeon Pfouts, Jacob Hammersly, and Tom Kyler. Others equally skilful were too modest and retiring to boast of their exploits.

Not all the large bears disappeared with the pioneer days. In 1946 Wayne Harpster of Port Matilda found a bear, dead apparently of natural causes. The skull measured 12 11/16 inches in length and 8 6/16 inches in width. When found it ranked fourth in the Boone and Crockett records. The 1964 edition showed it in fourteenth place. In 1965 a bear that weighed 550 pounds was killed in the same area (Black Moshannon) by Ralph Hughes. Unfortunately the skull was destroyed before it could be measured.

The bear is a paradox. He is at home in the remote, rugged mountains. Here among the rocks, evergreens, and thickets he finds food to supply his omnivorous appetite. His ears are sharp and his nose incomparable. Here he is shy and retiring. But when he forsakes the wilderness and lives near man he becomes a bold raider of bee hives, apple orchards, garbage cans, and cornfields. Occasionally he will help himself to domestic animals.

The animal quickly learns where he is protected. In certain state parks he becomes a nuisance. He makes nightly patrols, pilfering unprotected food supplies, scattering the contents of garbage cans in wild disorder. Occasionally he appears in daylight, to the delight of some campers and the consternation of others.

It is possible to live in bear country for years and never catch sight of the elusive beast. There are certain signs, however, that indicate its presence. They demolish ant hills, turn over flat rocks, rip apart decaying stumps, and wallow in certain wet sinks.

Oak trees often are scarred from their climbing. Before the acorns are ripe enough to fall, they climb into the trees and break sizeable branches in order to feast on the immature nuts. Beech trees are also marked in the same way and for the same reason.

Chokecherry thickets are often bent over and the smaller saplings broken where the bears ride them down to feed on the fruit. Trees in remote and abandoned apple orchards get their share of attention. Deer are forced to gather windfalls or be content with the fruit from low-growing branches but bears climb, either to gather fruit or to shake it down.

A city dweller parked his car and moved across a meadow that lay between the highway and the creek he intended to fish. Several apple trees grew beside his path. He was so intent on the business at hand that when a bear tumbled from one of the trees and with a frightened woof fled for the brush, the fisherman dropped his tackle and ran in the other direction. The native who recovered his tackle could not persuade his urban friend that fishing in the area was not hazardous.

Bears and berries go together like ham and eggs. The low-bush blueberry begins to ripen in early July. Then there is a succession of berries, including high-bush blueberries, blackberries, the viburnums, and many others, that continue to ripen until frost.

Last season I discovered a small patch of the sweet low-bush variety in the midst of a timber slashing. When the berries had had time to ripen properly I revisited the spot, intent on gathering enough for a pie or two. It was not full daylight when I arrived. I was startled as some large animal crashed away through the piled brush. I was late. The berries were gone. A bear had cleared the patch.

Blueberries indirectly led a neighbor of mine to a fine bear. Being an avid fisherman, he spent much time on a lake that is bordered by a blueberry swamp. On early mornings he often saw a bear come down a certain trail to the water before returning to the business of gathering berries. When the season opened he killed the bear as it followed the same trail to water.

Fields of corn adjacent to bear habitat suffer considerable damage. Native hunters are often successful when they drive the thickets in the vicinity of such a field.

"Bear trees" are found in most bear ranges. Some of these trees are used but once. Others are visited every season. I am familiar with a huge hemlock with claw scars and tusk marks on its trunk that date back for twenty years. Each spring or early summer new scars are added. What is their purpose? Are they range markers, scent posts, or just a good place to relieve an itch? We know that they serve as a focal point for any bear traveling in the area.

I walk the sand trail from the lake to the cabin. The rain of yesterday has washed a thin coating of duff over the white sand. During the night or early morning a bear has walked this way. His feet have picked up the duff and left each footprint clear and sharp. The pocket tape reads eight full inches from toe to heel without the claws. The front foot is five and three quarters inches broad. Some bear!

The squirrels are already cutting acorns on the hill. Has he chosen the cabin ridge for a feeding ground or is he merely passing through? I am resolved to hunt that ridge when the season opens.

I know that I am dreaming, but his hide would look well before the cabin fireplace. I'm aware that seeking to turn a bear into a rug is bucking the odds—but I might be lucky!

CHAPTER 2

Stalking Deer and Bear

BILL WALSH

When the buck lifted his body into the long, graceful leap of a whitetail showing his disdain for a four-foot barbed-wire fence, my crosshairs, steady and sure, were waiting for him. The trigger pull came fast but smooth. As the roar of the 30-06 punched the hush of early morning, I counted up one more deer for my eastern hunting record. I judged that when I circled the tumbled pile of beech-top slashing I'd find a blood trail of some 50 yards or so and a dead lung-shot buck at the end of it.

A doe, fat and sleek, had made the wire hurdle ahead of her antlered companion, setting him up for me. It was a break because, even though I'd spotted the deer some minutes before, they'd kept the tangle of logging rubble between me and a shot. I had immediately seen as they quartered toward me that one was a buck with a respectable though not outsized rack.

You know, I didn't find that so cocksuredly anticipated blood trail in the December snow. I did, however, find a powdered beech limb that had doubtless had a reciprocal effect on the 180-grain slug.

So when I tell you that I played bloodhound after those two deer you'll know it wasn't to salve my conscience on a bad hit. It was just that I had *seen* the rack; it was early in the day; the snow lay perfect for tracking; and another eastern whitetail buck had challenged a hunter as they've managed to do since the days of the prehistoric red men.

The first half mile breezed by as I trailed up and down short and ently sloping terrain astraddle crowned ridges. The deer separated from time to time but always came together again. They didn't mingle their tracks with those of other deer. Nor did one set of tracks differ in any way that I could tell from the other, so that I could tell which was his'n and which was her'n. I really didn't care!

As I strolled along, looking ahead, to each side, and even to the backtrail (the thing to do when dealing with whitetails), I got to thinking about the whole eastern deer-hunting situation. Such as how *good* it is for one thing.

Not that I won't hunt deer anywhere in the U.S.A. you can find them. Just last season I glassed some 74 western mule deer in California's high and dry Modoc National Forest in a fruitless hunt for the right kind of buck (the right kind would be what we call an eight-pointer in the east).

But when you look at the harvest record of deer taken in an eastern state—Pennsylvania, for example—and stack it against the west-of-the-Mississippi group with an eye for the kind of statistic that matters—harvested deer per square mile—well, it's clear that the easterners are riding a deer-hunting gravy train on which the rails are straight and level and the accommodations first class.

Just consider one statistic. The bow-and-arrow hunters in the Keystone State nocked killing arrows onto almost 10,000 deer in the three years just past. Frankly, I doubt if the bow-and-arrow Indians of Penns Woods ever did that well in the same amount of time. For one thing, there are more deer in the state now, and in most of the eastern states, than there were when the white settlers went on their first hunting excursions.

Pennsylvania regularly harvests more deer than California, a state some three and a half times larger. The 1969 harvest in Penns Woods came to almost 60,000 bucks and over 56,000 antlerless deer, and I am not going to convert that figure into pounds of venison, because I can get tired enough from dragging out just one 150-pounder, let alone contemplating whitetails by the ton. But back to my missed buck—also a Pennsylvania one.

The second half mile of trailing just about winded me. It twisted and turned and convoluted inside out and over again through a tangle of glacier-strewn boulders, laurel thickets, shade-tolerant hemlock jungles, and a few near-perpendicular hillsides without handholds. I suspect it was my persistence in following them that put them out of that section of the state-owned game lands and pushed them over a hill and straight across an open meadow into an area of second-growth beech and white oak. Easier going ahead, I told myself as I sank onto a downed log and got some breath back.

The game land on which I hunted is a favorite of mine. I shared a hunting camp with seven other fellows just at the edge of its 14,000 acres. My own hunting-license money helped to buy it and the million more acres of other game lands scattered across the state. Some are waterfowl areas, but you'll find deer on most of them. This one was all deer and a mile wide. I like it for that reason, of course, but also because I never have to ask anyone's permission or call ahead and make reservations to hunt on it. Neither do the many out-of-staters who go there to hunt, very successfully, every year.

Most eastern states have similar lands, owned by the hunters themselves, but Pennsylvania is ahead of the pack. It started piling up these tremendous chunks of real estate into a recreational reserve many years ago, when land was less expensive than now and before most other states even had the idea.

As I sat there resting, the sun came out bright and hard

against the snow. I put on my sunglasses—a necessary item for the eastern deer hunter moving over snow on a sunny day—and allowed my eyes to get used to the strain and the change. Then I made for the timber stand into which my deer tracks led.

It was easy to reconstruct the history of this corner of the game lands. The meadow was an abandoned farm pasture of 30 or more years ago; the timber stand was the new mixed growth that had followed the scalping of the loggers in the early 1900s. What had once been the virgin stands of hemlock, pine, and occasional hardwoods had now been supplanted by a magnificent assortment of beech, white oak, ironwood, and here and there a stand of small hemlock. How wise, I thought, of the game people to grab that land when the loggers had cleared it and thought it worthless, selling it to avoid paying further taxes on something they'd stripped. Of course Nature played the ultimate trick on these opportunists, for the current crop of timber, which includes now and then an extremely valuable wild cherry, is worth far more than the original timber, especially at today's prices.

Since the sportsmen now own it, they can and do sell it, under a carefully managed program of selective cutting. The money from such sales goes back into game-management programs, and the timber is only taken when its removal serves the interest of present or future game management. But back to my buck and his companion, neither of which I'd caught even a glimpse of since my futile shot.

Tracking became an impossible nightmare when I entered the timber. Great numbers of deer and large turkey flocks had recently pawed and scratched through the snow to garner the fallen acorns and beechnuts. Separating the new-made hoofprints of the two deer I followed from the network of thousands of others, some very old but some very new, became a step-by-step process that sent me frequently back to check and recheck my decisions.

Gambling that I might pick up the trail on a wide circle, I tied my backwoods red handkerchief to a twig and stuck it into the last print I had "positively" identified. I left it there and looped several hundred yards to the left. Like a pencil on the end of a compass, I made the complete circle. I should have saved the time. The same patterns of hoofs on snow, on leaves, on turkey **V** scratches, were everywhere I searched. And the stand of timber stretched on that way for a mile or more, I knew.

To be positive I was on *my* deer, I'd have to spend some 15 minutes or so on every hundred yards of travel. That would mean several hours of tedium to get through the stand. I gave it up. That is, I gave up that *method* of tracking.

Instead I moved quickly along in the direction the deer seemed to be heading, which was toward a small saddle in the opposite ridge that opened onto a bench and would take them almost back to the spot where I'd first seen them.

A half hour later I heard deer running ahead of me. The sound of delicate hooves breaking through the slight crust on top of the snow is distinctive and unmistakable. When many deer are involved, it is almost a sighing, as of a small wave on a sandy beach. This sound was from very few deer. It resembled a slight rustling, like silk against silk. I stopped and forced myself to munch one of the nut-and-fruit-laden chocolate bars I always carry into the deer woods. They give quick energy, and the natural fats and oils help keep a hunter warm in cold weather. And I checked my rifle.

Back at camp I'd taken the standard precautions for a cold-weather hunt—complete cleaning and oiling of all movable parts, followed by a meticulous wiping *clean* and *dry*, so there'd be no moisture to freeze or lubricant to harden in the subzero temperatures often encountered in snow country. Nevertheless, I racked out the cartridge in the chamber of the old but favored firearm and, depressing the magazine load with one finger, slammed the bolt home and dry fired it to make certain the pin moved.

For this type of cover, I flipped my variable to the low-range setting, the 3x. In the meadow I'd had it on the 9x.

As I'd explained to a western friend, with eastern deer guns, because of the variety of ranges and conditions under which you may bag your buck, you must either compromise or specialize. I had preferred to compromise.

I can take you to thicket-grown deer trails where, at

strategic points, hunters have killed their deer year after year at a range so utterly point blank that the hunter not only sees the whites of the animal's eyes but can tell before shooting whether the whites are bloodshot.

In the same county I can show you lookout points from which the hunter commands an almost omniscient surveillance over three separate deer trails through a meadow so devoid of obstruction that the only thing that might come between you and your target is reflection from the snow. A group of hunters I know have taken deer from this vantage point at ranges that have varied from 150 to over 400 yards. Yes, they're good shots, they have the rifles for the jobs, and they spend some preseason time shooting at long-range targets. But with the same arms they'd be helpless in the thick cover that surrounds that meadow.

If you specialize, you have either end to work at—close range or long range. In the meet-'em-head-on setup you are talking about iron sights and a cartridge with brush-busting capabilities, such as the still-depended-upon 35 Remington. Similarly, the 30-30 and the 32 Special (with their lower velocities) will bust more brush than some of the faster moving 300s, 308s, and 30-06s.

For long-range guns, the choice goes from the 270 through the 30-06, the 308 and after that down to the 243 and similar fast-moving stuff. Magnums are a matter of personal choice. Some hunters deem the eastern whitetail a mite fragile for the big wallop. But if you've been moving a Magnum caliber with effectiveness and you know you'll be shooting over open territory, then that's your gun.

The compromise rifle is one that will logically give you a sporting chance at close, middle, or long range. For my money it's a 30-06 with variable scope, 3x to 9x or something similar. A 30-30 with 4-power optics could also be considered an eastern compromise deer gun, though it's a bit weak in the long-range department. Such an arm should be sighted in to hit about three to four inches high at 100 yards to eke out every last inch of trajectory for the long shot. The rifle that hits dead-on at 100 yards will send its cartridge under the deer on the average long shot. Consult the trajectory tables for your own caliber and study them carefully before sighting in. Sight high at 100 yards and *memorize*, up to 300 yards, at least, where the bullet will be at major trajectory points.

Generally, eastern deer hunts take place between mid-November and mid-December. Yes, that's snow time. In Pennsylvania I have opened deer seasons in near-zero weather, in pelting rain, and on warm, sunny days that, by mid-morning, had my heavy outer clothing off, my back against a tree trunk, and the heavy desire for an open-air nap on my eyelids. Your hunting wardrobe had best be prepared for any kind of weather.

And if you're headed for the mountain wilderness of Maine or the Adirondacks of New York State, consult your local contacts regarding such specialized equipment as snowshoes. The need for snowshoes throughout most of the east, however, is a once-in-a-lifetime kind of thing. But when it happens you'll never forget it.

I remember a heavy snowfall that lasted throughout most of a Pennsylvania deer season in the late 40s. The local sports shop in our town sold out of every available pair of webfooters within 24 hours and placed an immediate order for many, many more. They sold all that came through, of course. But those that arrived after the season ended—it lasted two weeks at that time—are still amoulderin' on the shelves. In fact, the proprietor became known as "Snowshoe," and the name stuck for many years.

I remember the season because I had no snowshoes and attempted to get to a favored deer crossing by traversing a quarter mile of drifted meadow in my insulated duck-hunting waders (to keep the seat of my pants dry, of course). I was in good physical condition and in my late twenties, yet a couple hundred yards of that kind of wallowing in the thick, wet stuff, into which I often sank to navel depth, was too much for me.

My hunting partner and I returned to our basement workshop to "home make"—with what we later admitted to be limited equipment and even less know-how—two pairs of snowshoes.

We spent hours steaming strips of ash for bending and lashing into the proper snowshoe shape, and eventually we got a rough resemblance. Lacking rawhide for the webbing, we used yard after yard of ordinary shoelace material. Let me tell you, this does *not* work. After several steps these laces picked up so much snow that it seemed as though they weighed eighty pounds each.

Other hunters did no better. I heard tales of such outlandish solutions as waxed pieces of plywood and of shoes so large they would not fit between the trees where the hunter-wearer planned to walk. One genius hitched his three Labrador retrievers to a toboggan, but instead of pulling him they all gathered around to slurp their tongues across his face and over his eyeglasses.

"Take my rifle, quick!" he shouted to a companion. "I'll never forgive myself if I shoot these dogs but if I keep the gun I just might do it!"

At any rate, I'm sure you are getting the idea that you can have many different kinds of hunting in the eastern United States and enjoy many different varieties of terrain in the having.

One thing that's not commonly understood is that you can have much wilderness-style hunting in the deer-rich East if you want it. The Allegheny National Forest, for example, covers most of three Pennsylvania counties. Though it is crossed by major highways and many secondary roads, there are some areas where cars are forbidden; where shanks' mare moves you or you don't move; where men can—and have done so to prove it—get lost for days.

New York State's Adirondack wilderness also sprawls across some fine and outstandingly scenic deer and bear country.

This Adirondack wilderness is a reservoir of black-bear hunting that other states wish they had. In fact, the 595 black bears taken there in the 1969 season are many more than most states can boast for their entire areas. The rest of New York State accounted for 121 black bears.

Your first trip into any eastern backwoods country should be accomplished with Caution as your constant companion.

Carry contour maps and compass, and keep your wits about you.

After hunting the same hinterland for a number of years, however, a hunter can come to know his particular section of backwoods country as well as he knows his own neighborhood, though he should always carry map and compass just in case.

But you don't have to see how far from the well-traveled road you can get in order to collect an eastern deer.

I have always maintained that a stranger could drive into any good eastern deer state and have a reasonably good chance of driving out with a venison-decorated automobile without hunting more than 500 feet from the road. And without advance arrangements.

You can do this by taking advantage of the tens of thousands of free "guides" these states have placed at your service. Oddly enough, the "guides" usually come through the courtesy of the state's highway department rather than the conservation agencies involved with fish and game.

Sure, you guessed it. The "guides" are those highway signs that say DEER CROSSING or DEER AREA . . . or whatever tag the state in question uses to tell dusk-to-dawn motorists that a certain section of road offers hazardous driving because deer cross that road often enough to create a traffic problem. I believe the biggest and most eye-arresting of all such signs I've ever seen are those along the New Jersey super roads.

In some states there is a large highway kill of deer. In Pennsylvania, for example, nearly 20,000 deer annually fall victim to the auto and its driver. This is, incidentally, more deer than hunters kill in many a state that prides itself on its venison harvest.

So if you're inventive and ingenious, these signs may mean a deer trophy for you. Having selected the site with an eye to surrounding towns, farms, buildings, etc., a hunter then need only park his auto in a safe place near a DEER CROSSING sign, find the major trail the animals take, and follow the trail off the road a safe distance and take up a stand on it or, preferably, near it. In the short eastern deer seasons you will have plenty of help in moving deer to you—the other hunters who will be in the area somewhere, pushing in from another direction.

Incidentally, letting some other fellow drive your deer to you is one of the most popular ways of bagging venison in the East, although it is not an infallible method. The idea is to get into the woods in the vicinity of a known four-star crossing long before the shooting hour—and wait.

My grandfather collected almost all of his deer in this fashion, allowing the hunters who wouldn't enter the woods until daylight to push the animals to him. And this was when deer were not so numerous as they are now. His advice to me was, "When hunting the rump-on-stump method, follow these three important rules. One, Don't move. Two, DON'T move! Three, DON'T MOVE!" He also had something to say about "dudes" who couldn't keep their dadblamed mouths shut while in the woods, but I am assuming you know that the only time for deer-hunting shouting is when you are part of a noise drive, pushing deer to silent, waiting watchers already posted at strategic points.

In defense of Grandpa I'll say that he didn't rely on the other hunter until late in his life. Before that he tracked 'em down or came home empty-handed.

But he always let the other hunter push his bear to him. Bear? I'd forgotten to tell you more about the good bear hunting in the East. In Maine, for a starter, there are sometimes as many as 2500 black bears in the annual harvest.

I've already mentioned New York State's recent record crop of 716 bruins. Pennsylvania, with fewer and smaller wilderness areas, is cautiously curbing its bear hunting in order to preserve it for the future, but some Pennsylvania bear hunting takes place every year.

Not that the East is overrun with bears or anything like that. But considering that the East is overpopulated and highly industrialized, it should surprise a great number of folks to learn that a 521-pound black bear was shot in Pennsylvania's Clarion County in 1969.

What the eastern states have known for years and the western ones are suddenly realizing is that a black bear is still a glamorous hunting trophy to millions of American sportsmen.

Of course, stockmen, beekeepers, and timbermen may regard some of the black bear's shenanigans as destructive and bothersome, but a single animal is almost worth its weight in gold when one considers how many dollars are spent by so many hunters to bag so few bears.

Although black bears can adjust somewhat to civilization, they still require more wilderness than deer to keep up their numbers. Also, unlike deer, their reproductive rate is low. A sow bear gives birth only every second year under *optimum* conditions. That poor conditions are catching up with bear everywhere is reflected in the recent action of California in reducing the bear bag limit from two a year to only one.

Snapping out of my bear-thought reverie, I realized I'd probably not see any bears on my trek after the elusive deer I'd been tracking. Most bears would be in hibernation by this time, and I was hunting a bit out of prime bear range. Believing I'd given my buck and doe—if, indeed, the deer I'd heard were my quarry—enough time to move ahead and 'quiet down," I again took up the trail and found fresh hoofprints almost immediately. There were only two deer, as I could see from the tracks they had left as they had moved into and out of a small creek with unsullied snow on either side. Again I cautioned myself to take it easy. At such a time the pursuer of deer must take only a few steps at a time and look in all directions, even to the rear, for a glimpse of a tell-tale sign, such as the flicker of an ear, the flash of a white tail, or a patch of color not exactly like the tree trunk beside it. For some twenty minutes or more I stalked in this way.

As I moved along a ridge I suddenly came into an area where the timber was a little more open. Perhaps some thinning had taken place here in recent times but not enough to open up the growth of ground cover. I was able to see many more yards farther than before. Then I saw it—a movement along the limb of a tree, as might be made by a woodpecker or a nuthatch in climbing the trunk. Then it was gone. I switched my scope to 9x and with the safety kept on (for that motion could have been made by another hunter), brought the area into scrutiny in the *right side* of my scope, *not* in the center-crosshair section (this also for reasons of common-sense safety).

Whatever it was moved again. I leaned against the bole of a nearby tree to steady the rifle and the scope. On the third inspection I realized I was watching the ear of a deer. At a range of about 150 yards I was sure of that ear, but I was not sure of what appeared to be one half of a fairly decent set of antlers also sticking out of the side of that tree, as it were. Then the branch moved. I knew I had him if I could get him into the scope.

Then, because the hunting gods have always been good to me, as they were to 116,000 other Pennsylvania hunters who collected deer in 1969, the buck took two short steps into the space between a pair of white oaks and stood still, looking if not right at me then at something directly in line with me.

If he heard the safety click off the Model 70, he gave no indication. I lost sight of him as the rifle recoiled and the scope leapt upward, but there was that bit of memory picture in my mind that saw him lurch and begin to fall.

The doe sped quickly away, not pausing even once to look back. As she disappeared over a knoll, I sent my blessings to her because even though some antlerless deer are harvested each year in the East, instead of dying of old age or winter kill, enough are left to sustain the hunting of whitetails year after year. In the disappearing doe lay the continuance of a deer-hunting future that seems to know no end in the East.

Although Bob Bell's discussion of firearms suitable for the area deals with several types of guns, he devotes most of his talk to equipment used for big game. As the former managing editor of The Gun Digest *and currently editor of* Pennsylvania Game News, *Bell's mental storehouse is stacked deeply with enough technical dope about rifles and scopes to fill several volumes. Having hunted often enough with him to have some idea about what makes him tick, I am inclined to say that Bell is first and last a hunter in the most complete sense of the word. He deplores weaklings, cowards, and at times nonhunters. Yet despite his gruffness (yes, you are a little gruff, Bob), he is an amazingly gentle man who plays the hunting game like a gentleman, by the legal rules and by some he has made up himself. His advice and thoughts about rifles are based on 30 years of hard hunting experience.*

CHAPTER 3

Rifles, Shotguns, Handguns

BOB BELL

Only two big-game animals, the white-tailed deer and the black bear, are available in shootable numbers in the Northeastern United States. This simplifies the chore of selecting a rifle for the region because, as a general rule, the same one can be used for either. There are exceptions. For instance, the max-loaded 243 Winchester, which might be favored for open-country whitetails, wouldn't be ideal on a 525-pound bruin, whose layers of fat would tend to keep this light bullet from penetrating into the vitals. But such bears are so scarce we can pretty well ignore them and just look at the general picture.

Both whitetails and black bears have been taken with every available cartridge, I'm sure. Still, some loads are better than others, and an appropriate choice can be made on the basis of terrain and cover. In the Northeast, three general categories exist: thick cover, average woodlots and woods, and long range. The first will include small acreages of brush and slashings such as sometimes are found near run-down farms, rhododendron-grown ravines, and areas that have been cut and now are growing up. Most shooting will be done at ranges between 25 and 60 yards, with only an occasional shot through a "tunnel" to perhaps 150 yards. The second consists mainly of forested sections, pole stage or larger, interspersed with laurel, striped maple, and the like, with some small open areas of grass or low brush. Average shooting here will be at about 75 to 175 yards, with a chance now and then to perhaps 300. The third category includes all terrain that frequently offers shooting at 300 yards or more—farm country, power-line rights of way, or open hillsides. The second category is easiest to prepare for, as average problems require average answers. The first and last categories require specialization for top results.

To be suitable for a given kind of hunting, a cartridge must have enough energy to do the job required at the maximum distance it will be used; it must have an acceptable trajectory over that range; and it must have the accuracy needed to group well within the vital area of the target at the longest range in question. Many loads have more than enough energy at woods distances but do not qualify for long-range shooting, either because they cannot generate enough velocity to produce suitably flat trajectories or, probably through the fault of the rifles in which they are used, because they are not accurate enough.

It should be noted, then, that generations of experience have led hunters to the conclusion that approximately 1000 foot pounds of kinetic energy are required for consistent clean kills on whitetails or black bears. This information, which can be checked in ballistics tables, gives a reasonable basis to work from, though there is one group of cartridges to which it doesn't apply—the small-caliber, high-velocity loads designed for crow and woodchuck hunting. Some of these, notably the 224 Weatherby, the 225 Winchester, the 22-250 Remington and the 220 Swift, have sufficient KE for deer shooting, but give inconsistent results. On shots where the bullet gets into the lungs, they often kill like grenades, and sometimes they kill effectively even with paunch shots, owing to their explosiveness and massive shock effect, which simply overwhelm a highly nervous animal like the whitetail. Yet this does not happen consistently, not even when duplicate bullet placement occurs. And on angles where considerable penetration is needed, they often fail miserably. Their overall results seem unsatisfactory, probably because their bullets are thin jacketed and designed to perform reliably on 10-pound woodchucks or crows, rather than on comparatively large animals. Handloaders can overcome much of the weaknesses of these loads by using the Nosler Zipedo bullet, which has a heavy, solid base that insures penetration yet expands well. Hunters who do not handload but must for some reason use one of these cartridges would do well to choose the heaviest bullets available and then take great care in placing their shots.

Thick Cover Outfits

The 30-30, traditionally in the M94 Winchester carbine, is the standard short-range deer and bear outfit throughout the Northeast. Some three million of them have been sold, and I swear at times they must have all collected in northern Pennsylvania through some process of osmosis. I never knew a deer hunter who didn't own one at some time or another.

The 30-30 was the first popular smokeless-powder cartridge, and it had a reputation as a real heller at the turn of the century. Time has tamed its wildness, but it's with us yet and doubtless will be around when today's latest Magnums aren't even memories. The reason for this is simple. The 30-30 with its 170-grain flat-point soft-nose bullet is a fine deer and bear load at ranges within 150 yards, and that's where more than 99 per cent of these critters are killed. And this efficiency, wrapped in a six-and-a-half-pound, yard-long rifle that holds a hatful of cartridges, can be worked by flexing the fingers, and brings back boyhood dreams of the Wild West and the Great North Woods every time you look at it, simply has got to stay forever.

This outfit isn't perfect. Its biggest weakness is the sighting arrangement. The so-called "open" rear sight blocks out the bottom of everything you're looking at, in effect eliminating half your field of view; it swallows the front sight in bad light, resulting in high shots; it's almost impossible to zero in without hammering, filing, and assorted other operations; and the convex-faced front bead reflects light in such a changing manner that precise aiming is difficult at best. However, an adjustable receiver sight with a big aperture and a flat-faced brass-colored front sight eliminates all these problems, and the money you'd have spent for ammo to zero in the open sights will soon pay for the new ones. So fitted, you've got a thick-cover outfit that's easy to carry, gets on game right now, and does the job. These comments on sights apply to all unscoped woods outfits.

Nearly identical loads are the 32 Special, the 30 Remington, the 32 Remington, and the 303 Savage. All use bullets of about the same weight at about the same velocity. Obviously, results will be very similar, with a choice being determined by personal preference for one rifle or another. The 25-35 Winchester never came close to the popularity of most of this group, yet it was a pleasant load to shoot, and its 117-grain soft-point bullet performed reasonably well at the shorter ranges.

For brush-busters who want more power, the 303 British, the 348 Winchester, and the 35 Remington, among older loads, supply it. The 303 British has plenty of power to at least 300 yards with its 180- or 215-grain bullets, but the short magazine Lee Enfield rifles and carbines, though fine military weapons, are not noted for long-range accuracy. Neither will one's sleek lines keep a man up all night gazing upon it in a gunrack. Nevertheless, in the woods it also serves.

The 348, offered only in the M71 Winchester lever gun, no longer made and therefore currently demanding several times its last list price, and the M71 are quite likely the greatest woods outfit ever made, particularly if an occasional western elk or Canadian moose is on the agenda. It handles a 200-grain flat-point slug at some 2500 fps, and this simply overpowers game the size of deer and black bear. I used this combination for a number of years, never lost a deer I hit, and never had to hit one more than once in the body. Also took my first few elk with it. The Model 71, an updating of the old, grease-smooth M86, is in my opinion the best lever gun ever made. Mine has the aperture sight that's integral with the bolt and a flat-faced gold-bead front sight installed on a barrel cut to 21 inches. It's made ten-shot three-inch groups at 100 yards, and that's better than I can hold offhand. One example will illustrate the type of shooting at which it excels.

In 1946 I was hunting alone along Montour Ridge between Danville and Northumberland in Pennsylvania. I'd killed a few whitetails before, but never a big one. Spooking along a woods trail, I came to a spot overlooking a chopped-off hillside, and some 90 yards distant I saw the head and neck of a big buck, just visible above some thick brush. I tried to guess where his shoulder was. The gun roared, and he came out running, the far-side front leg swinging free. I'd smashed it just beneath the brisket. He was moving fast, in sight for only brief moments as he ducked among the brown-leafed oak tops and brush left by the woodcutters. But a fast flip of the lever had reloaded the 348, and I saw the gold bead against his shoulder as he flashed across an opening. The second 200-grain slug smashed through the forequarters, low down, and piled him up, and automatically—perhaps because of habits acquired in the then recent past in France, Germany, and elsewhere—I slammed another, unnecessary, bullet through the top of the shoulders.

He had a perfectly matched, eight-point rack, surpassed in size by only two whitetails of some dozens I've taken since, and the fast, natural handling of the M71 made it possible. Much as I like bolt guns, I don't think I could have worked one fast enough for this kind of shooting. Even now, decades later, I'd say that anyone with an M71 Winchester 348 needs nothing more for most any kind of big game in the woods.

The 35 Remington is another killer. Its ballistics aren't impressive—a 200-grain blunt-nosed bullet at some 2100 fps—but as with the 348, when you hit something with it, you take that something home. This fine load was helped by being offered in several slick-working Remington slide actions, the best being the once-popular M141, now also discontinued. This combination was my dad's favorite for deer. He had a Lyman Alaskan on his in Redfield Jr. mounts, and that gun would give two-inch groups at 100 yards. It's a real woods outfit.

Other good woods loads are the 6.5 mm Japanese and the famous 6.5 mm Mannlicher-Schoenauer, both loaded by Norma with 156-grain round-nose bullets. The latter has killed elephants, so it should find whitetails no bother. It has a velocity of some 2490 fps, about 400 fps faster than the Japanese cartridge. Both get good penetration with their long, slim bullets, and are dependable if not spectacular killers. It would be hard to find two rifles with more contrast than the rough Arisaka battlefield model and the super-refined Mannlicher-Schoenauer, yet so far as meat in the pot goes, there's not a lot to choose between them.

More modern woods loads, modern in the sense that they are of recent design if not recent concept, are the 44 Magnum and the 444 Marlin, both with 240-grain bullets. Their use of large-caliber heavy slugs rather than high velocity to gain energy is a sort of throwback but one I sympathize with, maybe in reaction against the never-ending speed craze. The 44 Magnum was developed as a heavy handgun load and later chambered in the handy Marlin M336 lever-action carbine and the Universal M440 slide-action Vulcan. The 444 is a sort of stretched-out 44, its straight-sided rimmed case holding enough powder to produce over 3000 foot-pounds of energy at the muzzle—almost twice that of the 44 Magnum carbine. The 444 is available only in the fine M444 Marlin Magnum lever gun, basically an M336. The Marlin lever guns have solid top actions which allow a scope to be mounted low and centrally, as it should be. Some early 444 loads did not perform up to expectations, apparently because they utilized handgun bullets, but that trouble seems to have been licked. Anyone wanting a powerful lever-action outfit should give thought to the 444 Marlin.

Some brush loads not seen often these days, but ones still capable of doing a clean job, are the old 38-40 with 180-grain soft-nose, the 38-55 with a 255-grain bullet, and the legendary 45-70 with its 405-grain bullet. These are most commonly found in lever guns, but a trapdoor Springfield 45-70 appears occasionally. Low velocity limits the effective range of these loads, but the big slugs kill well.

Iron-sighted woods rifles are best zeroed a couple of inches high at 100 yards, say at about the top of the front bead. Most shooters subconsciously aim with the center of the bead when they shoot fast, and such a zero will give a point-blank range of 150 yards or so, whereas one dead on at 100 will often strike too low on the occasional shot offered at the longer ranges.

Nowadays, most hunters prefer scope sights. The top-ejecting Winchester lever guns do not lend themselves to scopes, but the fine Savage M99, the Remington pumps, and the various bolt guns do. My personal favorite in the woods is a top-grade 4x, but those who don't shoot scopes regularly will do better with a 2½x or 1½-4x variable, because of their larger fields of view. During the past 30 years I've used scores of scopes, and there's no doubt that a good one is far superior to the best iron sights, but a poor one is worthless. Expect to pay a reasonable amount, get one from a reliable maker, mount it low and solidly, with Loc-tite on all screws, properly positioned for eye relief when wearing hunting clothing, zero it in carefully with ammo identical to that you'll use to hunt with, and you'll have a rig you can count on when things are tough. Get a *conspicuous* reticle—medium or heavy crosswires, post, big center dot (at least five MOA), or one of the newer four-posts and crosswires combinations.

A scope must be well sealed, because of the miserable weather often encountered in big-game season. Few are truly waterproof, in the sense that they can withstand indefinite submersion, but the good ones approach that condition. You can test them by completely dunking in water heated to about 135 degrees. The heat expands the air inside, causing it to bubble out at any leak. Don't leave it underwater too long or when the air cools inside the tube it will contract and draw in water through any aperture.

Open Woods Outfits

In more-open woods country, cartridges that give somewhat higher velocities than the preceding group are necessary. Their speed lessens the bullet's time of flight, thus flattening trajectory and making hitting easier out yonder. Some of these loads gain velocity by sacrificing bullet weight, and this lessens their efficiency a bit, in the sense that they're better at 200 yards than at 300; yet their accuracy often permits the precise bullet placement that can get by with slightly less power.

The smallest loads here are the popular 243 Winchester and 6 mm Remington, and the older 250-3000 Savage, all using 100-grain spitzer bullets. The 257 Roberts, unfortunately obsolete but still often seen in this region, also fits in here with the same weight bullet. (Handloaders can steam up the 117-grain Sierra boattail or the 125-grain Barnes until the 257 is far superior to the other three, but we're trying to avoid the handloading angle here, as space is limited, so we won't go into that further.)

Going up the ladder, the old 7x57 mm Mauser, particularly when used with Norma's 150-grain spitzer bullet at 2750 fps, is excellent. The 175-grain at 2500 fps offered by the American companies is fine to 225 yards or so, but doesn't reach out like the lighter one. The 8 mm Mauser is similarly handicapped in this country by being supplied with only the 170-grain bullet at some 2500 fps. This was the German military cartridge during both World Wars, and many thousands of rugged M98 Mauser rifles were brought back by GIs, so it's unfortunate that a wider choice of ammo isn't available. Nevertheless, it will do what's necessary in this bracket.

Three excellent 30-caliber loads fit in here too—the 30-40 Krag, the 300 Savage, and the 308 Winchester. When I was a kid, Krags were common in Pennsylvania. Now they are rarely seen, but I've got a hunch a lot of youngsters would be wiser to root around in Grandpop's attic for one of these super-slick, easy-loading-with-numb-fingers models than to insist on a Super Magnum to start with. Even that old 220-grain soft-nose that clears the tube with only 2200 fps or so manages to kill deer awfully dead with no fuss at all, and it's mighty easy on the shoulder. Some M95 Winchester lever guns also were chambered for the 30-40, but they've always been comparatively scarce. Neither it nor the Krag is ideal for scoping.

The stubby 300 Savage—sort of an '06 squeezed down to fit the M99 action—is always thought of as a lever-action load, though various other styles have chambered it. I always had the feeling it was favored by hunters not quite rough'n'tumble-backwoodsy enough for the 30-30. It's a fine load, accurate and with light recoil, and so close to the much newer 308 that it makes one wonder how far we've come in several generations. In the strong M99, it's an excellent choice.

The 308 Winchester is the commercial version of the NATO 7.62x51 mm military round-a 30-06 shortened to eliminate the airspace bequeathed to Granddad by today's powders. It's a completely modern case, strong enough for the high-pressure loads demanded by many. Anyone who wants a 308 can get it in a rifle to suit him—to name a few, the Winchester M70, the Remington M700, The Ruger M77 and Mossberg M800 bolt actions, the Winchester M88 and Savage M99 lever actions, the Winchester M100, Remington M742, and Browning autoloaders, the Remington M760 pump, even Ruger's fancy No. 1 Single Shot. Doubtless there are more, but you get the idea. It's popular.

I lean toward the 150-grain pointed bullet in both the 300 Savage and the 308, but wouldn't argue much with the guy who chooses the 180-grain in the 308. That weight is readily available in the 30-40 too, and shoots a bit flatter over the longer ranges than the 220-grain bullet. Handloaders would do well to try the 165-grain Sierra boattail or the Hornady spire point in these medium-size 30 calibers.

The 358 Winchester might be called a modern version of the 348, and it's come close to suffering a similar undeserved fate. Simply a necked-up 308, it is a small but potent woods package. When introduced in the mid-50s, it was offered in the Featherweight M70 and the M88 lever action, and at various times other rifles have been chambered for it, but no commercial rifle is currently being built for it. This is a shame. With a 200-grain bullet at 2500 fps, it has scads of power at normal ranges and has about the same trajectory over 300 yards as the 220-grain 30-06. It's never been a popular load, though, apparently because it doesn't attain the magic 3000 fps velocity that too many hunters nowadays believe is necessary. Nevertheless, anyone who has a 358 has a fine outfit for almost any North American game at reasonable range.

The 350 Remington Magnum is sort of more of the same thing. A stubby belted case designed to work through the short Remington M660 action, it also uses a 200-grain bullet—at a velocity of over 2700 fps. This is far more power than is needed for deer or black bear, but that's better than not enough. Another point in its favor is the lightweight bolt-action carbine that handles it. Its 20-inch barrel and six-and-a-half-pound weight make it exceedingly handy in the woods, and of course it will handle any game on this continent. Considerable test shooting with a 2½x scope gave me groups under two inches at 100 yards with factory ammo using 200- and 250-grain bullets, and that's pretty impressive with a cartridge of this power in such a light gun. Recoil felt about the same as a 338 Magnum in a nine-pound outfit.

The 350 Magnum is now offered in the M700 Remington. The longer action permits handloaders to seat bullets farther out, leaving more space for powder, which gives an even more impressive velocity, if that should be required.

Rifles in this bracket are best fitted with a good 4x scope. I feel, or a variable of 1½-4x or at most 2½-8x. These give all the magnification needed and yet are small enough that they don't give a tail-wagging-the-dog appearance. Medium crosswires are as good a reticle as any. A center dot should subtend about three MOA at the 4x setting of a variable, assuming it's the modern kind in which the reticle appears coarser at low magnification than at high. This will give approximately five MOA at 2½x and 1½ MOA at 8x, which is close to ideal. A large selection of variables in this power range is available. I've had good luck with Bausch & Lomb, Leupold, Redfield, Savage, Weatherby, and Wearer.

Long Range Outfits

Anyone who prefers to do his shooting at long range, or has to because of the region he lives in, has a different set of problems than the brush-busters and open-woods deer hunters. Where they lean toward light, easy-handling outfits, he can go with a longer, heavier rifle. In fact, he prefers it because of its steadier holding qualities, the improved accuracy that a heavier barrel usually gives, and the higher velocity gained by a longer tube. Here is where the medium-bore, 3000-plus fps, 55,000 psi cartridges shine, the place where terms such as "sectional density" and "ballistic coefficient" become important.

What might be called normal long-range shooting falls into the 300-to-500-yard bracket. I know there are some men, particularly in northern Pennsylvania—among them some serious experimenters as well as crackpots—who make a cult of trying for deer at nearly incredible ranges—anywhere from 800 to 1500 yards, and sometimes more. They use benchrest-type rifles chambered for the hottest available loads, target scopes, rangefinders, benchrests with sandbags or mechanical rifle rests, and other high-grade equipment. From experimental shooting, they know their points of impact at 100-yard intervals up to perhaps a mile. They shoot at quite a few deer, and because most are fantastic riflemen they hit some. But they don't kill all they hit, even when the bullet is placed in a vital spot. The reason is simple: at such ranges, velocity has dropped off so badly that the bullet simply doesn't expand. One of the proponents of this style of hunting has told me of firing several dozen times at a single deer at some 1400 yards. It finally lay down and was dead when he got to it, with four or five bullet holes, small, neat tunnels, through the chest. It just bled to death without realizing what was happening to it. If this deer had wandered out of sight after taking one or two bullets through the lungs, the shooter would probably have concluded that he'd missed it and gone on to try his luck on another, and the first one would have died wastefully. How many times this happens each year, I don't know. But I am not impressed with such shooting.

The basic problem here, from a mechanical standpoint, is the design and manufacture of a bullet that will give better than minute-of-angle accuracy and be strongly enough constructed to withstand the highest velocity that can be given it but that will nevertheless expand reliably when its striking velocity is less than half of its muzzle velocity. That's no easy chore, and this ideal projectile does not yet exist.

All of which brings us back to the suggested 500-yard maximum range for sporting shooting. This isn't an exact figure, of course, but in approximate terms, it's about the longest distance at which any of today's hunting bullets can be expected to perform reliably. One example should suffice. Take a 30-caliber 180-grain spitzer bullet loaded to 3200 fps, which is about all that can be squeezed out of the 300 Weatherby, the largest case readily available, at pressures you wouldn't be leery of resting your face near. This is a highly impressive load, giving better than 4000 foot-pounds of energy. However, at 500 yards it's left with some 2100 fps velocity and 1800 fp energy, or about the same as the 30-30 at the muzzle. In theory you can add another hundred yards of range and equal the old 30-30 at its typical woods distance, but there are all kinds of problems at even 500 yards that don't exist at 100, such as, for instance, placing that bullet. Zeroed at 200 yards, the 300 Magnum is a yard low at 500; with a 300-yard zero, it's some two feet low. Either sighting requires the shooter to aim at an imaginary point somewhere above the deer's shoulders, and maybe several feet right or left, depending on wind. Then there's bullet design. Built strongly enough to withstand its high muzzle velocity, and a rotational velocity of perhaps 200,000 rpm, these sturdy spitzers don't expand nearly as reliably at 2100 fps as the old flat-point softnoses. So 500 honest-to-gosh three-foot yards is one awfully long ways to shoot at any animal and expect to kill it cleanly. And if you can't expect to do this with at least 85 per cent certainty, you shouldn't be trying any particular shot.

The commercial cartridges most suitable for such shooting are Remington's 6.5 mm Magnum with 120-grain bullet; Remington 280, 150-grain; Remington 7 mm Magnum, 150- or 175-grain; Winchester's 270, 130-grain or the Norma-loaded 150-grain spitzer; Winchester 284, 150-grain and Winchester 300 Magnum, 150- or 180-grain. And of course there's always the 30-06 with 150- or 180-grain spitzers. The 338 Magnum, 200-grain, and 375 H&H Magnum, 270-grain, also would do if anyone wants to use one of these powerhouses for game as small as black bear and whitetails. The Weatherby Magnum series, from 240 through 300, also qualifies with appropriate bullet weights, as does the 7x61 S&H 160-grain from Norma. There are many similar wildcats, but these are handloading propositions.

Spitzer bullets should be chosen for all long-range shooting, as they maintain velocity and energy far better than any other style. Boattails add a little efficiency also. Zeroed at 300 yards with a maximum load, most of the cartridges in this group will be approximately four inches high at 200 yards, a foot to 15 inches low at 400, and 28 to 36 inches low at 500. Exact figures vary, and the only way you can be certain of your own combination is to shoot it at the ranges in question. If you do this a few times, you'll find that impact varies somewhat with changes in temperature, humidity, shooting position, light, the tension with which the rifle is held—and maybe according to what you had for breakfast that morning. So don't think that simply getting a hotshot Magnum solves all your shooting problems. It just moves them farther away.

Most small- or medium-bore cartridges of large capacity require slow-burning powders for best results, and these require at least 24 inches of barrel for proper burning. In fact, if you're building a rifle specifically for long-range hunting, a 26- or 28-inch tube is a pious idea. Adding length here is the easiest way to gain velocity at no cost. And don't insist on a featherweight barrel. The inertia of a heavier one makes life much simpler when you're trying to precisely place a slug at a quarter mile and the wind is almost lifting you out of your prone position in the snow. Another necessity is an adjustable trigger set for about three or four pounds, with all creep and backlash removed. Don't make it much lighter. You want enough resistance that you can feel it even when your fingers are stiff from the cold.

Most of my intentional long-range shooting has been done with a 7x61 S&H Magnum. It's nothing fancy—a 25-inch Buhmiller sporter barrel on a lengthened-magazine FN Mauser action with Sako trigger and plain-grained dense-walnut stock, glassed all the way. With 160-grain Sierra spitzer boattails and 62 grains of 4350 it occasionally gives five-shot one-and-a-quarter-inch groups at 200 yards, but that size is more typical at half that distance.

Many years ago I had the chance to try a shot at a farm-country whitetail while two carloads of other hunters watched. The deer was standing high on the crown of a distant hill. The range? I dunno. But I was zeroed three inches high at 100, which puts it on at almost 300, and from a solid rest I held the horizontal crosswire of the 4x Bear Cub just above the deer's erect ears as it looked at me, and hit it dead center in the chest, so the bullet drop indicates a distance crowding close to my self-imposed 500 yards.

Another time, an eight-point stood looking at me from about 300 yards, just the muzzle, top of head, and antlers showing. My outfit was the same, except that a 3-9x Redfield had replaced the 4x. Bedding the rifle down on a solid rest, with the scope set at top power—a decided help in such an instance—I placed the crosswires directly on the buck's nose. The bullet hit just under the point of aim, smashing the spinal column for an instant kill.

I don't describe these few shots out of self-praise but only because they're examples of what I call normal long-range shooting in Pennsylvania, and they were made with a typical hunting rifle. I've seen friends make more difficult shots a number of times and am certain many readers have done likewise. Such chances are not simple, but they are not outside the realm of probability, as I feel most of the 1000-to-1500-yard shooting is.

If all your shooting is beyond 300 yards, a good 6x or 8x scope will be ideal. But if you use the same outfit in the bush occasionally, a 2½-8x or 3-9x variable is better. The big 4-12x and 6-18x jobs have more magnification than is needed for big game, though they serve well on varmints if the same rifle is used on such game.

Test fire your variable from benchrest on a target, to see if the point of impact remains the same throughout the power range. Most vary a little, some a lot. If the change is well under a minute of angle, as is normal with the best American scopes, that's about as good as you can get. If it's a couple of minutes, trade it off to someone less particular. Since most long-range shooting is done with the scope at top magnification, zero in at that setting. If it moves an inch at 2½x when you're shooting offhand in the woods, it makes no difference.

I've hunted in Pennsylvania every year since 1940, except the 1943, '44, and '45 seasons, when I was in the Army. Many years I also hunted in other states. In that time I took deer with quite a few rifles. As the years passed, I constantly found myself wanting a lighter-weight rifle than whatever I happened to be carrying. A few seasons ago I even borrowed my wife's featherweight 257, a cut-down, restocked M722 Remington. It worked fine, which convinced me I needed another gun myself. I selected the 284 Winchester cartridge, put it on a M98 action, which allowed seating the long 160-grain spitzers only to the base of the case neck, and specified a 21-inch lightweight barrel. Trigger is a C-H adjustable model, stock the Mannlicher design from a crotch cut of Pennsylvania black walnut, glass bedded. It was topped with a Weaver V4.5 scope in Redfield Jr. mount. The dot reticle measures nine MOA at 1½x, three MOA at 4½x. QD swivels and sling complete the outfit. With handloads it stays under one and a half inches at 100 yards. A friend kidded me about choosing the 284 cartridge, saying it was no better than the near-ancient 270, which could well be true. But that's like

NED
SMITH

saying a new pro passer is no better than Johnny Unitas. For me, this little 284 is ideal—fast handling, accurate, powerful, and light enough for easy carrying but not so much so that it's muzzle whippy. I've fired it at five whitetails to date. All were instant kills with shoulder or chest shots. It might not be the perfect outfit for Pennsylvania shooting, but it's crowding close.

Thoughts on Shotguns and Such

Upland game and waterfowl require the use of shotguns, and the difference between an ideal quail or grouse gun and the best choice for Canada geese can be as great as that between an M94 carbine and a bull-barreled 300 Magnum, and the reasons for the differences are similar. One class of smoothbore game requires a light, short, fast-handling, open-bored model, while another needs a heavier, long-barreled tightly choked design. And then there are average shotguns for routine bunny bustin' and pheasant popping.

The question of range, gone into earlier with rifles, also has to be considered with shotguns. I prefer shotgun targets at between 15 and 30 yards (and most of Pennsylvania's upland game probably is taken between these ranges). An improved-cylinder barrel throwing one and an eighth ounces or more of shot will do all that's necessary here, though a modified or full choke will take game farther, of course. But 35 to 50 yards (those three-foot yards, that is) is getting out there a piece, regardless of choke or shot size, and beyond 50 yards I start thinking about a rifle. Anyone who needs any suggestions at all from a fella like me would do well to think likewise. I keep reading stuff by guys who blithely claim they routinely drop pheasants, mallards, geese, and what have you, at 60, 70, and even 80 yards, and maybe some of them do it, but they're out of our class and are best regarded as oracles to be pondered from afar rather than emulated.

If you have a given amount of shot, say one and an eighth or one and a quarter ounces, and shove it out of a given choke, it doesn't much matter what gauge you're using, results are going to be identical or so close to it that it would take thousands of test shots to prove a significant difference.

That being the case, it matters not a whit whether you prefer a 20-, 16-, or 12-gauge gun. Nor does the action design make any difference. Side by sides, over and unders, autoloaders, slide actions, even single shot—all will do the job if pointed properly. There's only one vital requirement with a shotgun—that you can hit with it. If you have one that performs well for you, hang onto it.

For generations the full-choke 30-inch 12 gauge was the standard in America, but in recent years, mainly as the result of the many informative articles published by several gunwriters, the virtues of the shorter, more-open barrels have gained recognition. Nowadays, 26-inch improved cylinder or 28-inch modified tubes are common on pumps and autos, while the same length in IC and modified is favored by many double-gun users. In average or thick cover most hunters find this length handier than the older favorite and do better shooting with it. I've gone even shorter with good results. My Browning Sweet 16 auto started life with a 26-inch IC barrel, but years ago I had it shortened to 22 inches, including the Polychoke, and the stock also has been shortened a bit. I have a number of shotguns that are more expensive, and probably all the others are handsomer than this bobtailed boomer, but not one is faster to get into action or more adaptable to my upland needs. My *compadres* call it "Old Ugly," but I call it my "Meat Gun." When I want to bring home some birds, this is the outfit I usually call on. I mention this because I want to emphasize that with an instinctive outfit like a shotgun, fit and feel are important, while looks are secondary and your buddies' comments don't matter at all.

Choice of shot size can be a problem. For upland game such as pheasants and rabbits, it's a tossup between No. 6 and No. 7½. For grouse, quail, and doves, 7½ is probably best. In a double gun, it's a simple matter to load the smaller size in the open barrel for the first shot at flushing game, the larger shot in the tight barrel for extra range if a second shot is needed. You thus have the advantages of both sizes. It's difficult to keep shells in this order in a repeater, since if the first shot gives a kill the chamber then holds the heavier size, which necessitates some juggling. It's simpler to use one size for magazine guns, the choice depending on the day's cover.

Routine upland shooting is fairly easy. Why shouldn't it be when you have a big pattern working for you and game at close range? Yet many of us do not do as well as we'd like. There are two fundamental reasons for this—a gun that fits poorly and lack of practice. Most of us cannot have custom-built guns, but there's no reason we can't alter the factory stock a bit if that will help, and usually it does. Simply getting the right length of pull will eliminate enough of the problems so that we can turn in acceptable performances. If we can swiftly shoulder the gun without having it catch under the shoulder when wearing regular hunting clothes and still have the stock long enough so that the point of the comb protects the nose from the thumb during recoil, it's about right. Next on the agenda is a dozen boxes of shells, to be shot up in conscientious practice on claybirds, pigeons, crows, or doves. This, plus daily handling of the gun—empty—at home, will do far more toward a heavy game bag than buying a Purdey or a Holland & Holland that will never be shot between hunts. It's strange how everyone realizes he has to practice if he wants to be a good golfer or tennis player, say, but refuses to "waste" a box of shells on claybirds, apparently assuming that as a true-blue American descendant of a long line of frontiersmen he just naturally is a good shot. It ain't true. It's the shooting that makes the difference. So burn some up. There's always more.

The same shotgun used by the upland hunter can also serve for close-range waterfowl such as decoyed ducks, which often are taken at under 35 yards. But for average shooting on geese and ducks, the full choke, longer-barreled 12 gauge has advantages. It swings smoother on passing birds and you can get up to one and seven-eighths ounces of shot in the Magnum 12 compared with one and a quarter ounces in the 16 gauge or 3-inch 20. The heavier charges give much denser patterns at long range. No matter what gauge or load is used, though, it's advisable to forget that 70- and 80-yard stuff and concentrate on the shots under 60—preferably ten yards under. Results will be much better.

Handguns

Handguns, as hunting arms, do not begin to have the over-all popularity of shotguns or rifles in the Northeast. Nevertheless, a certain definite percentage of outdoorsmen in this region does use them regularly, often to the exclusion of other arms. And tens of thousands of shooters use them for plinking and target work. We won't go into the last category at all, as paper punching is a specialty outside the scope of this book, and we'll hit only lightly on the other phases.

Since in Pennsylvania, the leading hunting state in the Northeast, autoloading handguns are illegal for hunting, there is little point in discussing them here, though various rimfire 22 autos such as the Colt Woodsman, Ruger, Browning, and High-Standard, all available in several models, are unsurpassed plinkers and pot guns where permitted. All have good triggers and comfortable grips and balance. For this use, a four-inch barrel is handiest, and adjustable sights should be selected or installed. It's just as necessary to zero in properly with a field gun as with a target model.

So far as our hunting goes, two cartridges stand out, the 22 long-rifle rim-fire and the 357 Magnum. The 22 will cleanly handle all incidental small game for the pot—rabbits, grouse, pheasants, what have you—if solidly hit. High-speed hollow points give more dependable kills than solids but are rarely as accurate as the high-grade target stuff. I used to carry a Ruger Single-Six for sitting cottontails and had no trouble concerning killing power with target ammo. The single-action revolvers, incidentally, are fine for such shooting, for if you miss (as I have been known to do), you can let the sixgun dangle from the trigger guard while you get the scattergun into operation without wondering whether the gun's weight on the trigger, or the recoil, will blow another shot out of the handgun.

For big game, the tendency for gun writers nowadays is simply to recommend the 44 Magnum and figure that takes care of it. A few plump for the newer 41 Magnum, but they apparently are becoming scarcer rather than more numerous. There's no doubt the big 44 is, on paper, the deadliest handgun load normally available. But in practice the 44 might not really be the deadliest load after all, the problem being the fact that in order to kill something with a gun you first have to hit it. Most run-of-the-woods handgunners do not hit much of anything with the 44 Magnum. Not that it's inaccurate. Elmer Keith can do wonders with it. So can a few others. But I know I am not Old Iron-Nerves Elmer, and I have a hunch you aren't either. Truth is, the 44 kicks. It kicks a lot in the Ruger single action, and it kicks more in the big Smith. I've shot both models more than a little, and you can take my word for this. Anyone who doesn't believe me should borrow one and shoot a few boxes of full-power loads when no one else is around (so he doesn't have to impress any friends with his toughness!) before buying. Might save some money that way. And then after this little experiment, he can go buy a 357.

Time was, back in the mid-30s, that the 357 Magnum was the hottest handgun heller in existence. People shot it at—and sometimes even killed—moose and mice and assorted other fire-breathing dragons, showing a lack of brain power matched only by those heroes who went grizzly hunting with the 220 Swift, usually from the far side of a canyon—a thoughtful precaution. Despite such shenanigans, the 357 was and is a fine load. (Come to think on it, so is the Swift!) It's noticeably superior to the 38 Special in stopping power and is accurate enough at woods ranges to group in a whitetail's chest if the shooter holds well enough. So placed, it usually kills deer-size game well, if properly designed bullets are used. Fortunately, these are readily available in factory loads, which is more than can be said for the 38 Special. Many good bullets are offered to handloaders too, including jacketed hollow points that will withstand all the velocity the case can deliver and yet perform well both as to penetration and expansion. And unlike that of the 44 Magnum, the recoil of the 357 is not at all objectionable. An ordinary shooter can, with a reasonable amount of practice, attain an acceptable level of proficiency with it. And since properly placed shots will kill well, what more is needed?

In the end, despite all the ballistics tables, gun-writers' opinions, articles, books, arguments, or whatever, the efficiency of any handgun, shotgun, or rifle depends on proper placement of the projectile. If you can put it where it belongs, you'll bring home game. That's something to keep in mind.

Dutch Wambold is a hunter too. Like Bell he has an intense desire to play the game well, but unlike Bell he chooses to do his hunting with a bow. He is a trophy hunter, interested in the outstanding animal. Because his choice of equipment is the bow, his wall hangers are more difficult to come by, yet Dutch's trophy list is impressive and no doubt it will become even more so.

CHAPTER 4

Big Game Bowhunting in the Northeast

H. R. WAMBOLD

Somewhere, sometime, someone said, "If the Indians had done no better with their bows and arrows than today's bowhunters, we would have had a heap of mighty thin Indians!"

Despite the comparatively low hunter success prevalent among our twentieth-century archers, the trend towards hunting big game with the bow and arrow keeps growing each year.

What is the secret behind this ever-increasing interest in a method of hunting that places the individual at such a decided handicap? One word will answer the question—challenge!

Wanting to master a shooting tool that requires countless hours of disciplined practice; making the sport of hunting more of a contest between the man and the animal; enjoying the outdoors at a time when Indian summer has changed the forests into crescendos of blazing color; being able to hunt in a less-crowded season; learning more about the animal being hunted, for most contacts with the animal during the bow-hunting season take place while normal movement patterns and other usual behavior remains unchanged—these are but a few of the many attractions that are causing more and more sportsmen to turn to the longbow when seeking a big-game trophy somewhere in the game lands of North America.

All of us who love to hunt have something within us that wants each stalk to be an exciting one. We want the entire hunt to be a contest leading up to a well-earned climax—the success of the hunter against nearly overwhelming odds.

When one starts bowhunting, an added edge enters the hunt. Patience, diligent scouting before the season, and the added excitement of completing a stalk to within an extremely close distance of the game being hunted, usually give more satisfaction than the actual kill.

If you have never stalked to within a matter of feet of some respectable whitetail buck, been able to control the shakes of a developing case of buck fever, and placed an arrow into the vital area of that trophy after having sweated several minutes of playing cat and mouse at a distance at which you could see the moisture droplets on that whitetail's nose—then you have never known what a great feeling it is to fill out your big-game tag and attach it to the antlers of that first buck taken with a hunting bow and arrow!

Like that old-timer said, "Any deer that will stand still and let one of them archer fellas shoot them splinters at 'im is either a mighty dumb critter or that feller is a damn smart hunter!"

Pennsylvania has become one of the leading states in total sales of hunting licenses. One million are sold annually. And in bowhunting the Keystone State is among the top three, with over 98,000 special archery licenses sold yearly to hopefuls.

The last unofficial survey conducted finds the majority of these archery-license holders lacking any appreciable amount of venison in their freezers. The percentage of archer-hunter success barely exceeds two and a half per cent each year!

What keeps them coming back? The weather, an obvious factor, is quite pleasant during the Pennsylvania archery season, which usually opens on the last Saturday in September and continues through the last day of October. No need to bundle up with the extra set of long drawers to keep the frost off your differential, or to fire up those hand warmers. In fact, during those Indian-summer days the sun is often warm enough for a most relaxing snooze along about the time when most respectable whitetails are enjoying a similar siesta.

Tree hunting is permitted in Pennsylvania, and there are a good number of bowhunters who practice it—one tree, dead center. But taking a stand above the ground really does increase a bowhunter's chance of success. Extremely close shots are commonplace. One bowhunter, a personal friend of mine, shot his buck at a distance of one yard. He almost had to lean backwards in order to make his draw.

The hot spots where the most deer are taken each year are in the northcentral part of the state. Potter County, located along the New York state border, records the largest harvest in the state almost every year. In fact, the combined harvests in Potter for the past three years come to nearly half of the entire state archery harvest for any one of those same years.

Although whitetail bowhunting is fair to good in most parts of the state, if one were to take a pencil and divide the state into three equal parts from east to west, the center portion would be the most productive. In this section the four northern border counties would be Bradford, Tioga, Potter, and McKean. Moving south, one would include Sullivan, Lycoming, Clinton, Cameron, and Elk counties. Clearfield and Centre would be the center-state counties in this whitetail belt, with the heaviest concentration tapering off in Huntingdon County.

In the northeast counties there are many private hunting clubs with large acreages off limits to public hunting. Pike County seems to offer the most open land, and it also has a fair share of the state deer herd.

A cluster of three counties located in the central portion of the eastern third of the state produce consistent harvests

NED
SMITH

each season. They are Schuylkill, Carbon, and Berks. Here the north and south sides and foothills of the Blue Mountain range provide excellent bowhunting.

Pennsylvania whitetail cover varies from hardwood ridges to hemlock and laurel thicket. Hunting terrain may be an apple orchard along the bottoms, open fields of farmland, or a high ridge where the ground acorns and beechnuts are staples of the whitetail's diet.

Although there are too many NO TRESPASS signs around, one can find excellent hunting on the many State Game Land tracts located throughout the Commonwealth. Over one million acres are open to public hunting. In addition, the Farm-Game Management Program sponsored by the Game Commission opens some prime acreage to public hunting.

Much of the posted land can be hunted if one asks permission. This universal courtesy goes a long way in gaining access to some of the finest whitetail country to be found anywhere.

The Pennsylvania whitetail herd crowds the number-one spot in the nation, so don't pass up the smaller patches next to the metropolitan areas. The influx of whitetails into some of the southern-tier counties makes bowhunting action possible within a stone's throw of expressways, turnpikes, and villages. In Pennsylvania, many veteran bowhunters do most of their hunting during the early evening. Shooting hours are from a half hour before sunrise to sunset. The last hour of legal hunting each evening proves the best time to spot that trophy working into some feeding area.

Although the network of highways and interstate expressways provides easy access to practically any hunting area, don't think that a high human population leaves no big country to roam around in. The Pocono Mountains in the northeast, the Broad Mountains slightly south, and the Blue Mountain range, extending through the center from the east to the Allegheny Mountains of the west, plus the ranges of scenic mountains of the northcentral region will provide you with miles to stalk without leaving the timber.

The topography of Pennsylvania to a great extent accounts

for the large whitetail herd. Ample range and feed combined with a fine management program have placed it next to the top-ranking whitetail states. Pennsylvania has a rather simple set of bowhunting regulations.

No bow that is held, drawn, or released by mechanical means may be used. No crossbows may be used. Poison or explosive heads are illegal. Only a single-shaft arrow may be used. No firearms of any type may be carried while hunting during the archery seasons.

Road hunting is restricted in that when alighting from any vehicle being driven on, or stopped along, a public highway or road open to public travel, one may not shoot at any game animal or bird if one is within 25 yards of the traveled portion of such road or highway.

Any type of shafting or hunting heads may be used. There is no minimum bow weight, and it is not required that a hunting bow cast an arrow for any prescribed distance. During hunting hours it is permissible to carry a strung or braced bow in a vehicle.

All species of large and small game may be hunted with bow and arrow during the regular firearms seasons. During other than the special archery seasons, a special archery license is not required for bowhunting.

Black bear are not open during the special archery seasons Bowhunters who wish to try for a blackie must hunt during the regular firearms season.

There are several other forms of bowhunting that provide additional recreation. About the most appealing is the spring gobbler season.

Limited to hunting by calling only, with electronic calls barred, this puts the hunting right in the bowhunter's class. The thrill of calling a gobbler within bow range is attracting more and more bowhunters each year.

No artificial blinds may be used, and that regulation excludes the use of piled brush, tree limbs, etc. Only natural cover, such as windfalls, depressions, banks, rocks, or brush piles, may be employed. The bowhunter may use a tree stand, providing it has no artificial screening of any type.

Shooting hours are from a half hour before sunrise to 10 a.m. each morning. All hunters must be out of the woods by 11 a.m.

Both resident and nonresident hunting license tags must be worn on the middle of the hunter's back, and they must have two game tags attached. In the upper right-hand corner is the tag that must be attached to a deer within an hour after it is killed and before the carcass is moved from the site of the kill. The lower tag is for wild turkey and is used in the same manner as that for deer.

If black bear is your bowhunting bag, the neighboring states of New York and Maine have excellent bear hunting to offer. Not only does the big country of the New York Adirondacks have an abundant supply of blackies, but it also harbors some mighty respectable whitetail bucks.

Although Maine is known as the 200-pound-buck state, many bowhunters think that it has a much greater attraction—its exceptional spring black-bear hunting, which has been highly successful for archers. Bait hunting is the most common method, although the use of dogs is permitted, and several guides run their hunts in that manner. Special spring bear-archery licenses for nonresidents cost $10. Numerous camps that cater to bowhunters offer room and board at reasonable rates. Guiding services are included. Best areas are inland in the northern part of the state.

Black bear are also abundant in the Canadian provinces of New Brunswick, northern Quebec, and Newfoundland. There are many pulpwood lumbering camps about in the upper regions of Quebec. Bears frequent the garbage dumps of these camps.

Getting back to whitetails, the southern tier counties of the Catskill Mountains of New York state are ideal bowhunting country. The hot spot continues to be Sullivan County and the country around Narrowsburg.

Westchester County, within commuting distance of New York City, should also be mentioned. Most of the real estate here consists of estates. This is the place where you can expect to see respectable bucks wandering around on someone's front lawn. Very little big country is found in Westchester, and on most of it you need permission to hunt. The many small patches are thick brushy swales spotted with heavy thickets. Here is ideal cover for some smart buck to really make a fool out of a bowhunter. Should you decide to try Westchester, you might find yourself taking home a deer plus an autograph or two, for many celebrities live there. You might wander into Jack Paar's back yard while tracking some wily buck, or step in Merv Griffin's tulip bed just when that deer is getting within range. Some of the best areas to try are Goldens Bridge and Sommers School. If you chance upon an irate homeowner who has just had her garden patch worked over by a whitetail, chances are you may get permission to sneak around the back yard in the hopes of eliminating the problem.

Upstate New York's Adirondack Mountain country is big and rugged. This is the home of some mighty fine whitetail bucks. One should not try hunting this country without the services of a guide.

The New England states all have a limited supply of whitetails. Vermont seems the most likely spot to have a fair degree of success. Maine has ample whitetails. It is not uncommon to walk into a Maine town and find everything closed on the opening day of deer season. The small sign in the window of the local barbershop or grocery store will read, "Closed today—went hunting!"

If you consider Maine for a whitetail, remember that the state has more timber land than open country. The deer have ample food in the countless hardwood ridges and swales. You must cover ground when hunting there, for the deer move little to get their fill. Most Maine woods have countless lumbering trails forming networks of squares for easy and quiet stalking. Apple orchards seem the best bet for catching the movement of whitetails into feeding areas, but the chances of finding a good buck are best in the big woods.

New Brunswick and Nova Scotia are two of the northeastern Canadian provinces that offer good whitetail opportunities for the bowhunter. Up until the past few years most stateside hunters were riflemen. The trick seems to be finding a Canadian guide who is able to work with a bowhunter. It will take a few years until a sufficient number of these men are experienced in this new form of hunting sport.

Eastern bowhunters are fortunate in that in the northeastern provinces of Quebec, Labrador, and Newfoundland they have close access to the habitat of two of the four species of North American caribou. Here one can hunt the newly named Quebec-Labrador caribou and the Woodland caribou.

Newfoundland has experienced one of the greatest booms in nonresident bowhunters of any province of our neighbor nation. The level terrain of most parts of the island are ideal bowhunting country. The sound game management of the caribou herds provides chances for excellent bowhunter success.

Caribou permits are issued on a first-come-first-served basis. The annual allotted number is determined by field surveys, and the areas are divided in total permits according to current populations.

Central areas seem most productive. One flies into such spots by bush plane, and camps are usually pitched along the shore of one of the numerous lakes that speckle the topography. Newfoundlanders prefer to call them ponds, and their maps are marked accordingly.

Hunting is done on foot, and a lot of country must be covered to find the good stags. Newfoundland is rain country with countless bogs to slosh through. Gear should include a lightweight rain suit and rubber boots.

The best time to plan a caribou bowhunt is during the last two weeks of September and the first two weeks of October. This is the time of the rut, when the stags are rounding up their harems and are on the prod. It is not unusual to find as many as 50 caribou being herded around by several record-size stags as each tries to steal the greater number for his own.

Large stands of fir and spruce form islands of timber around the many bogs, making ideal cover for a stalk within bow range.

Here, without any doubt, is one of the finest trophy animals any bowhunter can ever hope to hunt. If you are patient and don't try to crack the first stag you see, chances are that with a bit of ground cruising you will happen upon a record buster.

Newfoundland also offers some good moose bowhunting to make a hunt especially attractive. One may even find a good bull right in the same area where caribou will be hunted. Slightly smaller than their mainland cousins of Quebec and Ontario, Labrador moose still sometimes have spreads of up to 50 inches.

A bowhunter after the Quebec-Labrador species, now officially named as the fourth North American caribou, must make an extensive investigation to line up an outfitter capable of handling a bowhunt. For the most part, Labrador has been the home of the sport fisherman, and bowhunting is something new to most guides. If you are lucky enough to find the right man, here is the opportunity to combine some outstanding fishing with a bowhunt. Access to this country is by plane, and canoe travel along the many streams can get you right up to Hudson Bay.

Sound advice when planning any bowhunt away from home is to start planning in plenty of time, and write to references requested from your prospective guide or outfitter. Find out what the other hunters thought of accommodations, etc. Base your decisions on such comments, rather than on some flowery advertisement spiked with all kinds of guarantees.

At this point I'd like to make a few remarks on proper tackle, without getting into technical jargon, for countless good articles and books have been written on the subject.

Bow weights should never exceed the physical ability of the man who uses the weapon. Substitute accuracy at close range for heavy bow weights. Caribou *can* be taken with the same bow weights that are used for whitetails. Moose require a bit more weight in order to drive the shaft deep into the large chest area. For deer, a 40-pound bow is sufficient for normal-range shots. For caribou and moose, an extra ten pounds will do the job.

Concentrate on ample practice with hunting tackle. Be sure hunting heads are ultrasharp. Condition yourself so that the physical exertion does not hamper you when that big chance comes.

Remember how your hunting arrow kills—by profuse hemorrhage. No matter how big a trophy animal is, properly placed arrows in the vital chest area will down it in surprisingly short distances. This holds true of everything from elephants to field mice!

As to how to hunt whitetails with the longbow, one might sum that up as follows. (1) Whitetails leave plenty of signs to inform the bowhunter regarding their movement, feeding grounds, and avenues of escape. Take a bit of your hunting time to look such signs over caref lly. It just might pay off. (2) If it's possible, scout the intended hunting areas beforehand and find out where the deer are, and where a good buck may be at home. (3) Pass up the questionable shots, know your personal limitations, and shoot accordingly. This puts far more venison on the table than any other method.

As most sportsmen who have done any amount of bowhunting have learned, playing the game according to the book results in the most enjoyable hunts. Observe game regulations wherever you bowhunt.

You are one of the American sportsmen who enjoy our great outdoors and the countless hours of recreation there for the taking. Respect the environment that makes it all possible. Leave it as you found it, and the next bowhunter will drink the same clean water, camp in the same unlittered glade, and breathe deeply of the same cool, crisp, wood-scented air.

PART TWO
Upland Game Hunting

I think I invented the titles "King" and "Crown Prince" of turkey hunting to fit Roger Latham and Lou Stevenson. Latham was a biologist with the Pennsylvania Game Commission when that agency decided to bring the wild turkey back to the eastern hunter. He later became chief of the Commission's Research Division and was there when turkey hunting in the East reached fulfillment. He is the author of the standard The Wild Turkey *and is currently outdoor editor for the* Pittsburgh Press. *It is an honor to have him included in these pages.*

CHAPTER 5

The Wild Turkey

ROGER LATHAM

At the time the Pilgrims set foot on a now-famous rock in the New World, the wild turkey was one of the most abundant game birds in the forests.

This big, beautiful bronze bird was to become a staple food item for the settlers because it was readily found and easily shot, even with the crude firearms of the day.

This bird of early America was neither particularly wild, nor even very astute. A flock would allow the blunderbuss-carrying Pilgrim father to close within easy range and hardly fly even after he had shot. Early writings indicate that the turkey was little different in those days from the ruffed grouse now in the wilder parts of Canada.

Stories are told about how the good hunter could drop a whole flock of turkeys out of a tree by shooting the bottom one first and then continuing upward until the last one was dead. How things have changed since then!

When white settlers first came to North America the forests were practically unbroken over almost all of the eastern United States. In those mature forests of pine hemlock, chestnut, oak, beech, and hickory, the turkey found plenty of food and protection. It had no serious natural enemies, even though Indians, panthers, bobcats and lynxes, foxes and wolves, eagles and horned owls took a constant toll. Its range in that day covered the entire eastern seaboard from Florida to southern Maine and southern Ontario.

The white European with his civilization and industrial drive broke the peaceful "balance of nature" that had existed for centuries between bird, predator, and primitive man. At first, his little clearings in the forest created few problems for the turkey. But as the population grew and spread westward from the coast, the amount of cleared land increased greatly. Eventually millions of acres of mature forests were felled, the stumps pulled, and the land converted to agriculture. Thus, far more than half of the total turkey habitat in the eastern United States was destroyed completely.

With the growth of the cities and the beginning of the industrial age in America there came a tremendous demand for lumber, paper, tanbark, and other wood products. Eventually this demand resulted in the cutting of almost every last mature stick of timber in the entire region. This came very close to sending the eastern wild turkey to the same sad ending that had come to the woodland elk, the woodland buffalo, the heathhen, the passenger pigeon, the wolf, and the panther.

The wild turkey is a bird that thrives in mature forests, forests that produce great quantities of acorns, beechnuts, and similar fruits and seeds. When the timber was cut, the young sprout growth bore very few of these staples, simply because the saplings were not old enough or large enough. Those young brush forests were far better habitat for the ruffed grouse.

The situation was aggravated by innumerable forest fires. These kept tremendous acreages in this youthful stage far beyond the normal length of time.

NED
SMITH

Fortunately for the wild turkey, there were a few spots that escaped the farmer and the lumberman. The deep swamps and the precipitous mountainsides were not places where a man could grow crops or cut timber economically. So, a few thousand acres escaped the axe and the plow in this vast territory. In these widely scattered spots a remnant of the former great flocks managed to survive.

By the early 1900s, the bird was gone from all of New England, New York, New Jersey, and the lake states west of Pennsylvania. A few managed to hang on in southcentral Pennsylvania and along the high Appalachian ridges through West Virginia, Virginia, the Carolinas, and Georgia. Others survived in the swamps and coastal lowlands of the Carolinas, Georgia, Florida, and Alabama.

Through a period of almost 50 years, all those concerned about this bird virtually "held their breath." But gradually the crisis reached a peak and then slowly dissipated. Forests began to mature sufficiently to begin to produce enough food for year-round prosperity for the turkey. And the forests began to open up somewhat, so that this big bird felt more comfortable. The wild turkey is ill at ease, and in danger, when it is so closely confined that it cannot make maximum use of its unexcelled eyesight for protection.

About the time these second-growth forests were beginning to mature, people began to develop a concern for the country's natural resources. Forest-fire protection was one way in which this concern was expressed, and this contributed much to the return of the wild turkey.

Also, the profession of wildlife management came into its own during this period (about 1930). For the first time there were dedicated men who were determined to come to the aid of the wild turkey and other beleaguered wildlife.

The effort to restore the turkey followed the typical evolutionary pattern of game management. The very first move was to provide protection through closed seasons or greatly restricted seasons and bag limits. Concurrent with this control of hunting pressure, most state game agencies conducted campaigns against predators. Bobcats, foxes, owls, hawks, skunks, opossums, raccoons, and other meat-eaters were trapped, shot, and sometimes even poisoned by the tens of thousands. It was not then widely realized that such "predator control" would eventually result in a further deterioration of woodland environments.

Since these two management measures were begun shortly after the forests had been first lumbered, they had little chance to do more than maintain the remnant flocks that had survived. Significant expansion of the range or of the numbers of birds was not possible under the circumstances.

The third restoration and protection effort was to establish large refuge areas where the precious remaining birds would presumably be secure from harm from human hunters. These preserves probably had some limited value, but they were largely abandoned as the forests matured and the range of the turkey expanded.

The next step was the artificial propagation of wild turkeys and their release in the rapidly maturing forests. This appeared for a while to be the most effective management measure of all. Some of these releases seemed to produce almost immediate results in places far removed from occupied range. But one thing was clearly evident from the very first. The half-wild stock first used on the game farms was next to worthless. When they were released, they failed to go wild and would almost invariably establish a "home" in some farmyard.

Recognizing the deficiencies of this stock, the wildlife specialists of the Pennsylvania Game Commission decided on a scheme to induce the necessary wildness. They constructed pens in the forest where fine wild gobblers were known to live. In these pens, along about March, they placed game-farm hens that had been carefully selected for color, size and conformation. The wild gobblers responded beautifully and mated with the hens. The eggs which were laid were returned to the game farm and hatched.

The following year, the best hens from this mating were selected and placed in the breeding pens in the forest. This procedure was continued year after year, until finally the stock on the Pennsylvania wild-turkey farm was almost a pure wild strain.

These new birds lived up to expectations. Upon release, they went wild and stayed wild. No longer did they frequent the farms or walk the back roads where poachers could pick them off one at a time.

This stock was distributed widely, not only in the Keystone State but in other eastern states as well. These birds also formed a nucleus for propagation in other states.

As the years passed, however, biologists discovered that the wildness bred out of these birds in as little as two generations if no new wild blood was added annually. So to a large extent the propagation program was a failure. In its place, game managers adopted a trap-and-transfer program which produced amazing results in many places. These wild-trapped turkeys established themselves quickly and permanently where repeated releases of game-farm birds had failed.

The spread of the range in Pennsylvania was spectacular. The widespread introduction of the superwild game-farm stock, the trap-and-transfer program, and the natural spread of the native birds resulted in the occupancy of almost all suitable forest areas in about 20 years. Then as the timber matured in other areas the native birds continued to push into it.

These turkeys did not stop at the Pennsylvania border. Suddenly, New York had flocks spilling over into the state from the northcentral counties of Pennsylvania. This encouraged the wildlife managers there to establish their own restoration program, and for several years the Empire State has had both a fall and a spring season.

West Virginia and Virginia have had equivalent success, at first using good game-farm stock and then switching to the trap-and-transfer system in more recent years.

Maryland was able to build up substantial numbers in the western counties and is now attempting to provide hunting on the Eastern Shore through the stocking of wild-trapped birds from the southern states.

Almost all of the New England states are making some progress, although some, such as Connecticut and Massachusetts, do not have many large blocks of relatively unbroken forests for the turkey.

The northern parts of Vermont, New Hampshire, and Maine may be too far north, but all three states are experimenting with releases in their more southern regions. There appears to be considerable doubt that the turkey can establish and maintain itself in the northern spruce-cedar forests of these three states. Moose and wild turkeys may never mix!

It seems proper to mention that the current phase of wild-turkey management relates to habitat improvement. Good forestry practices keep a high proportion of the timber in a state sufficiently mature to support turkeys. Today, the cutting is done in blocks or strips, and there is no longer any widespread elimination of turkey habitat such as occurred over the turn of the century.

Habitat improvement may include the creation of grassy openings where hens may bring their poults for insects and green food. Plantings of grains or chufa may be made where natural food needs to be supplemented. Pipelines and power lines through the forests may also be planted with a permanent pasture mixture and kept limed and fertilized to provide clover and other valuable greens for the big birds.

The state game farm producing turkeys for stocking has all but disappeared, and the few that remain are expected to be phased out in the near future. Predator control appears to be unnecessary for the prosperity of the turkey, and this management measure has been abandoned for the most part. Also, few wild-turkey refuges still exist, simply because this wary bird appears to be able to survive without this protective aid.

Game managers are optimistic about the future of the turkey and the future of the turkey hunter in the eastern states. The range is constantly being expanded, more lenient seasons are being established, and hunting is getting better all the time.

A turkey caller and a little skill in its use are all a man needs for an introduction to one of the most challenging and rewarding forms of hunting in the world!

Lou Stevenson grew up with the wild turkey too, but unlike Roger Latham he was watching with the hunter's eye rather than the biologist's. Lou admits he hunts things other than turkeys, but he can't remember why. Turkeys are an obsession with him, and when he's not hunting them himself he's showing others how to do it. The list of dignitaries that Lou has successfully guided on turkey hunts would impress any name-dropper. If you have the slightest interest in the bird that Ben Franklin thought should be our national symbol, this chapter is for you.

CHAPTER 6

Wild Turkey Hunting

LOUIS W. STEVENSON

"It ain't the gobbler, it's the gobble." That's the way one old-timer expresses his opinion of turkey hunting. To him and to many thousands of other turkey hunters, the thrilling call of a wild turkey gobbler answering a call is satisfaction enough for a day's hunt, even though they don't see a bird.

If a dedicated hunter is asked whether he got a turkey, he may reply, with a great deal of pride, "No, but I had a couple of gobblers answer my call."

Turkey hunters, the ones who talk turkey all day and dream turkey all night, are peculiar people. They think nothing of getting out of bed in the wee hours of the morning, grabbing a few bites of breakfast if time permits, then heading for the hills and their favorite hunting grounds. Arriving at a predetermined spot, they will stumble through pitch-black woods, climb a mountain, wade a stream, if necessary just to be at a certain place before the first rays of dawn appear. Shivering in the cool hours before sunrise, they will sit patiently, not expecting to see a turkey but with ears keyed to every sound in order that they will not miss the call of a gobbler in the spring or of a lost turkey in the fall. A grouse, a squirrel, a fox, or any other animal or bird can safely walk in front of them. Under no circumstances would they shoot and thus disturb any turkeys in the vicinity.

The subject of turkey hunting in the northeastern United States can be broken down into three broad categories: Where, When, and How.

If a turkey hunt is to be successful, three conditions must be met—there must be birds to hunt, the hunter must be aware of the time when his hunting is most likely to produce a turkey, and he must know the fundamentals of hunting.

Although the wild turkey at one time could be found in all the eastern states, today the hunting of wild turkeys is no longer legal in New England, New Jersey, and Delaware. Nearly all of the states where turkey hunting is permitted have both a fall and a spring gobbler season.

In each turkey-hunting state there are certain areas that are noted for populations of turkeys. In New York this is in the southern area adjacent to Pennsylvania. In Pennsylvania the heavy population is in the northcentral part of the state, although turkeys are found in nearly every county. In Maryland it is in the western area.

If the hunter does not know the turkey areas in any particular state, he would be wise to consult the Conservation Department of the state involved and heed their advice on good turkey-hunting country.

Once turkey country is located, the hunter's next task is to pin-point the location of turkeys within that area. This can sometimes be accomplished by talking to local game wardens, farmers, or sporting-goods dealers. Don't neglect the small-town barber. He knows almost everything.

Don't ask for the names of well-known turkey hunters and then expect to get them to tell you where to hunt. Chances are they would direct you to anyplace except where they know there are turkeys. The exact location of flocks of turkeys or individual gobblers can be found to be as highly classified as the names and addresses of special agents in the C.I.A. It will be up to the hunter to dig out this information for himself. Knowing that he is in turkey country, he should get out early in the morning, before daylight, and listen for turkeys. He may hear a turkey gobble or the cracking of limbs as a big flock of birds leaves the roost and the subsequent clatter of the entire flock.

Traveling the back roads, he may be lucky enough to see a flock feeding in a grain field after harvest. He may see a flock feeding on grasshoppers on an open hillside in the fall. Occasionally he will see a flock crossing a road just ahead of his car.

He should get into the woods, travel along old roads and trails, and check the hardwood ridges, looking for signs of turkeys. There may be tracks of turkeys and perhaps spots where they have scratched away the leaves in search of insects, seeds, and other types of food. Scratching signs should be carefully studied to be sure they haven't been made by squirrels searching for nuts or by deer pawing the ground. In the latter case, deer tracks will very likely be found on the bare ground.

There may be turkey droppings and often turkey feathers. The number of such signs is a good indication of the number of birds about and whether they are regular visitors to that part of the woods.

Never fail to check the edges of oats, corn, buckwheat, and millet fields, particularly where they are bordered by heavy woods. These grains are favorite turkey foods. Turkeys have been known to visit such spots, day after day, as long as any grain remains.

Try to locate the nearest stream, spring, or pond that may be a watering spot close to the feeding area. Food and water near each other may mean that the turkeys are staying close in the area.

Look for ridges where there are acorns, beechnuts, wild cherries. Examine places where wild grapes are plentiful. Such spots are natural feeding areas and should be carefully studied for turkey signs.

In the fall there are quite often early light snowfalls. This is an ideal time to locate turkeys and find out where they are feeding and where they are ranging.

Once you have located a turkey flock or a gobbler, get away from the area as quickly and as quietly as possible. A flock of turkeys may feed, water, and roost in a small area and will remain there if not disturbed. If you hear a gobbler call in the early morning hours, don't try to attract him with a turkey call. Save that thrill for opening day. And last and far from least, keep your information to yourself. In turkey hunting it's every man for himself.

In these searches for turkeys, the hunter should carefully study the terrain and note special landmarks and hiding places, so that once he has decided where to hunt, he will be able to get back there, even in darkness. If a bird happens to call from a ridge a mile away, he should be able to get to that vicinity by the shortest and quickest route. A topographical map often proves helpful.

We have been talking about turkey hunting, not hunting for turkeys. There is a vast difference. The so-called road

hunter hunts for turkeys, but he is by no means a turkey hunter. He travels the back roads where side hills can be scanned with binoculars, and when he spots a turkey, he gets out of his car and with a scope-sighted varmint rifle blows the bird to pieces. He could have as much sport by driving to the nearest turkey farm, buying a bird, and shooting it at any range he chooses. We assume that the reader now understands something of *where* to find turkeys. We will next consider *when* to hunt.

When to hunt can mean either the fall season when all turkeys are legal game or the so-called spring gobbler season, when only bearded turkeys can be taken.

Bearded turkeys are mentioned because that is one of the positive means of identifying a gobbler. However, since some hen turkeys, particularly the older hens, may also have beards, game laws usually specify "bearded turkeys." It has been estimated that as many as one out of five older turkey hens will be bearded.

A turkey hunter must make up his mind that sleep is a secondary consideration during turkey season. This is particularly true during spring gobbler season, when the gobblers call and answer a call most readily immediately after dawn.

In the fall, when a flock leaves the roost every bird seems to want to tell the world that day has begun, and for several minutes the woods ring with their calling.

If a flock has been scattered and has not reassembled before going to roost, on reaching the ground the next morning the birds will continue to call until all have joined the flock. This is probably the easiest time to call a turkey into range.

A flock that has been scattered during the day will try to get back together before going to roost. It often pays to get to the place where they were scattered and try calling them in the late afternoon. Because of their habit of calling before flying onto a roost, early evening is often a good time to locate turkeys. If it is a still day, the sound of a flock of turkeys flying into a roosting tree can often be heard for a considerable distance.

Windy days and rainy days are the worst times for turkey

hunters. The woods are too noisy for the hunter to hear a turkey unless the bird is very close, and the range within which a bird can hear a call is also restricted. And if the hunter's call is made of wood, like the common box call, it may get wet or damp, which could result in a false call, and that might chase every self-respecting turkey into the next county.

If you are hunting on either a wet day or an exceptionally cold day, carry your call inside your shirt. Body heat will keep the call dry and the wood warm, so there will be the right vibration and sound when a call is attempted. Place a rubber band around your call, if it is a box call, to keep it from rattling while you move through the woods.

Where and when to turkey hunt are actually the easy parts of wild-turkey hunting. The subject of how to hunt covers a very wide field and a great deal of detail.

Guns should be considered first, since the type of firearm used will to a very great extent determine the success of whatever kind of turkey hunting a hunter chooses to follow. A hunter who hunts from a good hiding place, whether it be a clump of laurel, a downed tree, or in states where they are allowed, a blind, can use either rifle or shotgun.

When stalking birds in heavy cover, he will be better off with a shotgun. For hunting the ridges, a rifle is probably best. What rifle or shotgun should be used? Ask a dozen hunters and you might get a dozen different answers.

Although many turkeys are killed with 22 rim-fire rifles, cartridges of this type are not considered adequate for wild turkeys. It has been estimated that as many as half the birds shot with a 22 long rifle escape and are lost to the hunter and become easy predator prey.

There are two cartridges in the rim-fire class that do deserve mention—the 22 Winchester Rim-fire Magnum and the very new Remington 5 mm rim-fire. These little fellows, with a 40-grain bullet in the Winchester 22 Magnum and a 38-grain hollow point in the 5 mm Remington, are very accurate and effective in the hands of a good hunter who can place his shots.

The Remington 5 mm is still too new for its effectiveness as a turkey killer to be established. However, the 38-grain hollow point, with its muzzle velocity of 2100 fps, is still moving at 1605 fps at 100 yards. That should provide plenty of punch to down a turkey.

High-velocity varmint rifles with factory ammunition will kill a turkey at ranges of up to 300 yards, but usually the hunter ends up with a beautiful bird blown to pieces. Even with full-jacketed bullets these cartridges are too powerful for turkeys unless loaded down to around 2000 fps.

The 32-20 and 25-20 are excellent cartridges for turkeys, as is the 22 Hornet with a full-jacketed bullet. Full-jacketed 30-06 or 308 150-grain bullets will do a good job if handloaded down to around 2200 fps. Above that they do too much damage.

If a hunter has a pet scope-sighted rifle that delivers too big a wallop for turkeys, it would be well for him to find some full-jacketed bullets, have them handloaded to a reduced velocity, and then try them out for accuracy. And try them also for damage on woodchucks and crows before using them for turkey.

In some states the use of rifles for turkey hunting is restricted by law. In Pennsylvania, rifles are banned completely during the spring season.

What shotgun and what size shot should be used?

Probably a long-barreled ten-gauge Magnum would be the most effective shotgun, but we are not interested in carrying cannons. A 12-gauge Magnum with a full-choke 30-inch barrel, either double or automatic, loaded with a three-inch Magnum load 4s or 6s would probably kill any turkey if given a decent shot up to, and in many cases exceeding, 50 yards.

The most popular turkey shotgun is the standard 12-gauge in double or semiautomatic, with full-choked 28- or 30-inch barrels using two-and-three-quarter-inch Magnum shells in either 4s or 6s with 4s being the first choice. Magnum loads are available for the 16 gauge and the 20 gauge, and they are quite effective, but because of the smaller gauge they carry a smaller load of shot and consequently throw more-open patterns. There is a greater chance of a miss at extreme ranges. Turkeys have been killed with the 28 gauge and the 410, but they definitely are not recommended.

Some hunters think that 7½ shot is the proper size, and though it is true that 7½s give a dense pattern, they are not worth a hoot if you happen to get a shot at the north end of a turkey that is headed south. It is not always possible to get a head shot, and if the bird is flying high, the hunter needs something with punch enough to bring it down.

Number 2s and BBs and buckshot kill turkeys very dead when they hit, but the open patterns resulting from the small number of pellets in a load leaves too much to be desired.

Over-and-under rifle-and-shotgun combinations in many calibers and gauges are used by numerous hunters. Under certain conditions they are fine, under other conditions—no good.

Consider the hunter who shoots a flying turkey and knocks it down only to have it take off again, as happens in many cases. Lacking that second shot from a shotgun, the hunter usually loses the turkey. And what about the hunter who hits a turkey at 100 yards with the rifle, well beyond shotgun range, and only wounds the bird? He will probably lose the bird if it recovers and manages to get away before he can get into shotgun range.

So much for turkey guns. Now for clothing. The choice is wide. Many hunters wear camouflage clothing, including netting that can be drawn down to cover the hunter's face. Other hunters choose neutral colors of brown, khaki, or green that will blend into the landscape. Some hunters who are more cautious in their hunting prefer red or even orange hunting clothes. A few companies make red camouflage clothing.

Regardless of the clothing worn, it is essential that the hunter should be hidden from view as much as possible and should remain motionless. Camouflage and other inconspicuous clothing will not disclose a slight movement as readily as bright-colored clothing, hence the chance of a turkey seeing a camouflaged hunter is not as great. Remember that a turkey has very keen eyesight and can detect a strange movement at a considerable distance.

A turkey hunter's greatest satisfaction is to call a turkey into shooting range and to thus be able to bag a nice bird. To do so he must have a turkey call and understand how and when to use it.

There are many types of turkey calls available. All of them can be used successfully if handled properly. Some are easy to use, others have certain limitations.

The mouth-operated calls that have a rubber diaphragm are placed in the mouth and operated by causing the diaphragm to vibrate. Hunters skilled in the use of this type of call can imitate the yelp and call of a young turkey or hen nearly to perfection. And the hunter's hands are always free and ready should a bird suddenly appear.

Then there is the wing-bone call, made from the hollow wing-bone of a turkey. This type of call has had many modifications, including the use of hollow bamboo cane and combinations of bone and cane and sometimes even pipe stems. Calls of this type are widely used particularly in the Deep South.

Probably the easiest type of call to use is the common box call consisting of a wooden box with a movable lid. This call is known as the Gibson call, or Missouri call, and with it you can imitate every call of a turkey, including a gobble.

There are variations of the box call in which a piece of slate or of cedar is drawn across a lip of the box to produce the yelp of a turkey.

Turkey calls are available in nearly every sporting-goods store. The hunter should select the one he feels will be easiest for him to use and then practice with it until he has mastered every call necessary for a successful hunt. A visit to a neighboring turkey farm will be very helpful. The hunter should try to match the calls of the domestic turkeys. Their calls are practically the same as those of their wild cousins.

Now that the turkey hunter knows where to hunt, when to hunt, and is properly equipped, how will he go about getting a turkey?

If he should be successful in scattering a flock of birds or knows where a flock has been scattered not long before, he should get to that place as quickly as possible. Concealing himself as best he can or with his back to a big stump or tree, he should sound three or five low yelps with his call. Often one such series of calls is all that is necessary to bring in a turkey. However, if a reply is received from a considerable distance, he might well call again to determine whether the bird is headed in his direction.

Once it has been established that a turkey is headed for the hunter, by far the best procedure is to put away the call and be ready with the gun. Continued calling increases the risk of a false note that may alarm the bird. To use any call other than a mouth-operated one, the hunter must move his hands, and that may be detected by a bird and ruin all chance of a shot.

Spring hunting for gobblers involves a different technique. The hunter should be in the woods before daylight. As the first rays of light appear, various birds will start to sing. The shrill call of a pileated woodpecker, the hoot of an owl, the call of a crow may result in a gobbler giving forth with a throaty gobble. If no such call is heard, the hunter should give a hen call consisting of not more than three yelps given quite rapidly. If a gobble is heard in reply, wait. Don't call again for several minutes. Often a gobbler will call and call again without the hunter touching his call. As long as the sound indicates that the turkey is headed for him, the hunter should be very cautious with his calling.

If the gobbler comes fairly close but stays out of range and gives no indication that he will come closer, three very soft yelps will often bring him strutting into view.

Some hunters have heard gobblers calling and then heard hen turkeys yelping nearby. Under such circumstances an old gobbler is quite interested in his duties at home and will be very difficult to call away from that vicinity. The only course left for the hunter is a very careful stalk, although a successful stalk of a wise old gobbler is a rare occurrence.

If a hunter has been calling from a certain hideout and receiving no reply, he should never move quickly if he leaves for another location. He should look around very carefully. Many birds have been known to come into easy shooting range without ever making a sound. A turkey may be on the right, the left, or behind a hunter, and a quick move means he will immediately disappear.

One rule in turkey calling is not to call too often. In spite of the perfection of many types of turkey calls and the ability of hunters to use them, there is always the chance that something will occur to cause a false note, and away goes the turkey.

It is not necessary to be able to imitate, or be familiar with, every call of a turkey in order to be a successful turkey hunter. Full knowledge comes only after years of experience, and even then a wary old bird will make a sound that defies description and which sounds like anything but a turkey. By the same token a turkey may answer a sound that has no resemblance whatsoever to the call of a real turkey.

There is another thing that a turkey hunter should always remember. If he is successful in downing a bird, he should get to it as quickly as possible. A turkey's wings may give the hunter quite a beating if he grabs a wounded bird, but failure to do so has allowed many of them to recover from the initial shock and get away before the hunter knows that the bird is not as seriously wounded as first appeared.

There are other methods of turkey hunting that the hunter should know. One is stalking or hunting the ridges. In turkey country the hunter will walk slowly along the top of a ridge, pausing occasionally to listen for the sound of a flock of feeding turkeys. He will carefully approach the rim of the ridge and peer over the side for the sight of a bird or flock of birds. For this type of hunting, the rifle is usually the best firearm to use.

Some hunters travel slowly through turkey country, stopping every few minutes and giving a few yelps with their caller. If they get a reply, they will get under cover as quickly as possible and endeavor to call the bird into range. Occasionally a whole flock will come in answer to a call, but this is quite exceptional.

If there is a tracking snow, a hunter can quickly determine

whether there are turkeys in the area and, if any, in which direction they are moving. If they are feeding and moving slowly, he can often make a wide circle, get ahead of them, and wait for them to come to him. He also has the chance to follow the birds at a rapid pace, hoping to scatter them and then be able to call one into range.

There are several pieces of equipment that are important to the turkey hunter. One is a compass, and the hunter should know how to use it. If he happens to be following a turkey, he may be giving little attention to the distance or direction in which he is traveling. A compass, in such circumstances, can save a long hike or possibly a night in the woods.

Another important item is a pillow or something comfortable to sit on. To sit for several hours on cold, damp ground leaves a lot to be desired. Since the hunter must remain motionless, he must be comfortable in order to do so. One of the best seats is the so-called Hotseat available in most sporting-goods stores.

One insignificant but important piece of equipment is a short length of strong cord. A twenty-pound gobbler becomes a real burden if a hunter has to tote it for a mile or more, possibly over some steep ridges. A stick thrust through the bird's tied-together legs eases the burden considerably.

Although the wild turkey is rated as a very wise bird, and the expert turkey hunter is supposedly wise in the ways of the turkey, sometimes both outsmart themselves. The expert comes home empty-handed, and the 12-year-old boy next door proudly walks home with a big gobbler that he had spotted sitting in a tree while out squirrel hunting with his single-shot 22.

There remain two important requisites to make a turkey hunt complete—having a trophy to show and to remind you of a successful hunt and having your bird served as the main course of a delicious dinner.

An easy way to make an attractive trophy is to arrange your turkey's tail feathers in the shape of a fan on a thin piece of plyboard. The feathers should be dry plucked and glued to the board, the large feathers first, the others placed on top according to length. After securing the feathers in a fan shape, cover the base of the fan with a piece of birch bark, and, if your bird was a nice gobbler, fasten the beard to the birch bark.

To serve the bird, clean and prepare it as you would your Thanksgiving turkey. If you don't feel up to the job, there are many small butcher shops where the job can be done. Stuff the bird with your favorite stuffing and roast it slowly in a moderate oven.

Wrapping the bird in aluminum foil helps to keep the meat moist while it is roasting.

The writer has eaten many wild turkeys. All were excellent except for one old 20-pound gobbler. We roasted him all day, and he was still tough. Even the gravy tasted tough. A session in a pressure cooker tenderized him, but he was a tough old bird to bag and tough, to a degree, right up until the time when he was completely consumed.

It would be difficult to name a major outdoor publication that Ned Smith has not contributed to in the past ten years. His speciality, of course, is the wildlife portraits that have placed him among the world's finest bird and animal painters. He is equally skilled with camera and typewriter. Flyrod and shotgun are also used with artistry by this practicing outdoorsman. A walk in the woods with Ned Smith is a memorable experience.

CHAPTER 7

Hunting Grouse Without a Dog

NED SMITH

No one who has known the experience will deny that hunting ruffed grouse behind a capable grouse dog is one of life's consummate pleasures. Unfortunately, it is a treat accorded to relatively few of us. In the first place, good grouse dogs are hard to find. To handle Old Ruff with any degree of success, a dog needs a great nose, more bird sense than most dogs possess, and a meticulous manner that is better inherited than taught. Few dogs are so endowed. Then, too, not everyone is in a situation that makes keeping a dog feasible or even possible. The city dweller or apartment tenant usually has no place for a sporting dog, and many an avid hunter simply hasn't got the price of a good grouse dog.

What are the alternatives? Well, you might turn to some other game. Or you might use old Bowser on grouse, incompetent though he is. He'll probably find any birds you knock down, though if he's like most nongrouse dogs I've tried to hunt grouse with, he'll see to it that you don't get a shot in the first place.

The only remaining course is the one taken by most gunners. They hunt without a dog. Ignore the guys who say it's not practical or it's not fun. It's both. If it isn't, my friends and I have been wasting a lot of time over the years. But easy it's not. Dogless grouse hunting calls for a whale of a lot of walking, ususally through dense cover and over bad footing. It entails a working knowledge of grouse habits that would fill a book. And it requires reasonably good gun handling, too, if you hope to put a molar to one of those luscious birds once in a while.

Ruffed grouse are found in forested areas over most of southern Canada and the northern United States and south in the eastern mountains to Georgia, so it's not hard to find a place to hunt. The trick is to find a huntable population of birds, for they are not abundant everywhere within their range.

Old grouse hunters recognize good cover at a glance, but beginners must learn. Start by crossing off the open forests of big trees. Grouse like to have food and concealment handy at all times, and these are best provided by overgrown slashings, windfalls draped with grapevines, mixtures of scrub oak and pines, "wild" apple trees on abandoned mountain farms, close-to-the-ground evergreens near food plants, mountain brooks winding through thick hemlocks and laurel, and woodland edges of almost any sort. Food is harder to spot than cover, but the list is almost endless. Such favorites as wild grapes, beechnuts, acorns, greenbrier berries, hawthorn fruits, witch-hazel blossoms, wintergreen berries, and various ferns, green leaves, and berries attract the birds during the early part of the fall hunting season. As winter approaches, buds—aspen, birch, blueberry, apple, and so on—are more heavily relied on.

But good coverts are like tracks—you can't eat 'em. So the next step is to find the birds themselves. Without a dog's sense of smell to lead the hunter to the precise location of the game, the dogless gunner must cover the ground thoroughly, hoping to come close enough to any nearby bird

NED
SMITH

to flush it from its hiding place. The usual pattern is to wander from one promising spot to another, paying close attention to fallen logs, tangles of greenbrier or wild grape, laurel thickets, etc., and that's where the mileage accumulates.

Sometimes, especially on damp, overcast days, the birds hold tight, and it is necessary to practically kick them out. Many are passed by unknowingly. A trick often employed in these conditions is to stop suddenly and stand quietly with gun at ready. For some reason, nearby grouse cannot tolerate the inexplicable silence. Unnerved, they burst from cover, giving the waiting hunter an easier-than-usual shot.

Just as often, however, the birds are wild, flushing before the gunner can come within range. Many factors cause wildness, but very dry conditions, blustery winds, hunting pressure, and lack of cover are the most common. Stop-and-go hunting, like slow hunting, will only make them wilder. The solution, if there is one, is to keep walking at a moderate, steady pace; any break in the cadence of your footsteps will make the birds nervous. Walk as quietly as you can without actually sneaking. Being able to hear that first rustle of leaves as the grouse comes out of its hiding place will give you a tremendous advantage in terms of range, speed of flight, and the amount of cover the bird can put between the two of you.

No game bird knows better how to take advantage of cover than a ruffed grouse. For instance, hearing a hunter approaching, he usually hides on the far side of the handiest and best windfall, vine tangle, or other hideout. When the hunter gets too close he simply roars off, leaving the baffled fellow staring at an obstacle through which he can neither see nor shoot.

Any grouse hunter knows you can't completely eliminate this problem, and it wouldn't be grouse hunting if you could, but you can certainly tip the odds in your favor. The thing to do is to prevent him from using that screen. Always approach a likely hiding place from higher ground, if possible, in hopes of seeing over it if a grouse flushes. If this isn't possible, walk by the suspected hideout within easy shotgun range. Move as briskly as you can. If the bird thinks you'll go on by, he'll frequently stay put, at least until you pass his hiding place. Then, being more or less out in the open, he might fly, and will almost surely do so if you pause for a moment. It's because of such occurrences that grouse are said to be "smart" enough to flush behind the hunter's back. The *really* smart ones either don't flush at all or they scramble back through the windfall or tangle before taking wing on the far side.

One of Old Ruff's almost legendary tricks is to put a tree trunk between himself and the man with the gun. If the tree is some distance from you, there's little you can do about it; step to one side and the grouse will usually alter his course to remain out of sight. Certain ornithologists have pooh-poohed the idea that this maneuver is intentional, but they obviously are not grouse hunters. Anyone who has chased Old Ruff for a season or two has seen ample proof that this tactic is deliberate, and it's no more mysterious than the same bird's evasive dodge into thick brush ahead of a swooping hawk.

There's little excuse for letting a nearby tree get in your way if you plan your approach properly. When nearing a birdy-looking spot simply give large trees a wide berth. Even small ones can interfere with the swing of your gun, so if you must squeeze by them, do so in a way that will keep your barrels in the clear. Pass to the right of the tree if you shoot right-handed; to the left if you are left-handed. When crossing logs or tangles try to keep moving. If you must stop, do it before you get into an impossible position for a shot, and be ready for the flush that might result. Carry your gun at ready when you can. Try never to be off balance; you can't get off a shot while clutching a tree for support. If these seem like picayune details, remember that they account for most of the missed opportunities in grouse hunting. You'll not have to concentrate on them for long; the more you hunt the more these practices will become second nature to you, and you will then understand why so many birds escape unscathed from hunters who continue to make these "trivial" mistakes.

One of the grouse's most attractive habits is its normal reluctance to fly far when flushed. By following its line of flight, you can often put it up again, and when grouse are scarce you'll appreciate the extra opportunities you can get from one bird. Remember this the next time you miss one with both barrels; forget about reloading for long enough to watch where it goes. Even the line of flight of wild-flushing birds that get up out of sight can often be determined by the sound of their take-off and the slap of their wings striking branches along the way. If they can be found, these birds will usually hold better on subsequent flushes, and it's sometimes possible to jump the same bird three or four times or more.

Grouse hunting is at its best on pleasant, sunny days. The birds are usually easier to find, and they behave better, neither flushing too wild nor sticking unreasonably tight. Usually, that is.

If you're crazy enough to be hunting grouse on a rainy or foggy day (I've done it when I was too young to know better), you might think they have suddenly become extinct. The fact is, they are probably roosting in pines or hemlocks near their usual haunts, oftentimes high above the ground. Keep a sharp eye peeled as you approach such trees, as grouse have the sneaky habit of slipping out the far side without the roar that usually accompanies their take-off. Many times you won't know they've gone, and even catching them in the act doesn't necessarily mean meat in the pot. Few shots are tougher than that offered by a grouse that drops like a bomb from the top of a tall white pine and slants down the mountainside with the throttle wide open.

On such days, as well as when the ground is covered with snow, grouse frequently land in evergreen trees after being flushed. These birds present the same problems as those that have spent the night there—flushing wild, silently, or both.

Hunting grouse with one or more companions poses its own problems, chief of which is keeping track of each other. Few things are so irritating, if not downright risky, as a hunting companion whose garb blends into the surroundings. The minute you can't hear his footsteps you are out of touch. If he's the kind who barges on ahead, lags behind, or wanders erratically, you won't know where he'll turn up unless you communicate at frequent intervals by hollering at the top of your lungs. A fluorescent cap or vest goes a long way toward solving this problem, and when the birds start boiling out you know where your buddy is and he knows where you are.

Even though you are conspicuously dressed, it's still a good idea to stay abreast of each other under most conditions, primarily for reasons of safety but also to avoid becoming separated. "Staying abreast" in this sense doesn't mean marching straight ahead in military precision. Some fellows hunt that way, but they walk by a lot of grouse. Be sure your buddies understand that you intend poking into all the grousey-looking spots along the way. Then they'll understand the zigzagging that ensues and wait up when necessary. You, of course, will do the same for them.

A pair of hunters can move tight-sitting birds very effectively by *not* keeping abreast of each other. The technique could be described as the leapfrog method, I guess. One man advances a short distance, then stops. The other, walking parallel to the course of the first, passes him, then waits while the first man advances beyond him. This maneuver is repeated as they progress through the covert. It's a rare bird that can keep his cool through all those intermittent pauses; most of them make a break for it. Of course, when you use this method, you and your partner must stay in sight of each other at all times, or you'll soon be completely goofed up.

When you are hunting without a dog to find your cripples or recover birds that have dropped out of sight, remember that it is important that game be brought down as close to the gun as possible. I'm sure that the number of grouse that fly away mortally wounded is small compared with the number that are dropped too far from the gun to be found. If there's a sermon to be found in this chapter it is this—pass up the long shots if you don't have a dog to do the finding for you.

When it comes to actually hitting a grouse, many fellows are licked from the start. The roaring take-off of a ruffed grouse flashing through vines and foliage as though they didn't exist is surely one of the most demoralizing experiences a tyro hunter can undergo. While his mind is yelling

"Shoot! Shoot!" his arms are turning to stone. Later, still too shaken to recall exactly what took place, he can only conclude that grouse are the fastest things in feathers. Didn't that one fly clean out of sight before the gun reached his shoulder? If he has read a few colorful magazine articles calling grouse "winged bullets" or "brown bombshells" he's got an even higher psychological hurdle to clear. I'm convinced that this quick-draw obsession has ruined many a potentially good grouse shot. It has certainly caused me to habitually shoot too hurriedly.

Don't fall into that trap. Avoid haste while you are learning to shoot. Mount your gun smoothly, ease off the shot as you swing, and follow through. Don't hesitate or dawdle, but don't do it faster than you can do it well. As you become more proficient you can speed up the tempo. Eventually you'll become fast, smooth, and a deadlier shot than most.

Grouse are not hard to kill; two or three number 8s are usually all it takes. But a dead grouse can be almost impossible to see once it hits the ground. Even when lying in plain view its protectively colored plumage matches the dead leaves perfectly. Should your bird drop out of sight, lose no time in getting to where it fell. You'll often spot it as its wings flutter their last or, if it's wingtipped, while it is still too dazed to find a hiding place. If no bird is immediately apparent I usually hang my blaze-orange cap on a twig where I think the grouse should be and begin the search, taking into consideration the angle of flight and the momentum which often carries it beyond the estimated point of impact. Watching for the gray or white plumage of the bird's underside is a good gimmick, that being the only part that doesn't match the leafy ground.

Wing-tipped grouse seldom run far, although an occasional individual is recovered thirty or forty yards from where it struck the ground. Usually they crawl under nearby logs or sticks, into crevices between rocks, or in holes beneath stumps. Scrape the leaves away from such places and you may find your bird hiding there. Keep a sharp eye peeled for lost feathers; they frequently mark the bird's path or sometimes its hideout.

Some dog owners become quite outraged at the mere mention of hunting without a canine helper, usually snarling something about "cripples rotting in the woods." I have hunted over some excellent grouse dogs, most of them good retrievers, and no one appreciates their bird-recovering ability more than I. But in thirty years of grouse hunting, most of it without a dog, I have lost only a half-dozen known cripples. Anyone who cares enough to pass up long shots, carefully mark the spot of each downed bird, and spend the necessary time looking for cripples can do the same. On two occasions I have spent more than an hour looking for a winged bird before I found it. Usually the bird is turned up in a minute or less.

Grouse hunting calls for surprisingly little in the way of equipment. The shotgun is all-important, and even though there's no "best" gun for everyone there are certain characteristics to consider when you make your choice. Balance is an indefinable but essential quality. Gauge is a matter of personal choice, but because grouse take little killing and close shots are the rule, I can see no need to handicap oneself with a heavy gun. My pet grouse gun is a 20-gauge L. C. Smith double that weighs six and a quarter pounds with a smallish beavertail fore-end. The 26-inch barrels are bored improved cylinder and modified. "Elsie" has proven ample, to put it mildly, and even when hunting with dogs, when fairly long shots were justified, I've never felt undergunned.

Stock fit is most important. Because grouse guns are mounted quickly and often from awkward positions, excess length should be avoided. For the same reason, many grouse hunters dislike recoil pads. They tend to hang up on clothing.

Many hunters use shot that is too coarse. No. 7½s or, better still, No. 8s are best and will produce much denser patterns than the 6s many hunters carry.

Next to the gun itself, footgear is probably the grouse hunter's most important piece of equipment. Light moccasin-construction shoes with eight-to-ten-inch tops and rawcord or composition soles are very satisfactory except on steep slopes with dry leaves underfoot. Better in this respect are lug soles or soft, deeply cut ripple soles. Where wet conditions are encountered rubber-bottoms or lightweight ankle-fit rubber boots are comfortable and dry.

Gamebags are wonderful for warm-weather hunting. They offer great freedom of movement, pockets for shells and lunch, and a bloodproof game pocket in case you hit one of the critters. In colder weather or for thrashing through scrub oak and the like a conventional upland hunting coat will provide more protection and warmth. Whatever the garment, I find that leaving it open and flapping invites the butt plate to catch in it at the crucial moment; fastening one button keeps it neatly out of the way.

Gloves are sometimes necessary in cold weather. Woolen gloves are warm but are impossibly slippery unless made with thin leather-faced gripping surfaces. Thin buckskin gloves are usually enough protection, and they are least bulky of all. For colder weather try those with thermal lining.

When it comes to headgear many hunters like a water-repellent hat. I happen to prefer a cap because the visor forms a useful sunshade and catches fewer branches than the encircling brim of a hat. Mine is fluorescent blaze orange, which tells my companions where I am and announces my presence to anyone else who wanders into the same covert. Lacking such a cap, one would be wise to wear a fluorescent orange vest. Some models consist of little more than straps, permitting lots of freedom but still presenting a lot of fluorescent surface.

For field dressing your birds you'll need some kind of knife. A pocketknife is certainly adequate, but I've come to prefer a very small sheath knife only because it doesn't mess up my pockets and is easier to clean and keep in order.

Few game birds are tastier than the ruffed grouse, but it is unfortunate that not many reach the table realizing their full potential. Improper field care is where the trouble usually begins, but it's simple to do it correctly. A slit between the vent and the rear end of the breastbone (the latter can be felt) will permit removal of the entrails. Just as essential is the removal of the crop, the membranous sac situated where the bird's neck meets the breast. Slit the skin and remove it, along with the recently eaten food it usually contains. Depending upon its nature, this food often sours very quickly if left in the bird and is responsible for the acid taste frequently detected in grouse. Removing the crop has the added advantage of revealing what a particular bird has been eating, thus furnishing a clue to the whereabouts of other grouse. Many hunters keep a list of crop contents, noting the volume and incidence of each kind of food. Over the years such a list will reveal food preferences in the hunter's region and help him to find more birds.

If the bird is still warm when you arrive home, it can be dry plucked, but once the feathers have set that is out of the question. To loosen set feathers, you must dip the bird in very hot water, ruffling the feathers with a stick, especially on the sides of the breast beneath the wings, to be sure the hot water gets through to the skin. Pull out the flight feathers first, then the body feathers. Many hunters merely skin their birds and oftentimes keep only the breast. However, the skin imparts a measure of flavor and fat to the bird and should be retained when convenient.

The most common gripe about grouse is the dryness of their flesh. Several of my hunting companions held this low opinion of their favorite game bird, and for years they gave me all their grouse. Then in a loosejawed moment I bragged about my wife's special grouse recipe that has the juice running out of the corners of your mouth, and I must have sounded convincing. Jack's wife got the recipe from my wife, and that was the last grouse I could wheedle out of Jack. The secret is to add liquid of some sort, in this case the unlikely combination of vinegar, cooking oil, and sherry, with mushrooms and seasoning. One of my very favorite recipes calls for stuffing the bird's body cavity with a mixture of chopped cabbage, chopped sweet onion, and egg. It sounds terrible, but the onion and cabbage somehow beat one another into submission, the grouse is saturated with the juice that cooks out of the stuffing, and the whole mess is absolutely delectable.

Just plain roasting is one of the least satisfactory ways to prepare a grouse; the poor bird simply hasn't enough fat for that. If you like the flavor of grouse, unchanged and undisguised by any full-flavored liquids, sauces, or condiments, try broiling. It is simplicity itself, and the result is all grouse. Here's how it is done:

Remove the second joints of the wings and the drumsticks (they shrink to rubbery nothingness). Then open the bird down the back with poultry shears. Remove the neck and cut out a strip down the back so as to get rid of those razor-edged bones that will quickly burn if allowed to remain. Spread the carcass open, flop it on its back, and crush the body flat with the heel of the hand on its keelbone.

Now place it breast down on the broiler rack about four inches from the broiler. Baste frequently with butter and broil until the thin bone edges are beginning to char. Then turn it breast up, brush with butter and basting often, broil until it threatens to scorch. When the high spots are acquiring a nice brown tinge it is done. In our electric stove the whole operation takes a half hour.

That's all there is to it. The meat is saturated with natural juices, and you can cut it with a fork. The butter provides all the seasoning necessary.

To be sure of having tender meat I always reserve birds of the year (those hatched the previous spring) for broiling. These can be distinguished from adults by the sharply pointed tips of the outer primaries (wing feathers). The outermost primaries of older birds have rounded tips.

There are innumerable ways to prepare a grouse that will produce equally succulent and tasty eating. It all depends upon how you like them. But if worse comes to worst, and your wife simply cannot prepare a grouse so it's fit to eat, don't fret and don't give up grouse hunting. Just come by my house on your way home, and I'll get rid of those dry old birds for you. But please draw them first.

Woodcock on the Side

The big-eyed, long-billed timberdoodle, more properly called woodcock, is the favorite game bird of a small but dedicated group of gunners in the eastern United States and Canada. These chaps don't need advice about where to find woodcock or how to hunt them. They already own dogs that dig timberdoodles, they know all the best coverts within a day's drive of their homes, and they think nothing of driving to hunting grounds in another state or another country when the fever's upon them.

But many other hunters, if they see woodcock at all, come on them while hunting other game, usually ruffed grouse. These are the men who could derive additional sport from the woodcock shooting that is often available near, or sometimes overlapping, their favorite grouse haunts.

Woodcock are not always with us. The birds we find in hunting season might be local birds that have nested in the area during the preceding spring, flight birds that have stopped over on their southward migration, or both. Depending on the weather, the flights begin in earnest about mid-October and end about mid-November. After that, most of the birds have gone. This in itself is a clue to finding more of these birds. Do more of your early-season hunting in places where you might find woodcock.

And where might you find woodcock? That's a tough question, though not because woodcock cover is so very scarce or especially hard to recognize, but rather because so little of it is actually used by this pernickety little bird. Alder thickets along a stream or in damp bottomlands are by far the most widely acceptable haunts, especially if they're grassy. Wild crab apple or hawthorn thickets attract woodcock, and so do patches of young birch or aspen saplings on hillsides above bottomlands, and apple trees on abandoned hill-country farms. Moist soil is essential; without it the earthworms on which woodcock feed are absent or out of reach.

If any of these cover types occur near your grouse coverts, why not comb them a few times during the early part of the season? You might be surprised. Don't cross off a spot after one fruitless visit. The very next night a flight of timberdoodles might drop in on their way to Louisiana. Keep your eye open for woodcock sign. Their droppings, in the form of "whitewash," and the borings made by their long bills in probing the soft earth for food are proof that the spot attracts woodcock and should be revisited on subsequent hunts.

Woodcock usually sit very tight, and a dog is a great help in finding them. However, once you've jumped a bird, you'll seldom have trouble finding him at least once more, for they usually make extremely short flights. Oftentimes you can see almost exactly where they've landed. The first woodcock I ever shot at came zigzagging to earth almost in plain sight, obviously wounded. Almost immediately, however, the frightening thought crossed my mind that the season on woodcock might have ended. It *was* rather late in the small-game season. Almost afraid to look, I laid down my gun, took off my coat to withdraw the hunting schedule from the license holder, and checked the woodcock season dates. Praise be, they were still in season! I was stepping forward to pick up the bird, which I was sure lay a few yards from me, when the plucky fellow rose on twittering wings and flew away. I wasn't able to find him again, but I learned several things from that experience—one, that woodcock don't usually fly very far; another, that they often zigzag when dropping back to the ground (my bird was no more wounded than I). I also learned a number of things about remembering seasons and bag limits, and about keeping one's gun in one's hand.

Woodcock shouldn't be hard to hit, but they frequently are. Their flight is oftentimes slow and mothlike, at other times fast and direct. Sometimes they dart from side to side like a frightened snipe. At all times they are unpredictable and their speed deceptive, especially to those who hunt them infrequently. If they have a common pattern of flight, it is to rise almost vertically to clear the brush and then level off and get away quickly, but where the brush is not so thick it's anybody's guess what they'll do.

No special equipment is required for woodcock hunting. Your grouse gun will do admirably for these smaller birds, and so will your No. 8 shot. No. 9s are as good or better.

A surprising number of hunters don't recognize a woodcock when they see one. On the ground (where it is seldom seen) it is a plump, dumpy bird with practically no neck and very little tail. The bill is extremely long, the eyes large and dark. The undersides are a rather uniform orange-buff, the upper parts beautifully streaked, barred, and mottled with browns, grays, black, white, and buff. It usually flushes almost underfoot, the wings making an audible twittering sound with each beat.

The snipe is the only bird that is likely to be confused with it, but snipe are slimmer and more boldly streaked from bill to tail. They usually utter a rasping *scaip* when flushed and are nearly always found in open, brush-free situations. Soggy meadows and pastures are favored haunts.

By the time they are plucked and drawn, woodcock are mighty small objects, but an epicure might remind you that so are most diamonds. A few people don't care for their rich, dark meat, but most folks agree that a woodcock is something special—on the table or sideslipping through the alders. And as long as you've tried him only one way, you'll be missing half the fun.

Our other grouser offers an alternate approach to the problems posed by this finest of upland game. Jim Hayes is a no-nonsense hunter who makes an excellent case for some of his unorthodox techniques. Since Jim shoots a lot of grouse, his ideas must be listened to with care. He also happens to be one of the few people I have ever known who hunt these birds with a double-barrel muzzleloader. This involves cocking the hammer or hammers each time a grouse flushes. (I have a hard enough time getting off a shot with a modern shotgun when one of these unpredictable creatures decides to fly.) This section is essential reading for any grouse hunter.

CHAPTER 8

Grouse Hunting and Various Grousey Matters

JIM HAYES

Grouse Coverts

Anyone who has spent much time in woodland hunting has probably noticed that ruffed grouse are more frequently found in some places than in others. A walk along a ridge overgrown in wild grape may nearly always produce flushes. A nearby overgrown apple orchard may be another favored location. Yet other areas, though they appear equally "grousey," rarely or never contain birds.

The presence of grouse indicates that you are probably within a covert—a definable tract of mixed covers that will support birds throughout the year. To grouse, this is home.

Continuous and unbroken though it may appear, a grouse range is actually made up of a series of individual coverts, some of them fairly isolated, others overlapping. A covert may vary in size from ten to more than 100 acres. However, those areas frequented by the birds at all seasons of the year are much smaller. Within a 60-acre covert, their wanderings may be mostly confined to five or ten acres. When the heavy snows come they restrict their range even more.

By hunting a covert regularly and taking field trips through it out of season, you can quite easily learn to determine where the birds will be at various seasons of the year and under different weather conditions. By noting the location of flushes and watching where the birds land, you can get a fairly good idea of the size and perimeter of the covert.

Several years ago we made a photo blow-up of part of a topographic map and began marking Xs to pinpoint the location of flushes. We determined that 65 per cent of our flushes were within a quarter-mile radius of a certain knoll, which we then presumed to be the geographical center of the covert. Thirty per cent of our flushes were within the second quarter mile from this point, and only five per cent beyond a half mile.

The size and shape of a grouse covert is determined by the arrangement of the cover blocks, and also by the total area used by the birds on a year-round basis. Some coverts are oval or circular, but more often they are irregular, square, or in rectangular strips.

Assuming that you are in good grouse country, where do you look for coverts? The answer is, almost anywhere you find a concentration of preferred cover types, properly arranged. Most coverts are spread over different types of terrain—ridges, benches, knolls, slopes, and so on. Experienced grouse hunters develop an almost instinctive ability to size up covert locations. All it takes is a practiced eye.

There are several things to look for. First, and most obviously, look for birds. Look also for winter shelters, edgings, and a variety of interspersed cover types. Ideally, a covert should offer the widest possible assortment of preferred foods and cover types.

The size, arrangement, and proximity of mixed covers—slashings, overgrown fields, brushy edgings, mature woodlots, and scattered thickets—are also important. Areas of cover that are close together permit the birds to move easily from place to place. This makes for a close-knit covert. If shelter areas are far removed from feeding areas, with little protective cover between, the birds are more exposed to predators as they move from one place to another. Predator losses over the course of a year can make the difference between an ideal covert and a marginal one.

Most of our grouse hunting is done in overgrown rolling hill country and on abandoned farms with stands of pine, slashings, mature and intermediate woodlots, and scattered patches of wild grape. Any brushy country that is broken here and there with hardwoods, old pastures and orchards, and stands of pine, alder, willow and thorn apple is worth investigating. Such country, we find, is more dependable than mountainous and heavily forested terrain where deer may have browsed out much of the understory.

Grouse are rarely found too far from an edge or opening. Look for them in woodlots or slashings within 50 yards of the edge of a field. Walk the old logging roads that wind through the woods. Land that has been timbered or burned over and then grown up in second growth can be excellent for grouse. The presence of tall pines with little understory beneath, or a number of tall dead trees, can diminish the value of a covert. From such vantage points, hawks and horned owls watch over the surrounding countryside and launch attacks on unwary grouse, squirrels, and rabbits.

Within their coverts, grouse find the two things they require for survival—food and shelter. Since grouse requirements change from season to season, the habitat should offer the elements to meet those changing needs—for drumming, nesting, dusting, spring and summer feeding, and winter shelter.

Drumming logs and suitable nesting areas are essential. Both are usually found in mature woodlots. Drumming logs are fallen trees, frequently good-sized ones. Most grouse nests are located at the base of stumps or trees, again usually large trees, within 50 yards of an edge, opening, or old logging road.

Grouse spend most of their lives within their coverts, although their home covert need not necessarily be the same one they were born in. There appears to be an interchange of young birds between coverts, but once they settle in a home territory, they rarely leave. A cock grouse, for example, will usually spend his lifetime within a half mile of his drumming log.

When grouse are scarce, they tend to stay well within the covert, not far from what might be defined as its geographic center. When they're more plentiful, they tend to be more scattered. If you flush a bird on the outer perimeter of a covert, the spot may be worth revisiting. It's likely that something attracted the bird to that place, and it may draw other grouse in the future.

Of course not all grouse coverts measure up to the standards of ideal habitat. But the extent to which they do so classifies them as ideal, average, or marginal, and is closely related to their carrying capacity. In theory, grouse require five to eight acres of covert for each bird. Thus, 50 acres of suitable habitat should be capable of supporting between six and ten birds. During a peak year this may rise to more than a dozen grouse. When the population reaches the saturation point—about one bird for each four acres of covert—some of the birds will move out. Then you find them in surrounding coverts, some of which may be marginal, or scattered over the countryside. It seems doubtful that many of these grouse survive to the nesting season.

Of course, the quality of a covert is not the entire answer to productive grouse hunting. Although closely knit, variegated coverts have a consistently greater carrying capacity than marginal coverts, much depends on nesting and brooding success, which is related to weather. That's true of coverts generally, but especially so of smaller coverts, which may rely on the nesting success of a single hen.

Because of the uncertain productivity of any one covert, it is a good idea to locate a dozen or so coverts scattered some miles apart. When grouse are down to a remnant population in a particular covert, you can rest it for the season and hunt others. Unless the birds are in a general decline, some of your coverts should almost always support huntable populations. When grouse are exceptionally plentiful in a covert, a heavier-than-usual hunting kill may help offset the much sharper cutback of a natural decline.

The best time to scout for grouse coverts is during late winter when the heavy snow is on the ground. A large tract of woodland with little or no understory, and surrounded by open countryside, will support few grouse. An area showing pine plantations or hemlocks, wild-grape thickets, and wood lots strewn with vine tangles and blow-downs, is a much better bet.

After you have reconnoitered a series of coverts in one locale, repeat the process in another area 50 to 100 miles away. By putting distance between clusters of coverts, you guard against the possibility of an areawide decline and enhance your chances of having a successful gunning season.

The ability to locate and define grouse coverts, and then to study and hunt them as defined areas, has many rewards. For one thing, it enables you to assess the rise and fall of the population cycle. You get an idea of what is an average number of birds in a given area. From that you can determine years of scarcity and abundance.

Knowing the layout of a covert and the location of the different kinds of cover in it enables you to concentrate your hunting efforts on those places where you have the best chances of finding grouse. That's important in states where the season extends from early autumn through mid- or late winter.

There is little doubt that grouse hunting within defined coverts provides the most consistent action. You do not have to spend most of your hunting day looking for birds. You move from one productive place to the next. Considering how little of a man's lifetime can be devoted to grouse hunting, that's mighty important.

Grouse Hunting with Bird Dogs

Grouse hunting with a bird dog you've trained yourself is like dry-fly fishing for trout. There may be other ways to do it, but many sportsmen would agree that this is the best. It offers the best of two worlds. It involves the pursuit of a grand sport *and* the creative satisfaction of seeing months of patient training pay off in the performance of your dog. And most hunters would agree that grouse hunting with almost any kind of dog is better than hunting with none. A dog will find birds that might otherwise be lost.

Many of us have had the experience of getting off a shot at a grouse just as it pulled a wingover and veered out of sight. Was it a hit or a miss? We walk to the spot where the grouse might have fallen, spend several minutes looking around, and continue on our hunt. We assume that we missed. But did we? A wing-clipped grouse will run when it hits. It will take advantage of the least bit of cover. Its plumage makes it difficult to locate among weeds and leaves.

A dog will pick up the scent and track down cripples that a hunter would never find. Beagles are excellent for rooting out tight-sitting grouse and locating cripples. Almost any kind of dog will recover three times as many downed grouse as a hunter unaided by a dog. Bird dogs were made to order for grouse, and grouse are made to order for pointing dogs.

Many of our opinions on owning, training, and caring for bird dogs may sound like heresy to professional breeders and trainers. But there's a big gap between theory and practice, so let's take a down-to-earth approach.

If you want to pursue perfection in a bird dog, consider the highly trained show dog or field-trial dog. These dogs are lovely to behold; they may possess lengthy pedigrees, blue ribbons, and gold cups; they respond to command almost mechanically. But show dogs don't always make great field dogs, and a field-trial champion may not be worth its salt as a gun dog.

Many hunters are not interested in feeding and caring for a dog on a year-round basis strictly for the sake of hunting with it perhaps a dozen times a year. Many men want a combination house dog, family pet, and hunting buddy. According to theory, this is all wrong. Yet it can work out quite well.

Many bird dogs make excellent pets. This is somewhat more true of the long-haired breeds, such as English and Irish setters and Brittany spaniels, and less so of English pointers and German shorthairs, although there are frequent exceptions. A bird dog can be a gentle playmate for the children, living in as a member of the family. This need not detract from a dog's hunting capabilities.

The hunter has his choice of many breeds. He may prefer a small, docile, close-working Brittany. He may select an English, Irish, or Gordon setter. Perhaps a German shorthair, English pointer, or Weimaraner may catch his fancy. Any of these breeds can make wonderful grouse dogs. Some of them, depending on disposition, can make combination gun dogs and family pets. Any of them, improperly trained, or not trained at all, can drive a man stark, staring, raving mad.

The name of the game is control. This begins when the dog is a pup. Discipline is essential. The dog must be taught to stop, sit, come, walk at heel, and respond to a whistle or hand signals. Once the basic commands have been mastered, you may want to teach the dog to retrieve. There's no prettier sight than a bird dog trotting back to its master with a grouse in its mouth. But a dog that will pin down a fallen bird and stay with it until its master arrives on the scene (if it doesn't chew the bird up) accomplishes the same purpose.

Once a pup is under control, serious field training begins. Is the pup "birdy"? Does it take an interest in grasshoppers and butterflies? Has it made its first awkward point at a sparrow or field mouse? These are all good signs of hunting instinct, although instinct should not be of major concern if the dog comes from hunting stock.

A young dog should get field exposure to as many birds as possible. If you are so fortunate as to have a herd of grouse in a wood lot behind your house, so much the better. But most owners are content to have their pups flushing, and perhaps occasionally pointing, meadowlarks, robins, sparrows, pheasants, grasshoppers, and anything with wings.

Of course, you should get the dog started on grouse as early as possible. Preseason field trips enable you to scout for future hunting areas as well as train your dog. This is also an ideal time to teach your dog to work close to you. Keep it under control at all times. If necessary, keep it leashed to a long length of clothesline. Discipline the dog when it shows the first signs of running wild.

Probably the most common problem with bird dogs is keeping them under control in the field. Many of them tend to range too far. In grouse hunting, the dog should never range over 150 to 200 yards from the hunter. But many of them do, and the trait is difficult to break.

There are no simple answers. You can tie tire chains to the dog's collar to act as a drag. You can use a log drag. You can use a short chain connected to a block of wood. This will bump the dog's knees or flap around and bump its head when it begins running wildly. An electronic shocking collar can be effective. If all else fails, forget the whole deal and be content that your dog is hunting with you at least part of the time. Even a part-time bird dog is better than none.

Depending on how close you insist on achieving perfection in your dog, it's practical to take a tolerant view of at least a few faults. A dog that breaks point and bolts after flushing grouse may cost you an occasional shot in order to avoid hitting the dog. But the same dog will find and point grouse that you might otherwise never see.

It's not uncommon for a bird dog to jump a deer or rabbit and give sight chase for a hundred yards or so. If the dog returns promptly and settles down to hunting birds again, many hunters are willing to overlook such transgressions. But if the dog spends a great deal of its time running deer, or if it takes off for ten minutes or longer on a rabbit chase, it's worthless as a hunter. So is a dog that persists in chasing cattle or chewing up birds. When a bird dog becomes worthless as a hunting companion, much of its purpose in life ceases to exist.

There's a large element of risk involved in buying a bird dog, no matter what kind of pedigree comes with it. Bird dogs tend to be somewhat high strung. Compared with hounds, many of them seem up tight and perhaps even neurotic to varying degrees. Some of them are inclined to be gunshy. If this fault persists, you may find yourself spending more time hunting for your dog than hunting for grouse.

There are no sure cures for gunshyness. A method that is sometimes effective is to take the dog to a skeet range, tie it to the car, and leave it for several hours. Over a period of time the dog may become accustomed to gunshots. An even better way is to board the dog for a month or more in the fruit country where pneumatic air blasts are used to frighten away the birds. If this doesn't work, the dog is incurable.

Buying and training a bird dog is somewhat like getting married. A man is never certain of what he's getting into until it's too late. The experience can be highly satisfying or exasperating to an extreme. Selection of a good dog has a lot to do with it, but the final result depends to a great extent on what you put into the relationship. It requires a total commitment. All in all, there is no greater sense of satisfaction than in hunting over a dog you've trained yourself. Those of us who own bird dogs know what we're talking about. Those who never have, won't and perhaps never will.

Grouse Populations—Boom and Bust

Ruffed grouse populations are said to be cyclic. The birds may be plentiful for several seasons, then decline to a remnant population, and later increase again and appear to stabilize for several years at a moderate number before becoming plentiful again. In some years in certain coverts they may be abundant beyond a hunter's wildest dreams. You might flush 100 grouse in a day's hunt. Three or four years later you might be hard pressed to put out a half dozen grouse from the same covert.

Although we don't know all the reasons why grouse populations fluctuate as they do, we think we know some of the contributory factors. Grouse populations appear to vary from season to season. One might attempt to discern a trend over a period of years. Such a pattern might seem to prevail within specific coverts or in much broader areas or even over an entire state or several states. Whatever the trend, there appear to be definite and frequent exceptions to it.

As we write this, ruffed grouse are scarce in much of West Virginia. The Canaan Valley is down to a remnant population, although woodcock hunting there is as good as ever. In Pennsylvania grouse have been on the decline in the northwest part of the state and evidently on the upswing in some of the southwest and southcentral counties. Within several years this picture may change.

Many hunters will recall that 1960 was a fairly good year for grouse in Pennsylvania. That same year, Maryland, West Virginia, Virginia, and Michigan reported a decline. In 1966 Pennsylvania grouse appeared to have hit a low in their population cycle. On the other hand, Michigan rated its grouse hunting as good in 1965 and fairly good in 1966.

Since 1964 wildlife biologist Steve Licinsky has conducted an annual survey of grouse hunters in Pennsylvania. The average number of flushes an hour among cooperating hunters who hunt primarily for grouse were 1.62 (1965); 1.48 (1966); 1.66 (1967), and 1.61 (1968). The percentage of grouse flushed to grouse shot at remained fairly constant—about one-third. The ratio of grouse shot at to grouse bagged was also about one-third.

To date, Licinsky has been unable to establish any definite pattern in population cycles in various parts of the state except to determine that "the so-called cycle is not uniform throughout the Commonwealth." He further observes, "On a statewide basis it was obvious that there was a decline in the average flushing rate from 1965 to 1966 and an increase from 1966 to 1967. When broken down on an individual county basis, however, this pattern is not consistent. Flushing rates continued to decline in some counties, while in other counties there was a recovery from the 1966 low."

All of which leads us to the belief that there are two excellent ways for a statistician to blow his cool. One is to survey women shoppers and the other is to attempt to draw conclusions from a survey of grouse hunters.

One reason why these birds appear to be so susceptible to erratic fluctuations in population is a matter of grouse arithmetic. It starts with the nestings. About six out of ten hen grouse are successful in their first nesting. Foxes, skunks, raccoons, snakes, and other predators take a high toll of the eggs. After a nest is broken up, some hens will attempt a renesting, and some are successful. Nesting mortality probably averages about 30 to 35 per cent.

Most hen grouse lay between 10 and 12 eggs, which hatch in late May and early June. The first three to four weeks after hatching are critical for the grouselets. The young birds can't tolerate wetting and chilling. A prolonged rain accompanied by low temperatures can all but eliminate a brood. Even under favorable conditions, less than half of the young grouse can be expected to survive to the opening of hunting season.

Many parts of the Northeast are subject to highly localized weather conditions during this critical period of late May and early June. A chill rainstorm that sweeps down one valley may not affect surrounding areas. This can nearly wipe out the broods in a particular covert while young birds in nearby coverts might be unaffected.

In the case of a more widespread rainstorm, a covert fringed by a pine plantation might have a higher survival rate of young birds. If the hens manage to move their broods under such cover, fewer young may be lost. A neighboring covert lacking this protection may be hard hit.

In some grouse coverts predator losses may be significantly greater than in others. In other coverts an increase in the deer population may cause overgrazing of the understory. This can have a detrimental effect on the habitat.

It's noticeable that grouse coverts change from year to year. Conditions of optimum habitat may exist for a period of years and then decline. A cut-over or burned-over hillside that grows up in slashings will eventually become a mature wood lot again. Wood lots encroach on edgings until the forest becomes continuous and unbroken.

These are all factors that affect grouse populations. When you consider the relatively high percentage of nesting mortality, the even greater mortality of young birds, and all of the other factors, it becomes evident that we're dealing with a precarious balance.

Even under the most favorable conditions, grouse can be their own worst enemies. They can't tolerate crowding. Over successful seasons, ideal conditions may produce a peak population. For a year or two, grouse will be very abundant. But such periods are inevitably followed by critically sharp reductions. A surplus of birds carried over into the nesting season can be even more disastrous than a deficit.

It doesn't take many grouse to populate a covert. Let's start with a 40-acre covert containing a cock and two hens. If just one of the hens is successful in bringing off a brood of 11 grouselets, and four of them survive to the opening of hunting season while two of the adult birds survive, that's a total of six grouse. The population has doubled.

In all probability, not all of the young birds will remain in the covert. At 15 to 17 weeks of age, some of them will leave and move some distance in search of their own home territories. But they may be replaced by young birds moving in from nearby coverts. This interchange tends to place at least a few birds in most coverts, even those where nesting has been a complete failure.

Getting back to grouse arithmetic, let's assume now that two hens within a 40-acre covert have successful nestings. Let's further assume that weather conditions are ideal, predator losses are minimal, and the survival rate is 50 per cent. This can mean 10 to 12 young grouse and two or three adults—a bumper crop.

Grouse require an average of six to eight acres for each bird, even though their wanderings may be confined to three or four acres at any given time of the year. When the population begins approximating one bird for each four acres of covert, a reaction takes place.

First, some of the birds will move into less-populated coverts, while others scatter into the surrounding countryside. We have reason to think that there is a high rate of mortality among birds that move into marginal coverts.

Second, predator losses increase. Foxes, hawks, and horned owls will be attracted to areas where they can find a meal. An increase in the predator population will cut into nesting success and survival rates in subsequent seasons.

Third, and this is conjectural, a surplus of birds carrying

into the nesting season may have a detrimental effect on mating, fertilization, and incubation.

As we said before, we're dealing with a rather precarious balance. If not enough grouse carry over into the nesting season, that's bad. If too many carry over, that can be even worse. We've considered the one extreme; let's look at the other—little or no carry-over.

Let's assume that the prehunting season population of a covert is three adults and five young, a total of eight grouse. Let's further assume that hunters bag two, and predators and accidents remove two others. That leaves four. Now we move into the period from late January through March. Unless at least one cock and one hen survive, no nesting can occur.

A winter of heavy snows and extreme cold causes many hunters to become concerned over the survival of wildlife. In the case of grouse, deep snow covering the ground for lengthy periods is helpful. Grouse can go for long periods without food, but during extremely cold weather, they need shelter. If they can spend much of their time in snow roosting, they tend to stay fat and healthy. Lacking deep snow, they may survive but in poor physical condition. If this happens, they may fail to mate or they may mate but fail to nest.

Ruffed Grouse Management

Most wildlife managers are agreed that the prime objective in ruffed-grouse management (something of a misnomer) is to provide hunters with the maximum sporting opportunity consistent with the long-term well-being of the species.

Unlike pheasant, quail, and wild turkey, grouse can't be pen-reared for the purpose of stocking. This has been tried and has never proved successful. A number of attempts have been made to improve grouse habitat by cutting and clearing, although these efforts have been on a small scale and largely experimental. Burning on a fairly extensive scale can be an effective means of rejuvenating grouse habitat, but it's nearly impossible to justify forest fires because of possible long-range benefits in terms of grouse populations.

This leaves conservation agencies with one management tool—the regulation of seasons and bag limits. Unfortunately, such regulation brings under control one of the least significant factors affecting grouse populations: the hunter harvest. This is why we refer to grouse "management" as a misnomer at best.

Research studies in New York indicate that only 17 per cent of the available grouse are killed by hunters even in areas subject to the most intensive gunning pressure. Pennsylvania hunters probably take no more than ten per cent of the birds, according to the Game Commission (1956). Yet biologists believe that as much as 40 per cent of the fall population could be removed by hunting without hurting future hunting.

The folly of overly restrictive regulation has been proved time and time again. During the cyclic low of the 1940s, Wisconsin and Minnesota closed their grouse seasons while neighboring Michigan remained open to gunning. This made no difference in the recovery rate. The grouse kill in Michigan increased from 165,000 in 1945 to 570,000 in 1949.

In the 1950s, the Michigan Conservation Department surveyed two similar areas, one hunted and one closed to hunting. Postseason survival rates were approximately the same in both areas. Roughly one-third of the grouse present in the fall remained in the spring regardless of whether or not birds had been removed by hunting.

Since the test area received about four times as much hunting pressure as the statewide average and was not overharvested during a 41 day season, the biologists concluded that Michigan could safely have a grouse season of two or three months or possibly even longer.

Such research findings have led the more progressive conservation departments to take a liberal attitude in regulating grouse seasons and bag limits. This provides maximum sporting opportunity and offers several side benefits.

In most states the most intense hunting pressure for small game is in the farming regions. These areas attract great concentrations of hunters seeking pheasant and rabbit. Probably less than 15 per cent of all hunters specialize in grouse hunting. The upland wooded areas—the grouse country—draws far fewer hunters than the farming regions. Obviously, if more hunters can be attracted to grouse hunting by liberalizing the seasons and bag limits, pressure is eased on the hard-hunted farming areas where landowner resentment and posting of land is a critical problem.

Another consideration is the fact that ruffed grouse tend to be self-regulating so far as hunter harvest is concerned. When they become scarce, they become increasingly wild and difficult to bag. An experienced grouse hunter must count on flushing at least six birds and getting shots at three of them in order to bag one. If birds are scarce and he succeeds in flushing fewer birds, his chances of scoring are diminished. Furthermore, when grouse are scarce in an area, hunters become discouraged and go elsewhere.

Scoring on Grouse: Tips for Beginners

There are few game birds that provide so much sport and shooting with so little killing as the ruffed grouse. The mourning dove is a noteworthy exception, but there are damn few others.

If you're the kind of hunter who insists on coming home with a heavy gamebag or who feels like wrapping his gun barrel around a tree trunk every time a bird outsmarts you, then grouse hunting is not for you. But if you have a sense of humor and like challenges, grouse hunting can be the greatest sport in the world.

A grouse hunter's first requirement, even more important than shooting ability, is endurance. You'll often be hunting rugged upland terrain, and good physical condition is essential. As we've noted elsewhere, seasoned grouse hunters figure on flushing at least three birds to get shooting at one and on shooting at three "possibles" to bag one. Less-experienced hunters can double or even triple those ratios.

In order to flush enough birds and get in enough shooting to put grouse in your gamebag, be prepared to hunt hard. The ability to go an extra mile can make all the difference.

Scoring on grouse requires a high degree of concentration and alertness. Grouse can hit top speed almost at take-off, and they can get out of shotgun range in two seconds or less. A hunter who is out for a stroll in the woods and is admiring the autumn foliage can't be expected to react quickly enough.

Successful hunters carry their guns at ready position and are constantly alert for flushes. This enables them to throw down on a bird almost instantly. It also allows them an extra split second to make sure they're on target, allowing for proper lead, and making a calculated shot.

Probably the number-one reason for most missed shots at grouse is snap shooting. When a bird flushes, the hunter throws the gun to his shoulder and throws off a shot in the general direction of the target, all in a single movement. This is a great way to burn shells, but it doesn't scatter many grouse feathers.

Grouse are temperamental birds. Sometimes they will sit tight and go thundering out almost from underfoot; sometimes they will be skittish and flush far out of range; and sometimes they will run ahead of a hunter.

Experienced grouse hunters vary their walking pace until they determine how the birds are reacting. If the birds are sitting tight, stop-and-go hunting can be highly effective. If they're flushing wild, you may have to maintain a fast, steady pace. A hawk call can be effective in hunting wild-flushing grouse. If a grouse flushes far ahead of you, and you see where it went down, sound the hawk call as you approach the spot. This may freeze the bird to its position until the hunter is close.

If you find that you have to climb a fence, duck under a low branch, or otherwise get out of shooting position, come to a dead stop at the obstacle, wait a few seconds, and then take a couple of steps. This will frequently provide shooting at birds that might otherwise flush when you are out of shooting position. If you sit down to take a breather, be on the alert the instant you get up again and take the first few steps.

Now a word about grouse guns. Beginners are well advised to stack the odds in their favor. Start out with standard field loads (low brass), No. 7½s or 8s, in a lightweight 12- or 16-gauge shotgun. A pump gun with a variable choke is an excellent choice. Set the choke at open bore or improved cylinder. This gives a wide-flung shot pattern. A broad shot pattern is important because though grouse are difficult birds to hit, they're not hard to fold. A single No. 7½ pellet in a wing or in the head is often enough to bring one down.

Another good gun is a double side-by-side or over-under shotgun with 26- to 28-inch barrels. Whatever gun you decide on, practice swinging it to your shoulder and dry firing at imaginary grouse. If possible, work out on the trap and skeet ranges. Practice until your gun becomes almost a physical extension of your body.

Experienced skeet shooters develop a rhythm that enables them to "instinct shoot" at fast-moving targets. This ability can be effective in grouse hunting—sometimes. If you don't possess this ability, however, your shooting is likely to be more deliberate and calculated, and this need not be a handicap. At times it can be an advantage. The important thing to remember is *don't snap shoot*! Between the time the gun hits your shoulder and the trigger pull, be sure you're on target and tracking. After the shot, follow through.

Grouse hunting can be compared with golf; the idea is to keep improving on your score. Par may be a limit bag or it may be a double. It may be bagging two out of two or three out of three. However you care to keep score, you are competing against yourself. As your proficiency improves, you may be inclined to add handicaps.

After several seasons you may find yourself scoring well with your 12-gauge pump or double. Perhaps you are folding as many as one in three of your "possibles." So you decide to give yourself a handicap. You go to lighter gauges.

In hunting with a 20-gauge or a 410, you'll find that though you surrender a bit in quantity of shot and in pattern, you gain somewhat in lightness of gun and in speed of handling. And you're discovering the sport anew, which is the principal thing. Your first grouse with a little 410 compares with the thrill of the first grouse you ever shot. Now you're an expert. You scoff at those who use heavier gauges.

For the past several years, the author of this chapter has hunted grouse with a muzzle-loading shotgun. These old-time hammer guns are heavier and longer-barrelled than modern grouse guns. It takes longer to cock the hammer than to flick off the safety of a hammerless gun. You rarely get off a second shot with any expectation of scoring. But even a muzzle loader can have advantages. Most of them are open bored. They throw a far-flung pattern, perfect for grouse.

This past season, I missed a grouse on the first barrel, then downed it on the second–something of an achievement in muzzle-loader hunting for grouse. So we move on toward our next goal–the first double. And after that? Well, maybe we'll go to a 22 rifle or a slingshot or a bow and arrow.

In the final analysis, though, maybe it doesn't really matter. There's no more satisfying weight than a ruffed grouse in the gamebag, but it's the hunt that counts, not the score. We recall many an enjoyable day afield that failed to produce a single kill.

Action comes fast in grouse hunting. A flurry of wings, a glimpse of the streaking bird, the swinging gun, the shotgun blast, a puff of feathers, a plummeting bird—all in a split second. You find him in dry leaves and admire his plummage. The kill—a blur across the mind—is over. But it stays with you afterwards. It's part of the day, along with the pines, the hills, the blueness of the sky, a fencerow silhouetted against a November sunset—impressions that last.

Oscar Wilde was not a grouse hunter, but when he got off the line, "We always kill the thing we love," he was talking for a lot of us who are. But there's more to it than killing—a lot more. Ruffed grouse achieve their own special kind of immortality. They are remembered with pleasure. Men should do as well.

George Harrison considers each day spent in the field an event of major importance. Shooting game or catching fish is relatively unimportant to him. Oh, he takes home his fair share, but to him the chase is really the biggest part of the sport. Many hunters say this, but Harrison means it. His old setter, Berk, feels just about the same way, and they are about the happiest pair of hunters you'll ever meet. As managing editor of National Wildlife *and* International Wildlife *George has occasion to visit many exotic corners of the world, but I suspect he's always thinking about the cornfields of southcentral Pennsylvania, where the pheasants fly fast and run hard.*

CHAPTER 9

Pheasant Hunting

GEORGE H. HARRISON

If I were an artist assigned to paint the perfect hunting scene, I'd show a man and his son walking across an old field, shotguns held high, their black and white English setter on point. The sky is blue, the maples are red. Thick clusters of green, yellow and brown foliage round out this gorgeous fall scene. The final touch is a cock ring-necked pheasant exploding into the air ahead of the setter. It's a perfect moment; a perfect hunting scene.

My own first hunting experience was nearly that perfect. My scene was near Conneaut Lake, Crawford County, Pennsylvania, in 1950. I was 14 years old. It was a dark, threatening day as my dad and I were hunting an old apple orchard with our English setter, Andy. The pheasant, unlike most I've flushed since then, ran under the old apple trees for an amazing distance before finding the right opening to flush. He was a beautiful dark cock.

I remember that Dad held his shot until the bird rose well off the rich carpet of fallen apples and decaying leaves. That wonderful scene is vivid in my memory. I have often thought of that day as I downed my own pheasants during the years that followed.

Pheasant hunting is more often shared as a family sport than any other kind of hunting I can think of. For example, wives who don't generally like to get up before dawn to hunt, like pheasant hunting because it is good any time of the day. Young hunters who can't endure the extreme cold associated with waterfowl hunting from a blind can keep warm pheasant hunting because they are always walking and sometimes running. The terrain where pheasants are found is usually easy walking. The location is often near home or at least near Uncle Zeke's farm. Pheasants present a big target and are easier to hit than other game birds. Dogs work well on ringnecks; even nonhunting dogs are often helpful for hunting pheasants. And finally, everyone likes the taste of pheasant, and the eating is as much fun as the hunting. All in all, they're an ideal game bird for family fun and quality hunting.

Ring-necked pheasants do best in the northern half of the United States. Associated with agriculture, pheasants thrive in open grassland, cultivated fields, and in irrigated desert country. Though the best pheasant hunting in the world is claimed by the Great Plains states, opening days in Ohio, Pennsylvania, New York, and New Jersey are hard to beat.

In the East, Chinese ring-necked pheasants do well only north of the Mason-Dixon line. For some biological reason still argued among scientists, the so-called common ringneck does not propagate well in the south. For this reason, some southern states began experimenting with some success with other strains of pheasants, particularly the Iranian species. Working with Dr. Gardner Bump of the Bureau of Sport Fisheries and Wildlife, the state of Virginia stocked two strains of Iranian black-necked pheasants in the late 1950s. Today these birds have done so well that the first open season on Iranians was scheduled for the fall of 1970. Over 30,000 of these blacknecks have been raised and released in

NED SMITH

Virginia. About 60 of Virginia's 100 counties now contain populations of the Iranians and crosses of Iranians and Chinese ringnecks.

Importing any kind of animal life from other lands is always risky. The unhappy effect of the starling and the English sparrow on our native bird population is a good example, to say nothing of the economic calamities produced by the Norway rat, the Japanese beetle, the gypsy moth, and other undesirable foreigners. The Chinese ringneck, however, is the most successful game bird ever imported to the United States. The first transplant to the United States was made in 1881 by the United States consul general at Shanghai, who shipped 28 Chinese ringnecks to the Willamette Valley of Oregon. The terrain, climate, and feed of the region so suited the brilliant-plumaged foreigners that, with the help of some additional stock, their numbers warranted a cutback within 11 years. Fifty thousand birds were reported killed on the first day of the shooting season.

In most northeastern and midwestern states ringnecks are reared and stocked by the thousands from game farms. In spite of a healthy natural production, game departments load the fields and hedgerows with young cocks before the opening day and periodically through the season. Pennsylvania alone stocks a quarter of a million pheasants each year. This practice is also common in areas that are not capable of natural production. Here it is a pure and simple case of "stocking for the gun."

Without a doubt, the prime ring-necked pheasant hunting area in the East is in the Pennsylvania Dutch country. Southeastern Pennsylvania is as good as the prime areas of the Great Plains on opening day. Nearly every hunter gets some shooting. Most bag at least one cock bird.

In one of his "Walkin' Shoes" columns in the Pennsylvania *Game News*, Ned Smith observed that eastern ringnecks are a pleasing mixture of several species and subspecies of Asiatic pheasants but most closely resemble the Chinese pheasant. The males often exceed three feet in over-all length, owing to their extremely long, slim tails. The hens are somewhat smaller, and their tails are shorter. A big rooster will weigh three pounds or more, but the average is about two and three quarter pounds. Hens average a little over two pounds.

As anyone knows who has seen one at close range, a male ring-necked pheasant is a strikingly beautiful bird. Its plumage is a pleasing blend of the richest colors imaginable. The head is a dark, iridescent blue glossed with green and violet in certain lights. The crown is greenish bronze edged in gray. A brilliant scarlet wattle covers the side of the face behind the ivory bill, and a white band encircles the neck. Breast and chest are a rich, glossy purplish red, with each feather narrowly edged in metallic blue-black. The mahogany red of the chest blends into orange-bronze on the flanks, and the belly is black. The upper back is usually either straw-colored or brownish streaked with black, blending into purplish red or mahogany marked with buff and blue-black on the scapulars that overlap the wings. The rump varies from yellowish gray to golden green or powder blue, bordered on the sides with orange-red. The wing coverts are powder blue, the flight feathers dusky, barred with white or buff. The long tail is tan, centrally duskily speckled and edged with a purple-red fringe. All but the outer feathers are regularly barred with black. The feet and spurred shanks are gray.

The hen's plumage is purely functional, being perfectly designed to make her inconspicuous while she is incubating and brooding her young. She is chiefly a pale buff-brown, heavily mottled and barred with brown and black above, faintly marked beneath. Her only departure from utter drabness is a faint wash of iridescent purple that is sometimes apparent on the sides of her neck.

Fortunately for the future of the pheasant population, the cock bird sees in the hens something more than dull plumage. Each spring he sets forth across his rolling acres searching for willing mates. His call—two raucous crowing notes followed by a series of quick wing beats—is heard at intervals throughout the day. It is primarily a statement of territorial ownership, and should a rival male dispute his claim there is likely to be a fight. Participants are rarely injured in a pheasant fight, but the fierce-looking blows of spurred shanks and flailing wings soon determine who's the best man. The loser quits the scene and thereafter keeps his distance.

Crowing means "keep out" to other males, but to neighborhood females it says "come arunnin'." They don't come arunning, that's true, but the resultant meetings of cock and hen could hardly be called accidental. Being a polygamist, he plays the field; four or five hens are just about the right number to keep his life interesting.

While his courtship display is not so elaborate as the strutting of a prairie chicken, a ruffed grouse, or a wild turkey, the cock ringneck does attempt to show off his handsome plumage to the best advantage. Also, at this time of the year his wattles are fiery red and so expanded as to shield almost the entire head.

When mating has taken place each hen makes a nest in her favorite spot. It is a simple affair, a shallow depression in the ground lined with dried grasses or leaves. Hayfields seem to be the first (and worst) choice for nesting sites, and the losses of eggs, young, and incubating hens during mowing operations are incredibly high. Less frequently used locations are fencerows, old fields, woodland borders, and streamside thickets.

An average of about a dozen eggs is laid. They vary in color from pale buffy brown to pale smoky olive.

Baby pheasants chip the large ends off their eggshells on the twenty-third or twenty-fourth day. Wet and bedraggled at first, they are transformed into the cutest little creatures imaginable with the drying of the natal down. Their general coloration is buffy, tinged with brown above. The crown is rich brown and black, and there is a blackish streak behind the eye. Three dark streaks run down the middle of the back.

Baby pheasants just can't stay put. Almost as soon as they are dry they are hustling about beneath the hen's warm plumage, and before the day is out they have left the nest, never to return.

Little pheasants lead a precarious existence. Even before they emerge from the eggs they are in constant danger of being obliterated by mowing machines or devoured by snoopy skunks, snakes, opossums, raccoons, foxes, crows, or farm dogs. After leaving the nest, they are even more vulnerable. Wet, cold weather is particularly hard on infant ringnecks. If they escape foul weather, there are countless other enemies waiting. Cooper's hawks, foxes, weasels, raccoons, great horned owls, domestic cats and dogs, and some of the larger snakes are not averse to making a meal of them, and their small size and relative helplessness tempt many a predator that would ordinarily not bother anything larger than mice.

Even the old birds have their enemies. Man's automobiles, mowing machines, and shotguns are the principal ones. Goshawks and great horned owls pick off an occasional ringneck where their ranges overlap, and foxes account for their share.

But in their strange new world the chicks have little time to worry about danger. They roam the dry fields all summer long, sampling this food and that, investigating all sorts of crawling and flying things, hiding quickly at a warning signal from the hen, and enjoying life to the fullest as soon as the coast is clear. Food is abundant, and they dine heavily on ants, beetles, cutworms, grasshoppers, and other insects, wild berries, succulent greens, and weed seeds. Dust baths at their favorite bare spots along the field edges are a daily luxury.

The youngsters mature rapidly. At two months of age they can make speedy but abbreviated flights; in another month they can take wing like adults. Clothed in their juvenile plumage, the young all resemble miniature females, but by late August the males are beginning to show evidence of their sex. The red coloring of the wattles is one of the first indications. The appearance of purplish-red feathers on the breast and sides of the chest and a smattering of dark metallic-green feathers on the neck give the immature males a conspicuously patched appearance. It is not unusual in late summer for several hens to combine their broods, resulting in big flocks of 30 or 40 birds.

By the time the frost is on the pumpkin it takes a practiced eye to distinguish birds of the year from adults. When the opening day of small-game season rolls around they're *all* old enough and smart enough to give the gunner a run for his money.

Ring-necked pheasants have several characteristics that serve magnificently to perpetuate the species. One is the ringneck's propensity to run. A bobwhite will freeze on the spot at the first sound of footsteps in its covert, and a grouse might either freeze, sneak off a short distance and hide, or flush wild. But a pheasant's first impulse is to stretch out its spindly shanks and put a hundred yards between itself and the suspicious noise. This characteristic is especially prevalent in cornfields and sparse cover.

Another of the ringneck's nasty habits is that of ducking into ground-hog holes, drain pipes, and the like.

The conventional method of hunting pheasants is much like that employed for hunting rabbits and quail—simply walking through suspected cover until a pheasant flushes or your dog goes on point.

While this writer was editor of the Pennsylvania *Game News* we printed an article by Bob Carter describing an unusual method for hunting pheasants—running them up!

"We got our system started years ago in a season when rabbits were occurring at a rate of about one to the square mile," Carter reported. "Concentrating on ringnecks, we soon began to notice that most of the birds we spotted were flushed far ahead and out of range."

Carter concluded that a rapid drive through pheasant cover would be more effective than a slow approach.

"We began to kill more pheasants," he goes on, "and to our delight, began to see more pheasants. Further advancing our theory, we decided that we were seeing more birds because we no longer gave them time to choose the best escape route. We were actually herding and hustling them toward the end of the field, where they had to get airborne in a hurry or get stepped on.

"In the course of getting experience with ringneck psychology we have added a good many refinements to our system.

"We always hunt from the thickest end of cover toward the thinnest, crowding the birds, if we can, to a point where they must fly to escape. Occasionally, even on well-farmed land, you will find promising cover that merges into denser cover. In these cases it is best to spot a hunter at the end toward which the drive is aimed. If he keeps a sharp eye he will catch roosters scuttling along the ground and can make a short rush to flush them before they reach thick cover.

"When you spot an end man in this manner it is *essential* that nobody shoot unless he knows where his companions are. The end man should stay at a corner of the field so that everyone can shoot safely," Carter concluded.

As with most bird hunting, hunting ringnecks with a dog adds a dimension to the sport and often birds to the bag.

But pheasants are tough for pointing dogs. Many setters and pointers that are the acme of perfection on quail simply don't know what to do with birds that won't stay put. Many of them wind up as hopeless creepers. Little by little the pointing breeds are wising up to the Chinese sprinter, and some are becoming first-rate pheasant dogs, but it still takes a smart dog to cut off a ringneck's retreat and nail him to the spot.

Feeling that a mediocre pointing dog is not the answer, a growing number of hunters are using flushing dogs. Springer spaniels and Brittanys make perfect pheasant dogs, and several of the retriever breeds do a good job. Rabbit hunters have long known that a beagle or basset that takes kindly to trailing birds is as dependable as any breed around. The hunter's job is to stay with the dog. If he can do that, shooting is practically guaranteed.

I'll never forget the year my English setter pup, Berkeley, was ready for his first pheasant season. Opening day in Pennsylvania in 1962 was also the day our first child was due to arrive. Both right on schedule, the season and the labor pains arrived at the same hour. Fortunately, I was able to get out into Dauphin County and kill a brace of birds over my too-zealous setter before taking Hester to the hospital. We now have a son who will soon be accompanying me afield for feathered Chinamen himself.

Depending on your shooting ability, the best firearm to use on pheasants will range from a 12-gauge shotgun with number 5s to a 410 shotgun with number 8s. I like to use a 12-gauge double with 32-inch barrels and No. 6 shot. My 20 gauge with number 6s and 7½s works fine too. Frankly, a lot depends on the gun you like and use best for upland game. The shot I use generally runs a little heavier than the shot I prefer for grouse, but some shooters don't agree.

Pheasants are not easily killed, even with a good shot. One evening just before quitting time, a friend and I headed for the car by way of an alfalfa field. Berkeley went on point and we moved in, but nothing happened. This procedure was repeated four times over about a 75-yard stretch of the field. On the fourth point the cock flushed and I shot. The bird was jarred by the shot but kept on a straight course for more than a quarter mile. Almost out of sight, it flew over a blacktop road and collapsed. We ran to the road, hoping to get there before a car flattened our bird. There was our prize, "deader than a door nail," square in the middle of the white line! In an area of more brush or rougher terrain our cock would have flown out of sight, apparently unharmed.

A pheasant is not likely to be found exactly at the spot where you saw him fall. Here is where a good dog is essential. A crippled pheasant with two good legs is a lost bird without a dog. He will somehow sneak to a place where he will be unnoticed by a human eye.

Pheasants are famous for their ability to hide after the opening day. The smart ones leave their usual haunts to find seclusion in swamps, heavy brush, culverts, or anywhere you are not likely to look.

One late fall day Will Johns and I were floating the Swatara Creek near Hershey in his canoe, hunting for ducks, when we spotted an old cock pheasant huddled in the overhanging roots of a tree along the creek bank. Only from the water was this bird visible or flushable.

Eating pheasant is by no means the least enjoyable thing you can do with this beautiful bird. My wife pressure cooks our birds. After browning the sections in hot butter or margarine for about five minutes, she puts them in the pressure cooker, adds water, seals the cooker, and cooks for 20 to 30 minutes. Often she will cook onions and carrots with the pheasant.

Others cook pheasant by roasting or broiling. The best advice is to cook your pheasant the way you like to cook chicken.

Ringnecks can be enjoyed in a number of other ways if you do not enjoy hunting them. They are a great addition to the winter feeding station if you are near natural pheasant haunts. They eat the same corn or birdseed mixture you feed the chickadees and cardinals. I've heard of some bands of pheasants getting downright tame during a winter feeding season.

One of the best ways, however, for the whole family to enjoy these gorgeous birds is to see them at a game farm. Individually, they are spectacularly marked, but in flocks of hundreds at a game farm, they are a maze of unbelievable color, sound, and movement. Most state game-farm managers are happy to have you visit their facilities. If you are there at the right time of the early summer, they'll probably show you the egg-factory facility where buffy-colored pheasant eggs are in all stages of incubation and chicks are in various stages of growth. Be sure to take your camera along.

Yes, the ringneck has been a huge success in America, both as a game bird and as a colorful addition to our farm land. Its ability to adapt to man's demands on the environment has proved that it is here to stay. Perhaps only the use of DDT or other dangerous agricultural chemicals could destroy this fine bird.

Surely one must place it high on the list of all-time-champion game birds. As a friend of mine used to say, "We sure have a horn of pheasant plenty!"

PART THREE
Small Game Hunting

Thad Bukowski, biology teacher turned writer, takes us down the rabbit path. His chapter portion is more a story about a rabbit hunt than it is a treatise on how to hunt rabbits. This is the kind of material not often found in books, and I believe that The Eastern Trail *is richer for it. The cottontail rabbit is probably our most popular game animal, and millions of boys, and those who are still boys at heart, have strong feelings about cottontails. Thad certainly has.*

CHAPTER 10

Cottontails Back Home

THAD BUKOWSKI

Grandpa always said you could put a beagle in a "spicket" and he'd run you out a rabbit anytime.

I puzzled over that statement, and it was a while before I realized he meant a "thicket," but then I agreed he was right. The alder and hawthorn tangles back of his western Pennsylvania farm were ideal cottontail habitat. It would be difficult for a cottontail to hate wild crab apple lying near rickety rail fences, with timothy and alfalfa patches nearby, and ready-made hideaways worn away alongside the banks of the tiny creek that saturated the bottomland below.

I was introduced to Grandpa's version of cottontail hunting with beagles when I came courtin' to the old hillside homestead near Harrisville, Pennsylvania, years ago.

Our oldest youngster is now 20, so that gives you an idea of how many hunts have gone by since Mac, the sage beagle, gave me a thorough sniffing-over on my first date there and decided I had the right password.

On Thanksgiving Gramps, Chip, old Em, and a couple of other farm cronies always get together with a beagle pack while the womenfolk loaded the table and basted the turkey from sunrise to past high noon, waiting for us to come back from our stomp so that we might eventually attack the victuals.

I went along without a shotgun on my first trip, and we ran into a fair amount of game, so by next Thanksgiving I was ready for some shooting of my own.

When next turkey day arrived, I showed up with a license, knowing that an extra single barrel was always around for a neophyte who was interested. I inherited a 32-inch full-choke squirrel thumper to start with, and on the afternoon before the hunt I uncorked a few hasty shots at Chip's red hat to get the feel of the thing. After I knocked off a section of the brim as the hat rolled along the ground, the boys felt I had a reasonable chance for the next morning's jaunt.

Frost crackled under my boots as I climbed the little rise back by the barn where the chickens cackled. A couple of hogs grunted as I clomped through the nearby garden where pumpkins still lay scattered. The scent of hay and packed wheat in the barn and corn in the nearby cribs made me take a few extra whiffs. I checked a couple of patches of nearby orchard grass for bunnies because the smells and comforting animal talk were too enjoyable to pass up quickly. Then I turned and hurried over the hill towards the old apple orchard beyond which the rest of the party were disappearing.

The swamp hollow over the hill took in parts of three farms. It was bordered on the south by a railroad track. Haw made up a good section of the slope. Fallow fields of stiff Queen Anne's lace and goldenrod pockmarked the land and a chunk of stomped buckwheat stubble contrasted with rows of broken corn stalk going in the opposite direction. Fencerows of chokecherry and hazlenut bordered nearby tilled fields. An occasional jagged wolf oak spread its branches as it highlighted a fencerow.

The sloping hillside made for easy trudging down to the

brook, which sprouted tangled alder and willow in its slowed-down spots and cattails in the swampier places. The sun always poked up through the big hardwoods beyond the track as we headed for our favorite swamp.

The dogs were often on the chase for a half hour before a barreling cottontail exploded out onto a slope. But the beautiful sound of those bawling beagles describing a hot pursuit in a chorus of gravelly voices was enough to make a trip successful even if you never got a look down a cold barrel.

Old Em raised his big Belgian double and anxiously fingered the curled hammers for a shot as a bunny streaked past him. But before he got it off, the cottontail was gone and the dogs kept crying.

"Why didn't you let him have it?" Gramps yelled from a distance, and Em mumbled something about not getting ready soon enough.

I was for making off to greener pastures on my first hunt, but Gramps snorted a quick restraint. He had his broken straw hat in his hand by now and was wiping his bald brow. The suspendered denims didn't make him look like a polished hunter.

"Every time you jump a rabbit, you most always find another one around. They run in pairs," he said. Gramps had hardly let the words out of his mouth when he dropped the straw, whirled, and crooked a finger around the trigger of his 12 as he raised it to his shoulder. He belted a fat cottontail for a double loop.

"I get three, maybe four like this sometimes," Gramps called as he calmly gutted his kill. "You gotta let the dogs do the work. You can't hunt for them like a lot of fellas try to do."

I settled down impatiently as the pack crossed and recrossed the swamp, the stream, and the hawthorns, sniffing out every puzzling lead in ever-widening circles. I marveled at how the beagles came back and started their circling time and again from the last lead. After a couple of good runs all dogs were finally content, and we started them off along the railroad track.

I jumped my first cottontail alongside that track. I missed

my first shot, but the dogs took onto the cottontail and turned him quickly. The others passed up their shots and let him come to me again. The way those three cheered my first cottontail when I finally downed him you would have thought I had shot an elk.

Gramps insisted we hunt a few hillsides above the tracks. "Them rabbits sit on the sunny slopes in the morning," he called. As a youngster, I listened and learned. Almost invariably our morning jaunts roused a bunny off a southern slope where the nocturnal feeder had stashed himself after loading his belly on the previous night's foraging.

Rabbit hunting around the homestead always involved a jolly crowd. The never-ending availability of bunnies made each hunt interesting, and they were even more exhilarating because there were many shots and the ones you didn't get caused plenty of humorous talk later on.

Cottontail hunts are an easy way to learn about shotgunning, as there is some excitement almost every hunt. A farm, a swamp, a wooded thicket, an abandoned strip mine or stone quarry, a timothy or alfalfa patch, a few companions and beagles or basset hounds are the necessary ingredients.

Cottontails tend to thrive in a countryside that once was or still is under cultivation. They associate themselves with agricultural civilization so much they're one of the reasons for a primary safety regulation in Pennsylvania. They are great homebodies and tend to stay near human habitat. They congregate close to houses where lawn grass is abundant or where there may be a small garden of vegetables. Because rabbits can live in such close proximity to human dwellings, the regulations state that one cannot hunt within 150 yards of an occupied building.

A cultivated northeastern United States farm that practices crop rotation is also a great attraction, especially if it grows such crops as timothy, corn, oats, alfalfa, buckwheat and vegetables and has a fruit orchard, some fallow ground, and a wood lot. Such an area is ideal for rabbits, particularly if some of the fields have hedgerows for cover scattered at their edges. A farm that has a few low-lying swampy places with cover is even more likely to harbor a plentiful supply of bunnies.

Cottontails may be found scattered through any apple orchard. Their many trails are recognized in timothy patches, where trodden paths weave along the edges of the fields near fencerow areas. These are often woodchuck holes nearby, into which bunnies will quickly dive for cover. Fall husked cornfields are also good places to find strays, for the cottontail will feed on waste corn and any other succulent growth that may be there.

A research study shows that cottontails remain close to the place where they are born. Most rabbits cover only 22 acres of foraging in the summer and limit themselves to only 14 acres of travel in the winter. Young rabbits may find a satisfactory home within a mile of their birthplace, if food and cover are suitable, and remain there for life.

One of the outstanding places to hunt rabbits on a farm is in any overgrown pasture that has a stream running through it with a good scattering of bull thistle, Jo-pye, and ironweed and an infestation of first-growth hawthorn, commonly referred to as wild crab apple by hunters. Such overgrown areas are ideal for the coursing of hounds. They permit hunters to properly station themselves in circular fashion at edges of such fields for shots at rabbits that circle while being trailed.

Many hunters also jump-hunt the cottontail without dogs and get their share. Three to five will scatter in parallel lines 15 to 30 feet apart and trace and retrace fields methodically as they hunt. This is enjoyable but not as effective as similar tactics with dogs that will take up the chase on a rabbit and circle him back to the place where he was jumped.

A pup obtained early should be methodically trained and cared for. Proper shots against distemper, hepatitis, and rabies are absolutely necessary. An early visit to the veterinarian will set the pup on a proper inoculation and vitamin schedule. He should get vitamin supplements, particularly through his first year, for proper tooth and bone growth. Since a considerable amount of hip dysplasia is cropping up in the dog world, it would be wise to check that no previous litter from the stock chosen had this crippling hereditary defect, which affects a dog's hindquarters at about the first year.

A pup should be taken out to roam freely with its master in familiar surroundings. Between the ages of six to nine months he will begin to get excited about rabbits and progressively develop the latent instinct to trail that is within him. A hunter must have patience to develop a good dog. The two must learn to communicate with each other.

If a pup keeps quiet even on a hot scent, a chunk of rope restraining him when a rabbit is jumped will make him bawl to high heaven, and he'll never forget the trick thereafter.

A young hound learns well from others, and a hunter should try to hunt him with a more experienced dog or group of dogs, but be sure that they are compatible. A hunter should also fire a cap pistol over his young pup, first from a distance then closer, until he eventually ends with firing a shotgun in similar fashion. Firing during feeding time, first from a distance, then progressively closer, is a good idea, since shooting is associated with something else the pup likes to do.

A hound probably reaches his hunting peak when he slows down a little and gets the savvy of three or four years of experience under his belt. He will undoubtedly do his best hunting at the ages of five through eight.

Some dogs are like hunters. They hate to get into the brush. They must be directed from their earliest years to hit the brushpiles and thickets where cottontails are most likely to be found. Rabbits feel very secure in brush piles. Hunters fail to scare them out even by leaping up and down on top of the heap. That's where a nosy hound may be most effective.

If a hunter watches as his pup grows in experience in the field, he will learn from the way that the dog hunts that there are many signals a dog gives while on a trail. An experienced hunter can readily distinguish when his dog is hunting birds rather than rabbits.

A dog will almost always get played out more quickly during the early part of the season and hunt poorly. Seasons often come in with dry and warm weather, which causes problems for dogs. The wise hunter will toughen his dogs before the opener. Their paws may be tender and affected adversely if they are overhunted early in the season without conditioning. It may be a good idea if one owns more than one dog to hunt them alternately in the morning and afternoon during the first few days of the season.

Just as some hunters go afield in peculiar fashion, dogs also have their idiosyncrasies. Some are one-man dogs and will hunt only for their master. Some hunt for anyone. Some are strong willed and will hunt where they wish without thought for the fact that their master may want them to perform in a particular area. Some hounds even prefer hunting birds to hunting rabbits. Over the years, I've hunted with most of the above types.

Such hunting may be just the ticket for the many Easterners who like to investigate the small patches of outdoors still available in the immediate vicinity of their homes. Many long-time hunters would agree that without cottontails, woods and hedgerows might lose much of their magic for Americans.

The rabbit gun need not be anything special. Most shotgunners use the 12 as a popular gauge, but 16s and 20s are as effective. Low-brass 6s and 5s are probably best as a first shot, with high-brass shells in the same shot size loaded for the second shot. Undoubtedly, however, too many gunners wrongly believe they need a full-choke barrel to "reach out" or at least a modified for the first shot in a two-barrel gun. They would be far more effective firing improved cylinder, for the brushy rabbit shot is usually quite close.

Companionship, humor, and the opportunity to initiate youngsters to the hunt make the rabbit hunt an eminently satisfying experience. Cracker-barrel reminiscences of a group of rabbit hunters bring chuckles to almost everyone who hears them recalling their adventures. What's more fun than telling about what once happened afield while awaiting still another chance to get out?

I'll never forget a particular rabbit that made a fool of me early in my hunting days. I was still using my single 16 when a bunny climbed over a nearby hill out of a peach orchard and the beagles gave it some noisy tunes. Their crying trailed off into the distance, so I set myself for a shot and awaited the cottontail's return. The others also stationed themselves in good spots on a craggy hillside.

I stood with my gun across my hips. Finally, when that became uncomfortable, I decided I'd grab a seat on a nearby grass clump.

I looked down for a spot and saw a cottontail frozen between my feet. He had been there for the past 15 minutes. The thought of shooting seemed monumentally stupid, but I lifted the gun to my shoulder—and saw my foot in the sights. I moved the gun aside and puzzled over what to do, still frozen in my tracks. I finally put the bunny in motion by stabbing the gun barrel at his rump.

The gun stubbed the hard clay and my mouth gaped as the barrel fell away from the stock. As the rabbit bounded away I grabbed both pieces and tried to put the gun together. I broke into a lope through the orchard yelling, "Rabbit! Rabbit!"

For a moment I couldn't understand why my companions sat and rocked with laughter, but hightailing through those peach trees, yelling and waving two sections of shotgun, wasn't exactly the best impression I could have made on those old-timers.

Although I have never lived that one down, that cottontail pulled another smart trick on the rest of the group, and I was a bit mollified. He veered out of the orchard toward a nearby farmhouse and sat down in the middle of the front lawn.

A fat gal was doing chores on the porch.

The crew bore down as the rabbit began delicately munching individual grass slivers.

Gramps yelled to the fat gal that he'd shoot the hare for her dinner.

She turned and raised a menacing fist just as the dogs began bawling at the other cottontail they were trailing in the distance.

"Eli," she said, "I don't care if you are a neighbor, if you shoot that there rabbit, I'll have you arrested."

The rabbit continued his feast, first looking at her and then at us as the argument developed. Finally the rabbit won out and we turned tail.

I changed to a side-by-side double 20 the next season and couldn't shoot my way out of a cowstall. Then I learned that I was aiming cross barrel and was nearly four feet off on many of my shots. As a youngster I was left-handed, but someone made a right hander out of me early in my school days. Probably no one then knew about the fact that one's dominant eye usually parallels handedness, and there I was, shooting from the right shoulder with a dominant left eye. I hadn't started shooting with both eyes open, either, so I had to train myself to close the other eye. At every opportunity I practiced winking with either eye, and some folks undoubtedly thought I was going a mite peculiar when they noticed me in an unguarded moment, but I prevailed until I accomplished the feat.

I turned to a 12-gauge semiauto after that because sighting down one barrel was comfortable and I wanted to add duck hunting to my repertoire. I did even worse. I hit only three of 23 tries that season. It wasn't until the snowy Thanksgiving which followed that I learned the gun was bored so tight it only spread a fistful of snow on a middling shot, so I promptly sent it away for a Polychoke. But I suffered the whole season for not testing the pattern of that gun.

Ever since I've shot Polychoke at improved-cylinder for most of my small game and damaged almost no meat for the table. But strangely, many hunting folk I meet insist they need that modified or full choke to reach out for their small game. In the rolling eastern countryside, this appears to be a mistake, since the game is gone over the first hill or into deep brush before it gets even to modified range and sometimes even before you can get off a reasonable snap shot.

Improved-cylinder shooting may be switched to modified shooting late in the season when most hunting areas are much more open. Leaves have fallen and the first snows have bent down the higher timothy, goldenrod, wild grasses, and ragweed. My latest gun for cottontail shooting, and for grouse and pheasant too, is an over-under I've just unpacked. It's bored improved cylinder in one barrel and modified in the other.

I've found No. 6s and No. 5s to be more than adequate for bunnies, although some rabbits travel quite a distance before dropping, and in some circumstances the 5s are preferable.

My best evidence that a rabbit can travel a considerable distance after being hit came when I was being ribbed one day for having a bad dog. Orrie Mathews, a hunting crony, took a poke at a bunny that bounded over a distant hill on a good farm plot near my home. The beagle stopped bawling after it disappeared behind the barreling cottontail, and we decided the rabbit had holed up.

But the dog didn't return as he should have, and Orrie began to pull my leg. Even I began to wonder.

"How come that hound isn't coming back like he's supposed to if that rabbit has gone hidin'?" Orrie laughed. I suggested we weren't sure the rabbit was gone and said we ought to give the pup a chance. Finally, however, I tried to call the dog from beyond the hill, but he still didn't come.

My irritation suddenly changed into a wide grin when the hound lumbered awkwardly over the brow with a big buck rabbit hanging from his mouth, legs dragging on the ground. That's one of a very few times any beagle of mine did such a thing, but he must have been tuned in onto Orrie's criticism.

Strange things have happened on cottontail hunts. I have seen a cottontail swim only once, but I know they can do so very well. The dunk was interrupted when a companion of mine popped off the bunny as it was nearing the shore of a quarry pool. Our two beagles had backed the rabbit down to the water's edge, so he dived in and was going at a good clip when Jim Penwell stopped him with his 20. I watched the scene from the top of a limestone spoilpile at the edge of the quarry. I was miffed at my friend for taking a shot like that and gave him my opinion.

"Boy, you haven't hunted around here very much," he called back. "They do this around here pretty regular," he said and added, "This isn't the first swimming rabbit I ever got."

I have never encountered more cottontails anywhere than

in those limestone-quarry areas at the Pennsylvania-Ohio border, and that brings up a most interesting point about why game might exist in certain areas in abundance.

Gramps didn't understand why it happened, but he could repeatedly go to the same chunk of farm and get 10 to 15 cottontails a season from a corner you'd swear would never raise two, let alone a dozen. It appears, however, that every time one is shot out, another takes over such territory because it is favored for food, water, and cover.

The limestone quarries near Bessmer, Pennsylvania, and New Middleton, Ohio, might just prove the value of proper habitat quite conclusively. For years limestone mining has been the industry of these two communities and of nearby Hillsville, and the three towns are separated from one another by a few dozen miles. Many years of rock blasting have exposed limestone boulders everywhere. There are many lime spoilpiles and pits from which spring water oozes to form quarry lakes.

There are about 25 of these lakes and many smaller ponds in these environs, and the water and exposed lime have jumped the pH rating of the entire countryside. Not only does wild clover grow rank, but even alfalfa and other ordinarily cultivated legumes thrive wild in this area of abandoned land. The countryside is strewn with limestone rocks of all sizes. These rocks not only give the cottontails places to hide but also provide the sweetener for the crop that they love to eat. Here cottontails can readily hide from foxes and other predators and still have plenty of food and water nearby.

I remember one occasion when we ran onto 28 rabbits in a morning's hunt in the area, and that offers a lot of shooting. Nearby cleared farms may produce only two or three after a long stomp on what appears to be a perfect hunting day.

However, I have never been involved in any group that has shot 28 cottontails in a day. And anyhow, clean missing is almost as much fun, and I can still dubiously pride myself on being a lousy shot. There have been times we've sent a half dozen shots past a bounding rabbit without a pellet scattering any ground within three feet of him.

This might bring us to the philosophical point that it may

be almost as much fun hunting as shooting, depending on what you're looking for in the outdoors.

My viewpoint on how many rabbits I should have in the bag changed drastically one day when my beagle panted his way right between my legs. He was behind an eager cottontail who also zeroed in between my ankles a moment ahead of the dog at a time when I was peeking along a path to see just where they were. That cottontail looked like he was playing tag with the pup, so how could I deny the dog his joy by bowling over the rabbit at the peak of his pleasure?

Besides, hound music should be listened to.

I relaxed and sat back while the beagle wore himself out with the trying chase. The baying that dog went through was worth more than any fancy killing shot I might have made.

I am not implying that this is now the only reason that I hunt, but I can understand the answer I got the other day from a fox hunter when I asked why he got only three foxes during the winter with a pack of good dogs.

He raised a hand and cupped it to his ear.

"I like to listen to the dogs," he confided.

I'm not so old yet that I can't get full enjoyment out of a good shot or two, or even a dozen, but I'm old enough to measure a good hunt in more ways than just by counting the number of shots I put through the barrel.

Don Lewis is, has been, and always will be a woodchuck hunter. He pursues them with the same amount of vigor and determination that drives the Boone and Crockett record-seeker to track a full-curl bighorn ram. There isn't a varmint cartridge of today or yesterday that Lewis hasn't fired at a woodchuck at sometime or other. He is, in the strictest sense of the words, a gun nut, but there is nothing nutty about his approach to shooting. He knows each rifle's capabilities and limitations and, inspired by a wife who likes to shoot as much as he does (as a matter of fact, Helen, I think you're a better shot than he is), dearly enjoys writing about them. The Lewises are the East's number one varmint-shooting team.

CHAPTER 11

Rifles for Squirrel and Varmint Hunting

DON LEWIS

The sharp rocks along the edge of the creek cut into my bare feet as I tried to ease noiselessly toward a caved-in coal mine that was a favorite den for several large chucks. It took me five minutes of hard work to cover 75 yards and get within 30 yards of the forgotten mine. There was not a sign of a chuck; my work had been in vain. I watched the opening for about ten minutes and then decided to leave, since the bugs and mosquitoes were swarming all over me. Just as I turned, a large chuck appeared from nowhere. I was caught flat-footed. Worse yet, this was my first chuck hunt, and I think my blood pressure was near the boiling point when I realized that I was face to face with my first chuck. The single shot M60 Winchester seemed to weigh 10 pounds as I raised it to my shoulder. Sweat blurred my vision, but I froze the open sights on the chuck's head and squeezed the trigger. Nothing happened, and I thought I had missed. Slowly the chuck slid down the dusty bank and lay still. I had killed my first chuck.

This small episode took place not too long after President Roosevelt made his famous "nothing to fear but fear itself" speech. Back in those days the farm boy knew little of the outside world and he didn't have an array of imported gadgets for amusement. The farm kid made his own pleasures. He was walled in by rolling hills and splashing streams, so he took naturally to the out of doors. His heroes weren't TV stars and professional football players. The country kid had his own local heroes. One of the few men we looked up to beyond the limits of our own community was E. J. Dailey, a famous trapper. We followed him with pure reverence because most of us loved to trap.

I came from this climate. I trapped along the streams and hunted everything the woods had to offer. Although I had a good sampling of every type of hunting, the flame that was lighted the day I shot my first woodchuck never died. Almost forty years later it still burns, and the sight of a grizzled chuck frozen in an upright position raises the temperature of my bloodstream. So far as I'm concerned, other than squirrel hunting, there is no type of hunting that can compare with the precisioned skill of varmint shooting. It may seem ridiculous in this modern era of elephant safaris to Africa, Kodiak bear hunts in the frozen northland, and charge-account trips to the land of the mule deer to extol the pleasure of pitting your skill against the insignificant woodchuck, but that's how I see it. In truth, I've always been a varmint hunter, and it's too late to change now.

I recall this bit of nostalgia simply to lend some credence to what I'm about to say. Precision varmint and squirrel hunting has been my life. From the five-dollar M60 Winchester that I used to shoot my first chuck, I've fired practically every type and caliber of varmint rifle that ever existed. From the common 22 long-rifle shell to the modern Magnums, I've watched the growth of the varmint rifle. I used to stand in awe and watch a neighbor shoot a 250-3000 Savage. I believed the incredible stories that were told in the country store about this rifle. Not knowing anything about ballistics and the law of gravity, I accepted with a pure conscience the old yarn that the 250-3000 bullet was so fast it rose six or eight inches after it left the muzzle. When I shot my first 22 Hornet I was spellbound by the vicious crack. It never occurred to me then that I would see the day when this dreamboat of the 1930s would be relegated to the ranks of the unfit and unwanted. Perhaps it is somewhat antiquated now, but it killed a lot of woodchucks for me.

In the early 1900s varmint hunting was more of a necessity than a sport. Ridding the fields of crows, chucks, and foxes was not considered a hunting sport in those days. Since only an occasional hunter took varmint hunting in a serious light, there was no real demand for special equipment. Maybe the country kid kept varmint hunting alive with the Stevens Crackshot and the Remington M33 single-shot 22s. They were adequate for the short shots. But there is always a gunsmith or shooting enthusiast who dreams of something better, and here and there a gunsmith would create a "wildcat" that would increase the velocity, lower the trajectory, and give extra yardage. One of the earliest of these was the 25 Niedner. It was a 30-06 case necked down to the 25 caliber. Believe it or not, this early creation has survived the years. It was always popular with the varmint hunters, even though it was not turned out by a factory until Remington came out with it in the 700 Model. Before that, most of them were built on Mauser, Enfield, and Springfield actions. It is now known as the 25-06.

Down through the years, there were at least 2000 different manufacturers of automobiles. The same holds true of the early versions of the varmint rifle. Literally thousands of innovations were tried. I think every conceivable idea was attempted in modifying a cartridge case. Many of these homemades had genuine merit and filled a gap for the varmint hunter that the factory products didn't. It really didn't take too much to outdo the popular 25-20s and 32-20s of that era. Even though many of these creations never got off the ground, today's varmint hunter has benefited from this myriad of wildcats. I've already mentioned the 25-06, which at last got on the market. Others include the 6 mms and Jerry

Gebby's 22-250, which he called the Varminter. The trend to sharper shoulders that's so common today started with the wildcats.

In those early days when everyone was trying to outdo everybody else, velocity was the paramount goal of every gun builder. A rifle was considered an improvement if its velocity was 100 or so feet faster than the last creation. Driven by this mania for speed, all sorts of fantastic wildcats were turned out. I read of one cartridge that had a muzzle velocity of well over 5500 fps. It used a steel-jacket bullet. It wouldn't keep its bullets in a six-inch circle, and it just wouldn't kill. Winchester's famous 220 Swift with a muzzle velocity of over 4000 fps with the 48-grain bullet was the only ultrafast cartridge to get on the market until recently.

It finally became apparent that there was much more to a good varmint rifle than just sheer speed. At last the truth had been learned; too much speed kills accuracy. The short, lightweight bullet has limitations on how fast it can be pushed and still controlled. Sadder yet, the sizzling hot bullets cut the accurate life of a barrel very short. The thousands of scorched and burned-out barrels of the gaslight era are ample proof that man failed in his attempt to conquer muzzle velocity. The gun builders conceded defeat, and at this point the dream of a mile-a-second bullet was shattered and the quest for speed was over. Accuracy became the goal of a new era.

With all the fuss that was being generated by the homemade wildcats, it wasn't long before the arms manufacturers realized they were missing the boat. The 25-20 and 32-20 were the only calibers that had any semblance of speed, and they didn't offer too much. When the gun companies saw what some of the fellows were turning out in little shops in basements and garages, they took a second look at varmint shooting. The little 22 Hornet was brought out by Winchester in 1930, and it was the first commercial cartridge designed especially for the long-range varmint shooter. Actually, the Hornet is not a true modification of another case. It is another case with no changes made. It's the old Winchester

22 WCF case with a new-type bullet and a different powder charge. The Hornet made a substantial contribution to varmint shooting in its day. If nothing else, it proved beyond a doubt that varmint hunting is more than just potting a chuck at a few yards with a 22 rifle. Secondly, the Hornet's 200-yard range forced the hunter to use a scope, and the day had finally arrived when the varmint hunter could make precise shots at ranges never dreamed of before.

The 22 Hornet changed the ideas of the average hunter and made him think more in terms of varmint hunting, but it was not the only rifle to help the sport grow. The 218 Bee was formed by necking down a 32-20 or a 25-20 repeater. With a larger powder capacity than the Hornet, it offered a slight edge in velocity, a flatter trajectory, and longer range. Winchester brought it out in the M65 lever action and again in the late 1940s in the M43. I liked the Bee, but it just didn't have much more than the Hornet.

Harvey Lovell, a highly skilled gunsmith, necked the 25-20 to a 22 caliber and came up with a velocity of around 3000 fps. Naming his new offspring the 22-3000 Lovell, he made a real gain over the 2600 fps Hornet. His original load of 16 grains of 4227 gave the 50-grain bullet sufficient speed for 250-yard shots along with good accuracy. This version enjoyed a short span of life as a wildcat. Many of them were built on the Winchester High Side Wall and the Remington Hepburn, but the cartridge died when the 25-20 case was discontinued.

Just as soon as a new wildcat would get a little attention, some gunsmith would attempt to improve it. Lysle D. Kilbourn made his famous 22 K Hornet by increasing the Hornet's capacity. Knowing that brass will flow, he just straightened the chamber walls and fired a factory case in it. It blew right out to the exact dimensions of the modified chamber, and a larger case was the end result. Another grain or two of powder could be used, but the hunter didn't profit much by the additional powder charge. The ones I shot didn't give me the feeling that I had a lot more yardage than I had with the Hornet. Harvey Donaldson, father of the 219

Wasp, did the same thing to the 22-3000 Lovell. His work could be considered successful, but like the 22 K Hornet, it failed to make the varmint hunter shout for joy.

I've shot many 25-06s, and I have one that was "improved." In the regular necked-down '06 case, 58 or 59 grains of 4831 powder can be used. In my blown-out improved job, 61 grains of 4831 can be stuffed in without effort. On the chronograph, I couldn't see where the slight rise in velocity was worth the extra pressure and heat that the action and barrel were subjected to. In fact, I could never get the improved job to shoot as well as several regular outfits I used.

Since the wildcat cartridge is just a standard case that has been modified to new dimensions, it might clear the air a little to find out just how this is done. There are two popular methods. The most common is fire forming. A conventional loaded round is put into a chamber that has been machined to the size of the new case wanted. When the shell is fired, the pressure produced by the expanding gases forces the case to the fit of the new dimensions, forming a new case. There is a good bit of case loss sometimes if the brass is old and brittle. On some cases, I've used a small amount of hot pistol powder and filled the case with corn meal to cut down on case splitting. Most cases are modified by making the neck angle sharper and lengthening the case to get more powder capacity.

Cold forming is another way to change the case. The 243 Rockchucker is the 30-06 case necked down to 243. It requires two steps. The regular '06 case is forced into a 25-06 trim die, and the excess brass that protrudes is filed off. The reduced case is then resized in a 243 Rockchuck sizing die, bringing it on down to 243. Not all case modifying is necking down to a smaller caliber. The 30-06 can be necked up to the 35 Whelen and still retain the original 17°30′ shoulder angle. To bring the whole thing down to a cartridge that everyone is familiar with, the famous 270 Winchester is the 30-06 necked down to 270.

With all the fine varmint rifles available today, there is little demand for the wildcatters. This doesn't mean that every varmint hunter is satisfied with what he can buy over the counter. The world of the wildcat is fascinating. There's an allure about it that tugs at the heart of the varmint hunter. Even though his outfit is pinpoint precise at 250 yards, he dreams of a new creation that will give him another hundred yards of accuracy. As long as there are gunsmiths, lathes, and milling machines, there will be wildcats. That desire to create and improve just won't die. The factory can flood the market with all types of fancy long-range shooting outfits, but the true varmint hunter will still yearn for something better. This is what keeps the gun factories on their toes. Remember, they were pretty well satisfied back in the early years with the 25-20; fortunately for us today, yesteryear's varmint hunter wasn't.

With so many varmint rifles available, how can a hunter decide what is best? High velocities are common, accuracy has improved with the fine barrels and bullets we now have, and the prices are not beyond reach. Good results can be expected with almost every one of these new rifles, regardless of the make or model. It's a tough choice. However, there are certain requisites in a varmint rifle that should not be overlooked. I dropped a number of chucks with the single-shot 22 Hornet in the Savage M219. The M43 Winchester in either the Hornet or the Bee was a fair outfit. The old Savage 22 High Power in the M99 and some other old-timers were rather impressive. Notice I mentioned the model of the rifle. There's a reason for this. Sometimes the caliber is not always as important as the type or model of rifle. Of course, you can't successfully use a 22 Hornet for 300-yard shots in any model. What I'm getting at is that the rifles I just mentioned, along with a good many on the market today, aren't bad in the accuracy column, but they lack a great deal as real varmint outfits. The varmint rifle is far from the conventional hunting rifle. A good bit is written about the all-round rifle, the combination rifle, the one that works equally well on either big game or varmints. There is just no such rifle, however impressive the article or the advertising might be. A varmint rifle is always a varmint rifle. Several things lead me to this conviction. After a good many years of varmint hunting and benchrest shooting, I found out that not just any rifle will meet the high requirements of the varmint outfit. Few six-to-eight-pound hunting rifles with thin, short barrels can fill the needs of the varmint specialist.

One of the most overlooked aspects of the varmint rifle is the first shot. As far as I'm concerned, this is the first requisite of a good chuck gun. How it groups or shoots after it's warm is of little consequence. It's the first shot that counts with the varmint hunter. There aren't too many hunting rifles that will put the first shot on the point of aim. I've fired dozens that took two or three shots to get the bullet to hit where the rifle was zeroed in for. One rifle I tested shot the first two or three shots as far as four inches from the aiming point at 100 yards. As soon as it was warm, it laid them right in. The varmint rifle can't have this deficiency, regardless of how small it might be. Every shot from the varmint rifle is a precisioned, well-aimed shot, and there is no room for error. This one factor alone rules out most conventional hunting rifles.

This means that the varmint rifle must have a long, heavy barrel at least three-quarters of an inch in diameter at the muzzle. The long, heavy barrel cuts down on vibrations and allows the rifle to keep the bullets in a very small area. The extra weight makes the rifle easier to hold.

The hunting rifle's stock varies a great deal from the varmint job. On the varmint outfit, strength is needed along with a lot of wood. Unlike the thin, narrow fore-arm on the big-game rifle, a flat beavertail fore-arm will keep the varmint rifle from canting. The long, heavy barrel should be bedded in a lot of solid wood. This all adds up to a stock weighing four to five pounds. Adding this to a seven-pound barreled action and a two-pound target scope puts the varmint rifle in the heavyweight class.

Of the important ingredients that make up the varmint rifle, the trigger should rank high on the list. No rifle is any better than its trigger. It makes little difference how expensive the material was, what the caliber is, or how much painstaking labor was involved, if the trigger is poor, so is the rifle. As I see it, a high-quality adjustable trigger should be on every varmint rifle. No other type will meet all the requirements. A trigger that is crisp, clean on release, and has no movement afterward is by no means easy to come by. The three factors I just mentioned are very important to the long-range shooter. If a trigger has play in it and is not crisp, the shooter will be uncertain when the shot will go. The pull of the trigger depends entirely on the individual. I prefer a pull of about two pounds. A person with large, powerful hands might not find a two-pound pull to his liking. A four-pound pull might be better for him. In any case, the pull should be exactly what the shooter needs. Backward movement—override past the point of release—can cause a slight jerk in the trigger pull. Since the trigger should be as personal as your toothbrush, get it exactly as you want it. With a fine adjustable trigger, it won't take too many shots to determine just how it should be set for you.

I can honestly say that any type of rifle can be used for varmint hunting. I can honestly say it, but I won't suggest it. There are rifles that will give much better results on varmints than ordinary big-game rifles. I've mentioned some of the early jobs such as the Hornet, Bee, Swift, Lovell, and 219 Wasp. Not one of these rifles is on the market today commercially. They weren't discontinued because they were inadequate. In fact, the 220 Swift still remains superior in terms of velocity to today's products. But time has a way of changing things. Why worry about getting shells for a 220 Swift or some other discontined case when a modern product will give the same results. I can't fret over the loss of the Hornet or the 218 Bee when the 222 Remington is more accurate and offers another 50 yards. Much as I liked these old-timers, I'm not going to lose any sleep over them. Take the Remington M700 heavy barrel 22-250, for instance. I've shot a good many of them, and they have what I like: a good strong action, weight, lots of wood, and the adjustable trigger. Top it off with a 10x or 12x high-grade varmint scope, and you've got a rifle that'll shoot better than you can hold. By concocting a not-too-hot load, you can expect top accuracy and years of barrel life.

The 22-250, which lived the first 30 years of its life as a

wildcat, is probably the top 224 caliber on the market today. But the 222 Remington gets credit for upgrading varmint hunting to where it is today. It may be that it made its appearance at the exact moment needed, or perhaps it was the fact that it was a new design instead of a modification of another case that made it become so popular so quickly. Whatever it was, it was as welcome as the last day of your mother-in-law's visit. At last the varmint hunter had a cartridge that had a flat trajectory, sufficient speed for long-range shooting, and a report that didn't rattle the surrounding countryside. It was a great day for the varmint hunter when a rifle could be bought over the counter that offered all this.

The 222 was later upped to the 222 Magnum, but for my money, I couldn't appreciate the new version. Like other calibers that had been improved, the 222 Magnum failed to come up to expectations. It didn't fill a gap between the regular 222 and the hotter versions. The 222 is a 250-yard rifle, and the 22-250 can easily handle another 100 yards, so there is not much purpose in buying a rifle that has a 275-yard range.

I've always thought of varmint hunting, chuck hunting in particular, as a 22-caliber sport. The 224 bullets are hard to beat, but they have one serious drawback; they can't cope with wind when the shots get beyond 125 yards. I've shot the high-speed Swift, the 22-250, and several other fast-shooting 224 calibers when the wind was turning the leaves on the clover stocks, and there was no semblance of accuracy. An occasional hit only proved that I had the wrong rifle. This is where the 6 mms and 25 calibers show their stuff. The heaviest slug I ever fired in the 224 caliber was 63 grains. This helped some in the wind, but the velocity dropped severely. The 75- and 87-grain bullets in the 243 can be pushed out the muzzle at over 3000 pfs. Even the 90-grain bullet will rub the 3000 foot mark, and in severe wind the 105-grain slug will cover the yardage in a hurry when it leaves the muzzle at over 2700 fps.

Earlier I referred to the all-round rifle. I suppose the 243 Winchester and 6 mm Remington can be put in this category.

There is no question about either's ability in the varmint class, and the 105-grain bullets handle deer and black bear fairly well.

Unfortunately, the 257 calibers fell victim to the 6 mms. There are still a good many 257 Roberts outfits available, but there is no great demand for them. The 25-06 helped keep the 257 bullets available, and now with Remington and Ruger bringing out the 25-06 in a factory product, we may see something of a resurgence of the old caliber. The 256 that Winchester developed is more suited for pistols than for rifles. Marlin came out with the M63 for this shell. It's a fine lever-action rifle, but the cartridge has to be classed around 125 yards. This takes us right back to the Hornet and the Bee.

I suppose the ultimate in long, long-range varmint shooting is the Magnum. Winchester's 264 and Remington's 7 mm have really impressed the shooting world. There can be no argument against these rifles being used for a dual purpose. Both have the power and speed to handle all types of hunting in the Northeast. Although the 264 didn't catch on as well as the 7 mm, it's still a fine rifle. It's 6.5 bore size was it's worst enemy, I think. The 7 mm just squeezed it out of the picture.

Remington's 7 mm has created more stir in the gun realm than any other big cartridge. You can't shoot one without immediately feeling a sense of respect for it. I think I've fired more than fifty of these powerhouses, and I never seem to be able to shake that feeling. Its power and pressure require a strong belted-head case, and to give an idea of the speed this rifle can attain, the 150-grain slug can hit a velocity of 3260 fps! That's moving a big bullet real fast. The 7 mm Magnum has a slight edge on the 264, since the larger bullet diameter gives a greater efficiency in the hunting-length barrels. Strange as it may seem, the 7 mm Magnum offers a longer barrel life than the 264.

I see great promise for the 7 mm Magnum and the fine Weatherby creations in the field of long-range shooting. The long, heavy bullets have a better ballistic coefficient than the smaller, shorter bullets. Whether it be a mountain goat at 600 yards or a sneaking fox at 250, the Magnums offer precise bullet placement. Their recoil is severe, and the noise will make you unwelcome in some areas, but the Magnums are here to stay; we may as well make room for them.

The newest entry into the varmint line-up is the 17 caliber. At the moment, it is turned out for factory fodder in the Remington M700. Harrington & Richardson have the 17/223 Ultra Wildcat. This is the 223 Remington case necked down to 17. The regular military 5.56 mm case can be used. There is a difference between the 17 Remington and the 17/223 Ultra Wildcat. Remington pushed their case neck back .087 of an inch. It would be unwise to fire the Remington in the H & R rifle, since there would be excessive headspace. The testing I've done so far leads me to believe the 17 is not just a flash in the pan. Definitely a 250-yard outfit with its 4000 fps muzzle velocity.

Where does all this leave the varmint hunter? In mighty good hands, as far as I'm concerned. Never in the history of hunting has the varmint shooter had such an array of types and calibers to choose from. Whether it be bolt, lever, or pump, he can have a varmint caliber in his favorite type of action. The 700 Remington varmint gun comes in the 222, 223, 22-250, 6 mm, and the 243 Winchester. Winchester covers the varmint line with its fine M70 and M88. Mossberg offers the 22-250 and 243 calibers in the M800. Sako has a good thing going for them in the Vixen heavy-barrel 222 and 222 Magnum. Savage offers the 110 Model in the 22-250 caliber in either left- or right-handed actions. There are plenty of others, including Weatherbys, H & Rs, Brownings, and Rugers. In fact, the chuck hunter of today has so much to choose from, he doesn't know which way to turn. Almost every company offers a full line of varmint calibers in either conventional hunting rifles or special heavyweights. It's really a matter of determining what is best for the type of shooting you will be doing. Keep in mind that the calibers run pretty much the same in all models, but there can be a whale of a difference in others aspects. Stay with the idea that you need weight, plenty of stock, and a good trigger.

A varmint rifle is not much better than its sighting arrangement. A good rifle with a poor scope will always be a mediocre outfit. Any high-quality scope can be used, but the varmint rifle will perform to a higher standard with the target-type scopes. Don't go overboard on power. Ten power is probably the best, but a 12 power can be used.

Regular hunting scopes, including the fine variable powers, have internal adjustments. These are not always as dependable as they should be. In other words, the adjustments don't always meter correctly, especially in the variable powers. The target and varmint types have external adjustments in the mounts. Each click actually moves the entire scope. If the bases are mounted the proper distance apart on the rifle, the slightest correction can be made without difficulty. The varmint-type scope ranks with the fine adjustable trigger. It takes them both to make a fine varmint rifle.

I think if we take an objective view of varmint hunting, we will agree that there is no one rifle that would be best for all of us. Varmint hunting can be highly skilled. It demands the best from the hunter and his outfit, so we should not condone or condemn any one rifle. We should simply strive to reach a higher degree of excellence with the one we use.

Chuck hunting might not compare with stopping a Bengal tiger or downing a mighty Kodiak bear. On the other hand, only a few hunters ever get a chance at exotic big game. For the rest of us, varmint hunting will have to suffice. Well-placed shots are the mark of the skilled varmint hunter. Dropping a chuck at 300 yards may sound rather insignificant, but it's a lot tougher to do than hitting a Bengal tiger at a mere 30.

I suppose the main reason I took naturally to squirrel hunting is that it is varmint hunting in miniature. The calibers used differ, but the type of shooting is the same. It's plenty tough to place a bullet precisely at 250 yards in varmint shooting, and it's just as tough to steer a bullet through a maze of limbs and leaves, trying to connect on a squirrel's head at 50 yards. In either case, it takes an experienced rifleman with a good rifle to accomplish it.

Squirrel hunting has been greatly overlooked by the average hunter. The trend towards using the shotgun for squirrels may have led many hunters to think only in terms of blasting a squirrel out of a tree with a load of shot. That's not too hard to do. This is not the type of squirrel hunting I'm talking about. There's nothing wrong with using the shotgun for squirrels, and it goes without saying that more squirrels will be taken with the smooth bore. However, the scoped 22 rifle puts squirrel hunting in a class by itself. If you think it's easy, try it. You might come back empty-handed several times before you drop your first squirrel. The shotgunner can take a whack at a squirrel in almost any situation; the rifleman must wait until the squirrel stops and a clear shot is available. This can be quite a wait. It can become pretty nerve-racking to get the squirrel in this position.

Varmint hunting has so many variations in rifles and calibers. It's impossible to pick just one. This is not the case in squirrel hunting. The common 22 long-rifle cartridge is the only one. Center-fire jobs are too explosive and powerful for squirrel hunting, and they are a hazard in the woods. The 22 Magnum also has some drawbacks. For the 50 yards-or-less shots in squirrel shooting, the 22 Magnum is too fast. It literally tears the squirrel apart. And the copper-clad slug of the 22 Magnum is prone to ricochet. It's true the 22 Magnum might add a few yards to the squirrel hunter's range, but this is not as important as it may sound. The squirrel hunting that I have done usually offered me 35 to 50 yard shots. The common 22 long-rifle bullet will act like a professional up to that distance.

I was as mistaken as the rest down through the years in thinking that the squirrel hunter needs no better rifle than the old single shot or pump rifle. I had always used a standard rifle with high-speed ammo. This was what everyone else used. But I began to see a ray of light when I assembled a semi-target 22 with an adjustable trigger along with a one-inch high-grade target scope. When I pitted two or three of my old favorites with cheap scopes against the new job, I soon discovered that the old favorites weren't as accurate as I had always believed. When I switched the new job to target ammo, it was difficult for me to accept the results. The rifles that I had put so much faith in down through the years fell far short with their one-and-a-half-inch to two-inch groups at 50 yards. Target ammo improved them somewhat, but they still couldn't produce the dime-size groups that the new outfit shot with ease. I must have shot at least 20 different rifles before I accepted the fact that most bolts, pumps, and levers won't shoot the tight groups needed for good squirrel shooting.

I realize that you can't honestly compare the average 22 rifle with an inexpensive scope against the type of rifle I tested. I also know that to suggest parting with close to 200 dollars for a squirrel outfit will make a good many hunters think you've chased too many squirrels. Few of these hunters would blink an eyelash if you suggested paying that much or more for a big-game rifle. The trouble stems from the fact that most of these hunters never tried this type of squirrel hunting. Perhaps they shot a squirrel or two with the old pump or lever, but they never pitted their ability and their rifle against these wary targets for any great period of time. In other words, they never got down to the serious business of squirrel hunting with the rifle.

If the 22 rifle you have won't shoot to your satisfaction, there are a number of models on the market that will. The Browning T-Bolt, the Remington M581, the Winchester M52D with the standard-weight barrel, and the Savage/Anchutz M54 and M164 all fall into the category of fine-shooting rifles. I've had good results with Mossberg's 144-LS target rifle. Several old-time models to look for are Remington's 521T and Winchester's 75 Sporter. Either of these rifles will make the grade. Most of these rifles are a little on the heavy side, but the squirrel hunter, like the chuck hunter, does not travel much. Most of his hunting time is spent watching and waiting. A few extra pounds will not be any drawback, and the additional weight of these rifles will make aiming much easier.

If the run-of-the-mill 22 rifle isn't always suitable for squirrel shooting, neither is the ten-dollar scope. The squirrel hunter needs a good scope just as much as the varmint hunter does. In fact, his shots are just as difficult, even though they are shorter. To say that a six power is a six power regardless of the cost is not being fair. There is much more to a good scope than how much it will magnify. The ability to transmit light is the mark of a good scope. Since the squirrel hunter usually hunts in the early morning and into the gathering shadows of dusk, his scope must be capable of showing a clear, sharp image. To do this, it must transmit to the eye a high percentage of the light that the front objective lens gathers. Scope makers admit that each air-to-glass surface reflects part of the light back. The amount can vary from four to seven percent. In a scope having ten air-to-glass surfaces, the reflection loss could be fifty percent or more. The seriousness of this loss is not so much that the target image is dimmed but that the "scatter-light" or "flare" from these reflections makes the image look gray or dull. The answer to this problem is lens coating. However, this happens to be a highly technical and complex operation. Bombarding a coating of magnesium fluoride not much more than six millionths of an inch thick on each air-to-glass surface requires some highly trained specialists and a few dollars worth of equipment. A scope that is properly coated will transmit far more light than an uncoated scope. On inexpensive scopes, the two outside lenses are coated for appearances' sake, but unless each air-to-glass surface is coated, not too much is gained.

One of my favorite squirrel scopes is the Unertl 6x one-inch target scope. It has tremendous light transmission, and its reticle is very fine. At 50 yards, the reticle will quarter a 30-caliber bullet hole. Most reticles on the inexpensive scopes will cover the head of a squirrel at 50 yards. Another feature of the target scope is its external adjustments in the mounts. The important thing here is the mounting. To get a quarter-inch adjustment at 100 yards, the two bases of a target scope should be seven and two tenths inches apart. However, I like to mount them a little farther apart on squirrel rifles so that the smallest adjustment can be made.

If you don't have one of these special outfits, it doesn't mean that you're out of luck. The common 22 rifle will bring down a lot of squirrels, and a lot of pleasure can be derived from pitting your skill against these high targets. I would suggest using low-velocity target ammo instead of the super-speed stuff. Target ammo will make any rifle perform better, and it has plenty of killing power for squirrels, even on the long shots.

If you've been thinking all these years that squirrel hunting is only for the boy with the six-dollar rifle, give it a try. I'll wager that it won't be too long before you'll decide that it offers any hunter a real challenge. It's a good bet that after a season or two with the regular 22, you'll be slipping a few dollars away each month to get a rifle and scope that will produce one-hole groups at 50 yards. It may take quite awhile to save that much, but, believe me, it's a day worth waiting for.

Keith Schuyler is an outdoorsman and writer with many special hats in his closet. Author of the books Archery, From Golds to Big Game, Lures *(a much-sought-after collector's item), and* Elusive Horizons, *an account of his World War II adventures as a B-24 pilot, Keith lives life with a gusto that would leave many of us bringing up the rear. A serious student of the archery game, he shows the outdoorsman how to have more fun with the more common small-game animals that are available to all of us.*

CHAPTER 12

Bowhunting for Small Trophies

KEITH C. SCHUYLER

The classic picture of a bowhunter shows him drawing down on some species of big game, usually a deer. This is frequently a depiction of one of Robin Hood's men poaching one of the King's deer or of an American Indian crouched behind a bush at a water hole. Things haven't changed much, particularly in the northeastern section of the United States, where the white-tailed deer is the most sought after quarry of the bowhunter.

Too often overlooked, however, is the sport that may be had with what is usually classified as small game. Although chasing a rabbit around a briar patch with a bow and arrow is somewhat less momentous than the downing of a big-game species, it is no less challenging. It has always been my belief that any legal wild creature taken with the bow and arrow is a trophy of sorts. To me, this is true whether it be a water snake or a wild turkey.

This brings us to the subject of identifying just what might be considered small game. If we look at hunting around the world, or even just within the continental limits of the United States, there would certainly be some areas of question. For example, it would be difficult to classify a 40-pound peccary as *big game*, but it hardly fits into the same classification that includes rabbits and squirrels. And a 400-pound Russian boar, or even one of the big feral pigs of the Georgia swamp, could hardly be considered small game in any classification. The dictionary is of little help, since it merely classifies big game as the more dangerous types, such as lions and elephants, which are hunted for sport rather than food. Game, generally, is classified as that which is hunted for food rather than sport.

If we confined our discussion to upland game species, our trophies would be well defined but rather limited. They would be such creatures as the wild turkey, the cottontail rabbit, the snowshoe hare, the ruffed grouse, etc. Obviously we would not include predators such as foxes, great horned owls, and many other targets that are a challenge even to the gun hunter. Excluded also would be such creatures as water snakes, snapping turtles, and others that make the toughest types of targets for archers but which are not very challenging to gun hunters.

So let's just consider them collectively as *small trophies*. A bowhunter seldom shoots so often as to make the question of whether the target is edible much of a consideration. We are going to discuss in particular those creatures with which I have had a shooting acquaintance.

A bowhunting contest held by our local club throws some light on our subject. Each creature, whether a protected game species, a fish, or a predatory bird or animal, is weighted in the contest with points based on the availability of the creature in question as well as on the difficulty of finding it and the difficulty of shooting it.

The two species of big game normally found in my home state of Pennsylvania were quickly dispensed with by crediting 50 points for a bear and 25 points for a deer. Antlered deer score one extra point for each antler point measuring one inch or more.

No more than 50 points can be credited in any one category. This rule is to prevent someone from cleaning up if, for example, he happens to come upon huge schools of spawning carp in the spring.

Other species are weighted as follows: turkey, goose, or wildcat—20 points; great horned owl—12 points; fox or crow—10 points; ringneck, duck, grouse, quail, or dove—8; raccoon, porcupine, or woodchuck—6; gray squirrels—5; red squirrels, cottontails, snowshoe hares, skunks, opossums, and unprotected fish—4; unprotected birds such as starlings, grackles, cowbirds, kingfishers, blue jays—3; common rats—2; chipmunks, water snakes, copperheads, and rattlesnakes—1.

You could sit around for a month trying to work out the proper score for each of the above species and still not arrive at a perfect arrangement. Yet we had little difficulty in getting agreement on this method of scoring. All trophies must be taken in fair chase under existing game laws, and any conviction for a game violation eliminates the archer from competition.

As is true of all types of hunting and fishing, no one person has all the answers to bowhunting questions. I say this in order to encourage others to improve upon what is presented here. In what follows you will find successful methods of taking small game in season and other creatures usually unprotected by law. In each instance, however, it is important that you be aware of local or state regulations relative to such shooting.

Tackle for Small Targets

Hunting most small game requires very little refinement of archery tackle. There are exceptions, of course, but generally speaking you can go with the bow that you normally use for field-target shooting.

It follows that little special selection is needed in choosing hunting arrows. Anyone who has done much shooting with the bow knows that the same weight arrow that works well on the target range will work equally well in the field.

However, if a heavier head is used, a correspondingly heavier shaft will be needed. I recommend that you use for hunting the bow that you can score the best with on field targets. Any arrow that flies well for a particular bowhunter and his bow is suitable for small trophy targets.

Of course, top target archers are not likely to risk their finely tuned bows and arrows for *any* kind of hunting. Nevertheless, these archers will do well to use hunting tackle that generally approximates that tackle that works best for them on the target range.

Cottontail Targets

Among small-game bowhunters, as among gunners, the cottontail rabbit certainly rates as the most popular. It is top eating and an enticing target wherever it is found, which is practically everywhere.

There are two ways to take the cottontail with the bow, and either might be considered tops in sport. One way is to seek shooting ahead of a slow beagle. The other way is stalking. Any rabbit is a relatively tough target to hit, so you should have no compunction about taking them wherever you can get shooting. No sportsman deserving of the name would shoot a rabbit with a shotgun when it is sitting in its nest, but trying to hit one with an arrow is a special challenge under all conditions.

It would seem that any arrowhead would be suitable for taking cottontails. However, my personal preference is for regular field points. Any arrowhead has sufficient killing capability, but the amazing stamina of most wild creatures makes it advisable to use heads that will pin the quarry to the ground. Strangely enough, a broadhead arrow that can effectively dispatch a big-game animal will sometimes slice through a rabbit and skip off without holding the creature for quick dispatch. Any such wound is usually fatal, but the rabbit may escape to the nearest ground-hog hole or lose itself among the trees or vegetation before succumbing to the wound.

Over the years I have taken a great many cottontails with regular field points. Until the past season, none that were hit had ever escaped successfully. In the one unfortunate incident, I had made what was, for me, a fantastically long shot—43 yards by actual measurement. The rabbit carried the arrow to a hole where it struggled free. It undoubtedly died very quickly. Since successful shots are normally made at ten yards or less, the angle of the arrow will usually carry it into the ground. In this incident, the flat angle of the shot prevented the arrow from burying itself properly in the ground. Or it may have hit a stone. In any event, this one loss has not discouraged me from continuing to use field points on rabbits.

If you own or have access to the services of a good, slow beagle, hunting in the very heaviest brush can be most rewarding. In such areas, gun hunting is difficult because targets are frequently too close for good shooting without literally destroying the rabbit. But bowhunting requires close shooting for consistent success.

If you must go without a dog, open areas sometimes provide the best bowhunting. Clover fields and other crop lands adjacent to good cover are favorite places for rabbits to nest during the day. It doesn't take especially good vision to find sitting rabbits, but it is necessary to know how to find them. Any suspicious clumps of weeds or breaks in the normal pattern of vegetation should be suspect. Look for the black button that is the eye of the cottontail. It is best to follow a circular approach, so that it is not necessary to stop until a rabbit is actually located. Once a hunter stops, he is generally committed to shoot. The next step may send the rabbit hightailing it.

Hunting when the snow is on the ground is sometimes excellent because it is much easier to spot a rabbit's nest. Cottontails are inclined to be more nervous at this time of the year, and they frequently go out wild at the hunter's approach. But no matter when or where you find shooting with the bow at the cottontail rabbit, you will have a chance for game that is challenging as a target and rewarding on the table.

Hunting snowshoe hares, sometimes called white rabbits, is little different from hunting cottontails. Hunting with dogs is all but out, since the snowshoe is a great traveler and is unlikely to provide much shooting once it has jumped from its nest. Consequently, hunting snowshoes is purely a stalking proposition, as you seek to discover them before they take to their feet.

Bird Hunting

In general, trying to shoot birds on the wing with a bow and arrow is not encouraged here. The chances for success, unless shooting is done under absolutely controlled conditions, preclude the possibility that many archers will give up their gun shooting for the improbable chance with a bow. And shooting into the air with arrows, which must always come down, can be dangerous at the worst and annoying to other hunters at the least.

Shooting birds on the ground, whether they be game birds or unprotected species, presents an entirely different set of conditions, for there are birds that can be decoyed or called in to the bow.

The wild turkey presents the greatest challenge. Considered by many hunters as equal to or exceeding a deer as a trophy, the wily wild turkey is certainly one of the toughest targets to take with the bow and arrow. It is not only smart, it is big, and no bow is too heavy. The best broadheads you can buy are recommended for turkeys and for any of the larger birds.

Because the turkey is so cute, the chance of stalking one down is practically nil. Any bird shot in this manner would almost certainly be one that was freshly stocked. On the other hand, turkeys can be called in to the archer by means of an artificial caller. My favorite for this is the diaphragm caller that fits into the roof of the mouth, since both hands can then be kept free while the calling is done. The smart caller uses his audio lure sparingly, preferably no oftener than once every five minutes.

If he scatters a flock of turkeys in the autumn, the archer has an excellent chance to call one in to the bow. Such turkeys will be anxious to get back together, and they will frequently respond to an artificial call. Where spring hunting is permitted, huge gobblers may be easily called up, although getting them close enough for a shot is another story. Anyone who takes a turkey with a bow and arrow can be rightly proud of his achievement.

Ducks and geese can both be decoyed in for close shots if the archer is well hidden. Trying to get a shot off without alarming waterfowl is a difficult proposition at any time. There is no question that taking either of these birds with a bow would rate with the best among hunting accomplishments. But the possibility of doing so in most areas is so remote as to discourage most archers from even trying.

There are probably more grouse shot with the bow and arrow than there are ring-necked pheasants, although grouse are harder to hit. It is not unusual for grouse to be clucking about a deer stand, and in some of the more remote areas they are fairly tame.

Ring-necked pheasants usually must be found sitting in deep grass, clover, or heavy weeds. Such opportunities are extremely few and far between because of the ringneck's excellent ability to conceal itself.

There is much talk of fru-fru, or flou-flou, arrows for use in bird hunting, but they are largely impractical. There is always the possibility that special situations will lend themselves to pass shooting or jump shooting, but such situations occur so seldom as to be not worth considering.

If you are contemplating such shooting, I recommend that it be done only under controlled conditions where no possibility exists of harming or alarming other hunters. But the cost of arrows as well as the difficulty in obtaining shooting at birds is certain to limit wing shooting with the bow.

Squirrel Hunting

Hunting squirrels with the bow and arrow is sport of the finest. The difficulty that attends such hunting makes each success a momentous occasion. Nevertheless, squirrels can be taken. It requires patience, good shooting, and a special look at arrows.

Shooting broadheads at squirrels is certain to be expensive as well as impractical. However, if you have some old broadheads and you plan to take nothing but ground shots, do use them. A gray squirrel can take an awful lot of punishment.

From the standpoint of safety and practicability, however, blunts are the best heads to use on squirrels. They have enough shocking power to knock a squirrel from a tree or kill him on the spot. A miss can mean a lost arrow on an aerial shot, but a blunt is unlikely to stick in a branch or the main trunk of the tree. Flu-flu fletching is desirable for tree shots. The arrow is less likely to stray into unknown territory, and your chances of recovering it are much better.

If you have hunted gray squirrels with a gun, then you know how to *hunt* them with the bow. You can wait them out at a likely spot, which is frequently a sheltered hollow in the woods or a neck of timber leading to a cornfield, or you can walk quietly along, looking for strays. It is a good idea to work with a companion when moving along, since squirrels have a well-known tendency to keep timber between themselves and the view of a hunter. If you are alone, a squirrel can sometimes be brought in view by throwing a stick or stone to the side of the tree where the animal is hiding.

Your score for a day's hunt will very likely be low, but the satisfaction that comes with downing even one of these tree dwellers is well worth the effort.

Hunting Woodchucks

Certainly one of the favorite sports of bowhunters in the Northeast is shooting, or shooting at, woodchucks. Bring on your heaviest hunting tackle, for these clever clover burrowers are very tough, and it takes a fast arrow to get them before they get under ground.

Hunting chucks with the bow is mostly a waiting game. Occasionally, close shooting can be found by walking through chuck-infested fields, but your best bet is to find burrows that are being used and make a stand near them.

A bodkin head is a good choice for these fellows, since it will inflict heavy damage while providing a certain amount of shocking power because its mass is greater than that of the average hunting head. If these heads are squared off at the back, so much the better. I do not recommend this type head for big game, because it is difficult to remove. However in shooting woodchucks this is a plus value, since it is sometimes necessary to make a mad dash and grab the arrow before the chuck gets into its burrow.

Just after sunup and just before sundown are the best times to take chucks. And, where legal, they provide hunting throughout the late spring, summer, and early fall months. Properly prepared, the young woodchuck is good eating.

Most farmers will be glad to give you permission to hunt, since woodchuck burrows are frequently dangerous to farm animals and machinery.

Submarine Shooting

Most states provide shooting at certain species of rough fish, but I think that all of them permit shooting of carp, though a fishing license as well as a hunting license may be required. But whatever you have to pay, it is worth it.

There are two tackle systems that are used for taking carp. Either can be used for other species of fish that are legal, including rays and sharks.

The most common system is the conventional equipment sold by most archery dealers. It consists of a large stationary spool that is fixed to the bow. The spool is wrapped with about 30 yards of line of up to 80-pound test to which the arrow is attached. Regular fish arrows are made of solid glass to give them weight. The heads are barbed. Fletching is unimportant, since shots are close. Some manufacturers provide rubber fins to serve as fletching.

The simplest method of hunting is to find a carp, shoot it, and drag it in.

To vary this a bit for more sport, particularly with large carp or marine species, join the bow-reel line to a fishing line. This is, in turn, attached to a rod and reel. After the shot is made, the heavy line will strip from the bow reel and you can then play the fish with conventional fishing tackle. The only part that archery plays is in getting the barb into the fish.

Another system that works well is simply to tape a spinning reel to the bow. The line from the reel is, of course, attached to the shaft or to the arrow head. In this manner the bow serves both in its usual capacity and as a fishing rod, since the quarry is played directly from the bow.

We use this system on smaller carp, snapping turtles, water snakes, and other legal aquatic targets. Junk wooden arrows can be fitted lightly into heads to which the line is attached. The loosely attached shaft will usually float free.

Stalking carp is much like hunting any other type of small game under normal circumstances. They are extremely wary except in the spring when they are spawning and can easily be approached in shallow water.

The main problem in shooting fish in deeper water is that of refraction. They always appear farther from you than they actually are, and you must make allowance for this in aiming. You can demonstrate this for yourself simply by placing a pencil or a knife in a glass of water. The object appears to bend at the point it breaks the surface.

Shooting fish may seem a long way from hunting, but it requires most of the same skills and it matches much of the excitement found in the woods.

Scatter Shots

Practically all of the other off-season targets use one or more of the requirements for species already discussed here. Raccoons, opossums, and foxes require the same tackle as the woodchuck.

Archery has an excellent safety record across the nation. All of us who hunt with the bow and arrow have an individual responsibility to maintain that record. Safety, respect for the landowner, and proper consideration for living targets are musts. This is little to assume in return for the enjoyment of a sport that will ever be a challenge to those who enjoy hunting at its hardest.

PART FOUR
Fishing

Boyd Pfeiffer, outdoor columnist for the Washington Post, *and John Plowman, full-time fisherman and part-time insurance salesman, here combine words to give the novice some basic information about fishing tackle. This isn't the sort of information that you'll get out of tackle catalogues but sound stuff that's based on actual fishing experience. For the beginner hitting the tackle store for the first time, some guidance like this is needed. The neophyte who follows the advice given here will be sure to avoid being saddled with equipment he'll never use.*

CHAPTER 13

Fishing Tackle

BOYD PFEIFFER and JOHN PLOMAN

We've come a long way in America since our forefathers had to "fish or go hungry." Few of the original settlers of this nation had ever wet a line in Europe, where sport fishing was reserved for the gentry and nobility. Thus the American pioneer learned most of his fishing techniques and obtained most of his "tackle" from the Indians, who employed a great variety of fishing methods, all aimed at acquiring the most fish in the least time. They speared big fish, sometimes using a lance with a detachable head attached to a leather thong, and they built weirs across tidal streams to trap salmon, shad, and other fish during the annual spawning runs. Nets were popular, as were basket traps set in small streams or along the shorelines of lakes and rivers.

Slowly, however, fishing as a sport became popular as the white man settled America and found ways to fill his larder with cultivated crops and domesticated meat. Early residents (*c.* 1700) of Boston, New York, and Philadelphia spent a great deal of time fishing, but it was not sport fishing as it is thought of today. Their tackle was crude. The rod, if one was used at all, was a cane pole 18 or 20 feet long. Frequently saplings along the stream or lake were cut for rods and fitted with a line of plaited horsehair (preferably the tail hair of a white stallion) to which was tied a hook baited up with whatever live bait could be caught.

Today anglers are still interested in "getting the most fish in the least time" but not through necessity. Most modern fishermen fish because no other sport offers them as much fun or as much challenge. A knowledge of fish habits and fishing waters and different fishing methods must be mastered if one is to consistently outwit the quarry. And unlike the hunter, the fisherman can always release his trophy unharmed to offer the same challenge another day.

Perhaps the greatest appeal of sport fishing is the variety of methods and equipment available to participants in this healthy, relaxing, and entertaining avocation.

Bait-Casting

Truly American in origin, the bait-casting outfit has undergone remarkable advances since its inception in the early 1800s. But the basics have not changed. Bait-casting outfits were originally designed to cast large baits—frogs, minnows, salamanders, etc.—that the fly rod could not handle. Spinning was many decades away at the time that bait-casting tackle was developed.

A look at a Snyder or Meek reel from the early 1800s would disclose a line-holding device not unlike today's reel in over-all appearance, but there the resemblance ends. The early reels, like those of today, had a handle on the right side to turn the spool and reel in the line and were made wide to hold a quantity of line. Some of these early reels were geared, so that one turn of the handle would turn the spool several times—the so called multiplying reel that is still in use today. These reels were simple devices, lacking the level wind, drag, and antibacklash refinements that time and technology have brought.

Today casting reels contain drag and antibacklash controls and are available with either a wide or narrow spool and with or without a level-wind device. They can be used with braided or monofilament line, will cast lines from about 4-pound test up to about 20-pound test, and, within reason, will handle any fish that the angler chooses to tackle.

It is ironic that the popularity of the more easily used spinning gear has caused a decline in the use of bait-casting equipment at a time when the manufacturers of bait-casting tackle have made more and more improvements. At some point in the near future anglers will "discover" bait-casting again, and there will be a rebirth of the old art of flinging out a bait or lure into the waters with this truly American tackle.

An average bait-casting outfit, if there is such a thing, starts with a five-and-a-half-foot semistiff hollow-fiberglass rod. The rod shaft itself is of one piece, with a metal joint, or ferrule, at the butt where it is joined to the rod handle. There are four or five guides and a tip guide at the tip end of the rod. They are made of chrome-plated nickel and are quite small in contrast to the large guides seen on spinning rods. The handle has a collet to hold the metal ferrule of the rod butt securely. This device acts very much like the chuck of a drill to hold the rod so that it will not twist or turn. Just below the collet on the handle is the reel seat, which is fitted with clamping devices to hold the foot of the reel in place. Usually this reel seat is offset—placed lower than the handle and the rod shaft—so that the reel will be in a more comfortable position for casting. At the lower end of the reel seat is a hook for the index finger to make it easier to hold the outfit and to turn the rod for casting and playing fish. A cork handle below the reel seat provides a secure grip of the hand.

A typical reel for use with this rod is a wide-spool model with a foot for clamping to the rod. The handle is on the right side, and there is an adjustment on one side of the reel (sometimes on both sides) for adjusting how "free" the spool will be. The spool is adjusted according to the weight of the lure to be cast. If the reel has a drag, it will be a star drag or a similar type. The drag is adjusted by a knurled ring or star-shaped wheel on the handle shaft. The level-wind at the front of the reel keeps the line evenly laid on the spool to prevent knots, loops, and similar problems. The spool itself is of aluminum or a similar light alloy and will probably be of large diameter to turn easily and freely when the cast is made. Twelve-pound-test braided or monofilament casting line should fill the reel to within a fraction of an inch of the spool edge. A lever or button on the top of the frame throws the reel into "free-spool." This means that the handle and level wind will not turn to create friction while the cast is being made.

The above outfit would be suited for most fishing conditions in the Northeast. It would be excellent for bass fishing and fishing for panfish, walleyes, smaller river catfish, and similar species. But there are many situations in which you would want to vary your casting outfit in one or more ways. Maybe it should be lighter or heavier, shorter or longer, or have a different-type reel or even a different rod action.

Casting rods are available in lengths of from four to six and a half feet. The shorter rods will generally be those with stiff actions and are for use with rugged tackle on tough fish. The longer rods, usually lighter and softer in action, are designed for use with light reels, lines, and lures.

Hollow-fiberglass rods are made by wrapping glass cloth around a tapered steel mandrel, coating it with an epoxy or phenolic resin, and baking it. As with other fishing rods, casting rods can be made of materials other than hollow fiberglass. Before hollow-fiberglass rods were developed, solid-fiberglass rods were used. These are still made, but mostly in the shorter lengths and in less-expensive models. This does not mean that these rods are no good. They serve as ideal rods in tough fishing situations and for big fish. Solid-glass rods are heavier then hollow-glass rods and have a slow action that could be described as sluggish. They are fine rods to use for catfish and carp when soaking a bait on the bottom for long periods at a time, but they are not the rods of choice for repeated casting.

Steel, beryllium copper, split bamboo, and other materials have also served as the blank material for casting rods, but these have all almost disappeared from the scene. None of these materials has the advantages of strength, light weight, and good action that hollow-glass can give.

Every rod company uses different terms to describe the actions of their rods, and often these terms are difficult to understand. Some companies use charts to show rod action. That is, they show the type and degree of deflection of the rod when it is placed in a horizontal plane with a uniform weight hung from the tip. The actions of casting rods fall into three general categories:

(1) *Slow, or classic.* A rod with this type of action bends slowly and evenly right down to the handle. There is no sharp bend anywhere in the flexed rod; the action is progressively smooth. This action is most commonly found in light rods of medium length or longer. They are ideal for accuracy casting and for casting light lures and bait. Sometimes this action is referred to as parabolic action.

(2) *Progressive taper.* This action is not as slow as the classic action, but there is still a smooth taper from tip to grip—that is, there are no areas of sharp bending—but it takes a more severe pull to flex the rod all the way to the grip. The tip bends more easily than the butt. This is the action most often preferred by experienced casters. It is smooth, and casting is easy. With this action one can handle a wide range of lures yet still have the stiffness to work a lure properly and to strike a fish hard.

(3) *Fast tip, or fast taper.* These rods are easily detected, since a flexing of the rod back and forth causes the tip section to bend sharply with relatively little bending in the rest of the rod. In the early 1960s this action was quite popular with the rod manufacturers. The main advantage of this type of action is that it can cast lures in a wide weight range, from small spinning lures up to heavy muskie plugs. Its disadvantage is that it is almost impossible to work a lure properly with it. In working certain surface lures, jigs, or any other lures to which live action must be provided by the angler, the tips of these rods may prove too limber to effectively bring out the lure's action.

Rods also come in "tournament" models. These are designated as either 3/8-ounce or 5/8-ounce rods. These rods are designed for accuracy casting in casting tournaments. They are of the classic, or slow-action, type, which allows for the maximum in accuracy. Don't think that these rods are only for the tournaments, however. They make ideal casting rods for "spot fishing."

Fittings on rods can vary and, like much else in life, depend upon cost. It is most important to have good-quality guides on the rod. Carboloy, chromed nickel, chromed stainless steel, or heavy foulproof wire guides are the best. As important as guide quality is the number of guides. Guides should be placed evenly *for the action of the rod* and spaced so that in normal bending of the rod, as in playing a fish, *no part of the line* will come in contact with the rod blank itself. Line contact with the shaft of the rod reduces rod and lure action and quickly wears out the line, whether braided or mono.

Reels also vary quite a bit from our "average" reel. The most common variation is the narrow-spool type. These are essentially the same as the standard models except that the spool is only about one and a quarter inch wide compared with the one and three quarters inch width of regular models. Many manufacturers make narrow-spool versions of their better quality reels. All major manufacturers have at least one narrow-spool version in their lines.

Another common variation of reels is in the type of drag. Usually the lighter narrow-spool models will have a simple drag, very often nothing more than the knob used to adjust the "looseness" of the spool for casting purposes. Heavier reels often feature a star drag, which is a series of plates and washers tightened or loosened by a starfish-shaped control on the side of the reel. The star drag can bring tremendous pressure to bear on the spool axle to slow or stop big fish. These reels work so that the spool can turn without the reel handles turning, making it easier for the angler to maintain control and keeping the hands free of injury when a big fish takes line.

Plug-casting anglers today can be divided about equally into two groups—those who prefer monofilament and those who prefer braided-nylon casting line. The braided-nylon line is traditional, easier to cast, softer, and easier to handle. Mono, on the other hand, is cheaper, tougher, and doesn't require a leader as must be used with braided line. Mono line puts greater pressures on the reel because of the stretch in the line, but this is compensated for in modern reels designed to use mono. Casting line can vary from about four-pound test for light bass and panfish, to up to 20- or 25-pound test for heavy pike and reservoir bass fishing.

Each angler develops preferences in tackle for particular species of fish and types of water, baits, lures, and other variables. Take bass fishing, for example. Bass, both smallmouths and largemouths, can be found in rivers, lakes, large streams, and ponds. Although an angler might fish for bass in any of these waters, the "best" outfit for each area and for each type of fishing would vary.

In river fishing, the "average" outfit described earlier would be just right for casting artificial plugs. But for live-bait fishing, some changes would be in order. Popular river baits such as minnows and crayfish are lighter than plugs and would require a lighter rod to cast them properly. And casting live bait requires a special technique. When using artificials, the caster starts the forward part of the cast immediately after the backward part, so that a sharp bend is put into the rod and the lure is cast accurately and forcefully. But the same sharp snap would throw the live bait off the hook. A softer rod and a softer, slower cast are needed for live-bait casting.

Fishing rivers is frequently a matter of spot-casting—picking a good-looking spot and then dropping the lure or bait right on it. These spots can be logs, undercut banks, stumps of old trees, rocks above the water, rocks under the water, riffles, rapids, eddies, and all the other places that spell BASS in capital letters. The soft-action rod helps here also. Because the rod is soft, the lure goes through a higher, more parabolic arc and as a result takes longer to get to the target. This is an advantage. It allows the caster either to slow the reel by "thumbing," if the lure seems about to go past the target, or to reduce tension on the spool to get a little more distance.

Stream or large-creek fishing is much the same as plug-casting a big river. The lures or bait will be light and small. A long, slow, limber rod helps to control the cast and to get the light lure out to the fish. Narrow-spool reels are a distinct advantage in this fishing. They permit the casting of light lures, since the spool is narrower and weighs less, and less inertia must be overcome to start it revolving. This narrower spool also makes the entire reel somewhat lighter and as a result more pleasant to use in a full day of fishing. And small reels and light lures call for light lines; the slow, limber rod helps to absorb the shock of the strike and the fight of the fish, thus easing the strain on the line.

For some bass fishing, extra-heavy casting tackle is necessary, not so much because of the size of the fish but rather because of the tough, brushy places where they are caught. Man-made lakes throughout much of the East are tough to fish. These lakes are formed by damming rivers and flooding rolling farming country or mountain areas dotted with a few small towns. Sometimes these areas are lumbered before the construction of the impoundment, but even if this is done, the job is frequently haphazard and incomplete. The result is a fishing lake filled with trees, stumps, fallen timber, foundations of old houses, and similar debris. This makes ideal cover for both the largemouth and smallmouth bass with which the lakes are usually stocked, but it also makes it hard for the angler to get the fish out. Some anglers who specialize in areas like this use bait-casting tackle almost exclusively. Their tackle? A heavy, stiff parabolic-type rod and a star-drag casting reel filled with 20- or 25-pound-test monofilament line. The bass they catch are big, and heavy tackle is needed to get those lunkers out of the debris. The bass are horsed out into open water and can then be played in a more gentlemanly manner.

Big northern pike and muskies require the same type of tough tackle, but here it will be needed not so much for the brush as for the fish. Another hard-fighting fresh-water fish is the coho, recently introduced into Lake Michigan and Lake Erie. These are often fish in the 20-pound class. Large rods and reels are the choice here also. Fishermen after big catfish in dammed lakes or below spillway pools also need tough casting tackle for their quarry. Both heavy fresh-water and light salt-water outfits are used.

Spinning

Spinning tackle, by far the most popular of all modern fishing equipment, has been on the scene the shortest length of time. Developed in Europe, spinning did not become popular in the United States until after World War II, when importers started to bring the new equipment into the country. The idea instantly caught hold, and spinning threatened to make both bait-casting and fly-casting obsolete. It hasn't, of course, but it does remain the most popular form of fishing tackle.

The idea of spinning, that of line cast in loops from a fixed spool, is very old. Primitive examples of the type are found in various cultures all around the world. Modern spinning reels retrieve line by means of a rotating cup that revolves around the spool when the handle is turned. The spool has an in-and-out reciprocating action that lays the line evenly on the spool. This feature is the spinning equivalent of the level-wind on a bait-casting reel.

An average reel holds about 200 yards of 10-pound-test line. This is more than enough for all fresh-water and much light-tackle salt-water angling. A drag adjustment on the reel, usually set in the front of the spool, makes it possible for the fisherman to control the tension of the line coming off the spool when the fish is big enough to have his own way.

A simple antireverse lever or button on the side of the reel housing prevents the reel handle from going backwards and rapping knuckles when a fish takes out line. The gears of most reels retrieve three to four revolutions of the spool with each turn of the handle, although some fast-retrieve models retrieve five revolutions.

The reel spool is filled to within about an eighth of an inch of the spool lip. Spools on most reels are easily replaceable, making it possible for the fisherman to carry spools with different pound test lines for various sorts of fishing.

The average spinning stick is a six-and-a-half-foot two-piece hollow-glass rod. The four to six guides are large, high-bridged, and placed below the rod. The high supports on the guides are needed to prevent the line from slapping against the rod blank, thus causing friction and cutting casting distance. The importance of guide size is exaggerated. Several years ago, one major manufacturer introduced several rods with small high-bridged guides. They cast as well as and perhaps even further than rods with the regular guides, but anglers had become so accustomed to large guides that they just wouldn't accept the new type, and in a season or two the rods were off the market.

Several styles of spinning guides are used. The main types are Carboloy, bridged chromed wire, and foulproof. Carboloy guides are by far the hardest. They just can't be grooved by the line, but they are more brittle than the others and too heavy to be used on light rods. Carboloy guides on a light or ultralight rod will make it sluggish, as many an amateur rod repairman has discovered after replacing light-wire guides with Carboloy. The chromed bridged guides are the most popular on most types of spinning rods, though the foulproof types are lighter and more flexible.

The number of guides on a spinning rod can make the difference between a rod that will perform well and one that is sloppy both in casting and in playing fish. A typical six-and-a-half-foot rod will have four or five guides and a tip top. The more guides, within reason, the easier and smoother the casting. The guides reduce the strain on the glass blank, the line running over the guides, and the guide itself. The average rod has a fixed reel seat that clamps the reel foot in place by means of a knurled ring. Cork grips both above and below the reel seat make the rod easy and comfortable to handle.

Spinning gear is often used improperly. It is not uncommon to see anglers holding reels on top of the rods, reeling backwards, or changing hands between casting and retrieving—all of which is unnecessary. The outfit should be held with the guides down and the reel below. The stem of the reel goes between the index and middle fingers. Right-handed anglers hold the rod (and cast) with the right hand and turn the handle with the left. There are left-handed reels and reels with changeable right and left handles for the 20 percent of the population that is left-handed.

There are probably more variations in sizes and types of spinning rods and reels than in any other type of freshwater fishing tackle. Outfits can be as small as the ultralight one-ounce four-and-a-half-foot rods sporting six-ounce reels filled with two-pound-test line. At the other extreme are the tough pool-cue-action seven-foot rods with heavy reels and fifteen-pound-test line that are the choice for rough bass fishing, muskies, heavy carp, and big catfish.

Spinning rods are most frequently made of hollow fiberglass, although some split-bamboo spinning rods are still manufactured. The various actions of spinning rods parallel those of bait-casting rods, i.e., slow, or classic; progressive taper; and fast-tip, or fast-taper. And as is the case with bait-casting tackle, the progressive-taper type seems to be the most popular. It is a good average action that avoids the extremes of the slow tournament action or the ultrafast tip that used to be popular.

Most spinning rods come center-ferruled, but a few are made with the ferrule closer to the rod butt. Some manufacturers think that, since most of the casting and fish playing action is in the upper part of the stick, a center ferrule interferes with the rod's action. Thus they place the ferrule lower. The only disadvantage of this is that it makes for two unequal sections and requires a longer rod case.

Fittings can vary on spinning rods, and typically this is a function of the length of the rod and the type of fishing for which the rod blank was designed. On the ultralight rods of four-and-a-half to six feet, light foulproof guides are best, since they bend with the rod and allow it to flex fully in casting and playing fish.

Although most rod handlers are equipped with a fixed reel seat, some lighter rods have only two metal bands on the cork grip to hold the reel in place. The two bands slip over the ends of the reel foot. Cork under the hand is more comfortable than a metal reel seat, and the bands are not as heavy as a reel seat, but the reel is not held very securely and in time the bands tend to chew up the cork grip.

Placement of spinning guides is not quite as critical as it is with bait-casting tackle, since the guides are under the rod and at no time does the line come in contact with the rod.

Heavier rods of from six to seven feet often have the large high-bridged hard-chromed guides, to prevent wearing and the need for quick replacement. Since Carboloy guides are heavy, they are usually found only on rods so stiff that the extra weight will not affect the action.

Reels vary from the small ultralight models up to light salt-water models and even ocean-fishing models. Though they vary in size, the best have all the features of the previously mentioned average reel.

All have an antireverse and an adjustable drag, and practically all today come with the full-bail line pickup. Some few, usually in the larger models, have a manual pickup, in which a simple roller guide on the rotating cup takes the place of the bail and roller pickup. Casting is just as easy with these, but it takes some practice to learn to flip the line manually onto the roller guide, rather than merely flipping the bail over with a turn of the reel handle.

Rollers on the manual pickups are usually better made and larger—this makes it easier for them to revolve—than the rollers in the bail pickups. Maintenance of all rollers is critical, since a roller that doesn't turn will quickly abrade the line. All it takes is to keep the roller clean and lubricated with the lightest machine oil.

It is important to pick a reel that fits the hand, so that it can be feathered while casting. Feathering is the shortening of a cast by placing the index finger lightly on the spool edge while the cast is being made, so the finger hits the loops of line coming off the reel to slow the lure. It is the equivalent of the bait-casting angler's thumbing his reel to slow a lure and cast accurately, and it is the only way that the spinning fisherman can control his cast once the line has begun to go out. Unfortunately, some reels are made with a long stem—the shaft from the reel foot to the housing—that makes it difficult for any angler to reach the spool to feather the line and for the angler with a small hand, impossible! Test a reel for this before buying it.

Most drags are controlled by a small knob on the front of the spool, some few by a knob on the back or underside of the housing. Adjusting the drag on a spinning reel is even more important than on a casting reel, where the position of the star drag allows it to be changed quickly. Many anglers adjust the drag by pulling some line off the spool and turning the drag until it feels "right." Then when they hang a good fish, they find that the drag is too tight, and the fish is lost before they can turn the drag knob. The proper way to adjust the drag is to run the line over the roller and out the guides and tie it to something stationary. Then raise the rod to a fish-fighting position about 45 degrees and adjust the drag until the line just pulls off the reel. Remember that as a fish takes out line the diameter of the spool is decreased, thus *increasing* the drag without changing the knob. It is better to have a light drag and to add additional drag by lightly touching the spool with the index finger when needed (the importance of reel-stem length again) than to have it too tight and risk losing a fish.

Spinning line is almost universally monofilament today, although a recently introduced braided line (Micron) looks like it should work better than mono in the heavier sizes. Lines range from 2 to 20 pound test, depending upon the size of the spinning outfit and the quarry. It is extremely important to match the size of the line to the size of the spinning outfit. For example, a heavy line on a light outfit will cause nothing but trouble. The light lure cannot carry the heavy line, and the light reel, with its small-diameter spool, will cause the heavy line to come off in tight coils. The tight coils hit the guides, create friction, and cut casting distance considerably. It is especially important to place the line on the reel properly. To do otherwise causes a twist in the line that is impossible to get out later. Follow the directions packed with each spool of line.

Spin-Casting

Although modern spinning tackle is European in origin, spin-casting is an American adaptation of the basic spinning principle. Spin-casting utilizes a rod essentially like that of bait-casting tackle and a spinning-type reel with a metal cone that fits over the line spool. The reel sits on top of the rod as in bait-casting tackle.

An average spin-casting outfit consists of a six-foot hollow fiberglass rod with the guides, offset reel seat, and action of a casting rod. The main difference between a spin-casting rod and a bait-casting rod is that the average spin-casting rod has a lighter action. Otherwise, spin-casting and bait-casting rods can be (and sometimes are) interchanged.

The reel is quite different from the regular spinning reel. Like a bait-casting reel, it sits on top of the rod with the handle on the right. The line is held on a narrow spool underneath the cone, and a small pickup rod that rotates around the spool, or in an indentation in an outer cup, picks up the line much as do the rotating cup and roller guide on a spinning reel.

An antireverse lever or button serves the same purpose as it does in spinning and bait-casting. A star drag controls the tension under which line can be pulled off the reel by a fish.

A push button at the back of the reel releases the line for casting. Pushing in the button releases the pickup mechanism while simultaneously catching the line against the inner part of the cone and the spool, so that the line won't drop in front of the angler. Releasing the push button on the forward part of the cast releases the line, which pays out through a small hole in the center of the cone. Turning the handle at the finish of the cast engages the line pickup again. Line is usually packed with the reel and is available in a variety of sizes, usually from 6- to 15-pound test.

Spin-casting is generally the easiest method of casting for beginning fishermen. There is no bail to fool with, and the line comes on the reel ready for use. The tackle is relatively inexpensive. Some disadvantages are that the narrow spools hold too little line for fighting really big fish, the cone cuts casting distance, accuracy casting is more difficult than with spinning tackle, and the tackle must change hands between each cast and retrieve.

Plug-casting equipment was originally designed for casting large natural baits, but more and more anglers today are going to artificial lures. Spin-casting and spin-casting equipment were originally designed to cast small spinners and spoons. The numbers of these lures are legion, but fortunately they fall into basic categories.

Plugs fall into surface, subsurface, medium-running, and deep-diving lures.

Surface plugs are designed to float on the surface of the water and create the impression of some type of natural bait. Many of them have popping faces that make a surface disturbance; others rely on spinners or similar hardware to kick up a fuss and attract fish. Used with casting tackle, these are basically bass lures. Larger versions work well for muskies and northern pike. Smaller sizes are made for panfish.

It is important to remember that though surface lures come in a variety of color schemes, the fish does not really see the top of the lure, only the bottom. Thus many experienced surface-lure fishermen choose their lures by the color of the *bottom* of the plug. No matter what the color of the top of the lure, most surface plugs have only one of three colors on the bottom—black, yellow, or white.

The right type of rod is essential for the effective use of surface lures. A fast-tip casting rod, for example, will not let you wiggle, dance, and pop the lure along in the proper fashion. A stiffer parabolic-action rod is a better choice for fishing surface lures.

Subsurface lures are those that travel from several inches to several feet under the surface. Frequently they float when at rest. Most are designed to imitate minnows. One of the most successful of the subsurface types is the balsa or plastic minnow. The Rapala, Hellcat, Rebel, and Cobra are examples of this type. Each of these popular models has an individual wobble, which together with the flash of their sides, makes them irresistible (we hope) to fish. Try to make these lures look like an injured baitfish, frog, salamander, or some similar fish food. You'll find that fishing success will be markedly increased over just casting out and reeling in the line.

Medium-running plugs run well down in the water and are best used in fishing for pike, bass, coho, and other species that travel deep in large lakes. Most medium-running plugs have a metal lip to provide a built-in wiggle, though some action can be added by the fisherman.

Deep-diving lures are those characterized by heavy lips that cause them to dive far down when retrieved rapidly. These lures, like the medium-runners, have a built-in action designed to attract fish. Although the deep-runners are usually thought of as lake lures, they can be used on rivers to scrape the bottom or to fish deep holes that could not otherwise be reached.

Spinners are basically lures having a shiny metal blade that revolves rapidly around a shaft when the lure is drawn through the water. Spinners can be used in large sizes by the plug-caster, but they are more frequently the choice of the spin fisherman because of their light weight. They are extremely effective lures for all sorts of fresh-water fishing. Trout, largemouth and smallmouth bass, panfish, catfish, pike, and pickerel are just some of the gamesters that will attack this lure with a vengeance.

Spoons are one of the oldest lures known to man. They have been fashioned from metal, pieces of seashell, and many other materials. The standard red and white spoon with a treble hook attached is one of the old reliables for northern pike and other members of the toothy pike family.

Jigs also have a long history. Basically a painted lead head with a fur or feather tail, jigs have probably accounted for more fish than any other lure. It is important to realize that the jig has no built-in action of its own and that the angler must manipulate the lure in an enticing fish-catching action.

The soft plastic and rubber lures are the newest class of artificials available to the angler. The plastic worm is the most important, but eels, minnows, crayfish, and insects are also available. They come in all colors, sizes, and even smells. Theories of rigging and retrieving worms properly are endless, but suffice it to say that the slowly fished worm hooked with a single weedless hook through the head is one of the most deadly lures of the bass fisherman. Learning to use these lures requires a longer apprenticeship than any other form of lure fishing, but the results are well worth it.

Other basics of the bait-caster and spin fisherman are determined by the individual angler's preference in fishing water and his degree of interest in fishing. Tackle boxes, for example, might vary from the huge containers used by the lake-bass specialist to the small single-compartment lure box stuck in a pocket by the casual fisherman out for a few hours along a favorite shoreline.

Fly-Casting

Fly-casting as a way to fish has always been a joy to some and an enigma to others. "Why," the puzzled group asks, "flail around with a long rod and coarse line to catch fish that can just as easily be taken with light spinning tackle?" People who ask this question are usually those who find fly fishing and casting difficult to learn.

The question is sometimes difficult to answer, but the truth of the matter is this: under some fishing conditions and in fishing for certain fish, flies properly presented are far more effective than any other type of lure or bait. The difficulty of using the equipment frequently stems from a misunderstanding of the principles involved and a poor choice or rod, reel, and line.

The basic principles are relatively easy. Fly-casting is not really fly-casting; it is line casting. The fly just goes along for the ride. The line is heavy in order to provide weight to flex the rod and to carry the fly to the target. The underlying principle is the same as that used in plug-casting or spinning. It is impossible, for example, to cast with a spinning or plug outfit using just a small worm or cricket threaded onto a light hook. There is no weight to flex the rod, and the lure or bait will not cast. In spinning and plug-casting, weight to flex the rod is provided by the plug, spoon, spinner, sinker, float, or whatever. In fly-casting the weight is provided by the line. It is equally important that the right weight line be used for a given rod and vice-versa. An ultralight spinning outfit with two- or four-pound-test line, light four-and-a-half- to five-foot rod and miniature reel would be completely inadequate for casting three-quarter-ounce lures. Casting, if it didn't break the rod or the line, would be sloppy and inaccurate. Conversely, it would be equally impossible to take a heavy musky outfit and cast small trout or shad lures. The weight of the lure would not be enough to flex the rod.

Fly-casting works the same way. The weight of the line must match the power and action of the rod. Several excellent publications deal extensively with fly-casting techniques. If all this sounds like it is getting complicated again, let's take a look at an average fly-fishing outfit and then see how it can be varied for particular fishing needs and wants.

An average fly-fishing outfit in most parts of the East consists of a two-piece eight- or eight-and-a-half-foot hollow-fiberglass fly rod with a progressive action from tip to butt. The small light-wire guides, called snake guides, are placed on the underside of the rod. A light-weight tip top is fixed to the rod tip. The guide nearest the reel seat (the stripping guide) looks like a typical casting-rod guide. The smooth cork handle is approximately eight to nine inches long. A light-weight reel seat designed to hold the reel under the rod is fitted to the end of the handle. Just above the handle on most rods is a small ring called a keeper ring. The line does not go through this ring. It merely serves to keep the fly out of the way when not in use.

Most likely the fly reel will be a single-action model about three and a half inches in diameter. This size reel is adequate to hold the fly line and some "backing line," which is usually Dacron casting line attached to the end of the fly line. If a big fish is hooked and takes out more than the 100 feet of fly line, the backing is there to play him further. With a single-action fly reel one turn of the handle will turn the spool around once. A typical spinning or plug-casting reel will retrieve anywhere from three and a half to five turns of line with each turn of the handle. A single-action reel is a simple device, basically just a spool with a handle on it that is held within a light-weight frame. Usually there is a click or a drag (or sometimes both) with an adjustment on the side or edge

NED SMITH

of the frame. A foot, or flat plate, at the bottom of the reel serves to lock the reel on the reel seat. Spools are interchangeable, so that different lines can be carried on spare spools.

The line for fly fishing is heavy. Depending upon the angler's preferences, fishing interests, and pocketbook, the line can be either level, double-tapered, or weight-forward tapered. The level line is the least expensive. As its name indicates, it is level from one end to the other. This is a good line for beginners, for pan-fishing in which a delicate presentation is not too necessary, and for bass-bugging at short distances. A double-tapered line is the typical choice of the trout angler. A double-taper is level throughout most of its length but tapers to a smaller diameter at each end. This type of line is more difficult to make and costs more than a level line. The advantage of a double-tapered line is that the smaller diameter end lands quietly on the water and makes for a more delicate presentation of the fly to wary fish such as trout and smallmouths in small streams. The third type of line is variously called a weight-forward taper, triple taper, and torpedo taper. It has a heavy level section (called the belly of the line) up near the front of the line. This heavy section tapers to a thinner diameter at the line points, where the leader is attached. The heavy belly section is concentrated near one end of the line. The rear of the belly section tapers quickly to a thin-diameter running line. This heavy front concentration of weight makes the line easier to cast over long distances. Weight-forward lines are also made in "bass-bug" or "salt-water" tapers. These have an even shorter belly section, so that quick, long casts can be made with a minimum of false casting. Attached to the end of the fly line is a leader. Fly leaders range in length from about 7½ to about 12 feet. The best leaders are tapered from a heavy butt section (which is tied to the fly line) through successively smaller segments down to a tippet section to which the fly is tied. This tippet might range from as heavy as 10-pound test in fishing for largemouths in heavy cover, to as light as one- or two-pound test for delicate trout fishing with small dry flies on clear, quiet brooks.

Fly-fishing tackle can vary greatly, both in cost and type. Although most fly rods are made of hollow fiberglass, there are still a few companies that offer high-quality split-bamboo rods. Fly rods usually range from seven feet to nine and a half feet, but some of those on the ultralight side get as light as one ounce and as short as five feet. These are specialized rods, but they do have their uses.

I still remember one late-summer trout-fishing trip on the Yellow Breeches in southcentral Pennsylvania. Don Ebright, a young Harrisburg fly tyer, was showing me his success with a small ant imitation that he ties. On this part of the Yellow Breeches, massive trees overhang the wide stream and in some areas low limbs almost touch the water. I was using a light seven-foot rod, while Don, familiar with the stream, was using a short rod of only five and a half feet. This seemingly slight difference meant that my casts were often caught in the trees, while Don was able to keep his casts low and fish far more effectively and easily. The results in numbers of trout caught and released by the end of the day reflected this difference.

Action is just as important in a fly rod as it is in any other type of fishing rod. The actions of fly rods fit into the same categories as those of casting and spinning rods, that is, slow (or classic) action, progressive-taper action, and fast-tip action. The slow, classic action is usually found today only in bamboo rods, and for this reason it is sometimes called "bamboo action." The rod bends slowly and evenly right down to the grip. This action is ideal for bass-bugging and handling long lines with large flies and bugs.

The progressive-taper is the action most commonly found in fly rods. The progressive action of the rod bends evenly as more work is put on the rod. The rod takes the increased flexing necessary without the tip collapsing, as would happen to a fast-tip rod, and without the entire rod straining severely, as would a classic-action rod.

The fast-tip fly rod is a tool that is loved by some anglers and hated by others. This type of rod action has definite pros and cons. The chief advantage of the fast-tip rod is in dry-fly trout fishing. The relatively stiff butt section and the rapidly flexing tip section make it possible for the angler to false cast rapidly, which is often necessary to dry the fly. The main disadvantage in this type of action is that, if long casts are attempted, the tip will collapse, leaving the unsuited stiff butt section to do the casting.

Fittings can make a great deal of difference in a fly rod, even though they may seem all alike. Guides should be of good quality wire, and there should be enough of them. If there are not enough guides on a rod, the line will tend to catch on each guide and will come into excessive contact with the rod, preventing the line from flowing freely. The line may be exactly the right size for the rod, but it will feel as if it is too light because it won't "shoot" properly.

Grips and reel seats on fly rods are pretty standard. On some very light rods, a couple of rings may be used to hold the reel in place. This "skeletal reel seat" has the advantage of being light in weight. Ferrules are of great importance on a fly rod, since the fly rod is subjected to much more casting strain than any other type of rod. One of the most unusual advances in recent years is the invention of the glass-to-glass ferrule first developed by Fenwick Rods. Almost all the companies now have similar models in fly-casting and spinning rods.

The advantage of this type of ferrule is that the glass bends and there is no "flat spot." The glass ferrule is an integral part of the rod, so it's impossible for a glass ferrule to come loose.

There are two types of fly reels—the single-action, already described, and the automatic. Most anglers use the single-action reel. Single-action reels are cheaper, lighter (important when you are casting all day long), hold more line and backing (important when playing big fish), have fewer mechanical parts to break down, and are less bulky. The automatic reel is spring loaded (much like a carpenter's measuring tape), and a touch of a lever will retrieve line. For panfishing, or for the handicapped angler, automatics are fine, but for most fishing the single-action is far better.

Often a fly reel is discounted as nothing more than a storage place for the line, and the importance of quality in a reel is summarily dismissed. Fortunately, some good single-action fly reels can be obtained at a nominal price. When buying a fly reel, be sure to get one that will hold the size line that fits your rod and, if you feel that you need it, enough backing for the fish that you are after.

The weight of the line for a particular outfit is particularly important, since without the proper-weight line, the tackle will be mismatched. All fly-line manufacturers now conform to a standard system of weight designations. The lines are numbered according to weight in a scale running from 1 to 12, though only 3- through 11-weight lines are normally made, since these fit all standard fly rods, from ultralight wands to heavy salt-water sticks. Once the proper-weight line for a given rod is determined, stick to it, for any line of that weight, regardless of line type or manufacturer, will properly balance the rod.

A floating line is the choice for bass-bugging, pan-fishing farm ponds, and for most stream trout fishing. But there are definite uses for the other types. Most notable, and the first of the speciality lines to be developed, is the sinking line. There are now three different types of sinking lines, each with a different rate of sinking. The fast-sinking line would be the choice in lake fishing, while a slow-sinking line, which would avoid snags, rocks, and other obstructions, would be better for river fishing. Fly-tackle companies market these lines under various names that indicate their sinking properties. But this is not the end of the line picture. One major manufacturer makes an intermediate-density line that will float when dressed but will sink very slowly when not dressed. There are also lines in which the terminal 10 feet sink while the rest of the line floats. At least two makers market a line the first 30 feet of which sinks. Backing placed on the reel before the line should be Dacron line of about 20 pound test. Mono and braided casting lines have a way of stretching that creates a tremendous strain on the reel spool. One problem in using any type of backing is in knowing how much backing to put on the reel before adding the fly line. The answer to that is to first wind the fly line on the reel, then tie on the backing and fill the spool up almost to the rim. Cut the backing line at that point, take off all the backing and the fly line, wind the backing on the reel, and then add the fly line. Be careful when doing this with a weight-forward line. Don't get the wrong end of the fly line attached to the backing! The best knot for attaching the backing to the fly line is a nail knot. You'll find it illustrated in any number of fishing-tackle catalogs along with clinch knots, barrel knots, and other knots important to fishermen. An alternate method is to splice loops in the ends of the backing and the fly line and then interconnect the loops. An advantage of this method is that you can change your fly line without retying knots.

The leader, that monofilament connection between the line and the fly, hook, or other lure, is an especially important piece of tackle for the fly angler. The leader can be nothing more than a level piece of mono, but the tapered leader is much superior for almost all sorts of fishing.

There are several important reasons why a leader must be used in fly-fishing. First, it would be impossible to put the heavy fly line through the small eye of the hook, and even if this could be done, the heavy line connected to the fly would make most fish extremely wary. Fish aren't used to finding their meals attached to a piece of heavy cord. And the leader tippet is very flexible, so that the fly can drift quite freely, in a manner similar to natural fish foods. There are formulas for building leaders, but most anglers soon find that with a little common sense they can build a leader that works well. A good way to begin is to tie the butt section to the line with a nail knot and then coat the knot with several applications of Pliobond. Pliobond stays flexible even when dry, protects the knot, and makes it smoother. Successive lengths of mono are then tied together with barrel knots. Commercial tapered leaders are available ready made in either knotted or knotless styles for the angler who doesn't want to make his own. Sometimes knotless leaders do not have a heavy enough butt section. It helps to tie a heavier butt section between the leader and the line. A heavy butt section is needed to prevent the leader from falling back on itself when a cast is made.

Just as spinning and casting lures come in categories, flies can also be classified. The basic categories are dry flies, wet flies, nymphs, streamers, and floating bugs.

Dry flies are tied so that they will float on the water surface. They are most often used by the stream trout angler. They come in innumerable patterns, all designed to look like a real or imaginary water or land insect floating in the stream. These flies are comparatively easy to fish because they are visible to the angler, so that a strike can be instantly detected, and no action need be imparted to the fly (indeed, such action would look unnatural and would make fish shy away.) The main disadvantage to dry-fly fishing is that fish feed on the surface only part of the time. Even surface-feeding fish find the bulk of their diet well below the surface.

Wet flies, streamers, and nymphs are all designed to be fished under the surface. Each of these types is designed to imitate a different category of fish food. The long streamers or bucktails are fished across and downstream in an erratic and jerky fashion to imitate an injured minnow. Wet flies are fished up, down, or across stream, but usually with little action. These flies are tied to resemble drowned land or water insects that are constantly drifting through the water and that make up much of the diet of many fish.

Nymphs are similar to wet flies except that they imitate live aquatic insects. These can be fished with some movement or without any movement at all. Nymphs are tied in very "buggy," lifelike imitations, since the fish will often look these flies over for far longer than they do other flies.

Bass and pan-fish bugs are either made of shaped cork bodies or tied with deer hair. Deer hair, being hollow, floats. They come in various sizes. The small ones are used for pan-fish, the larger ones for smallmouth and largemouth bass. Most bugs have a popping face and are fished like a miniature equivalent of the plug or spin fisherman's surface lure.

There is no end of accessories for the fly fisherman. Some of the more useful ones are: a fishing vest, to carry fly boxes and other gear; the various fly and bug boxes; fly-line cleaners; dry-fly floatants; clippers, for cutting mono when making leaders; and waders and boots, to get the angler out into the streams and rivers.

It would be hard to find two more qualified fishermen-authors to write about trout than Dr. Alvin Grove and Sam Slaymaker. Grove's place in angling literature was established 20 years ago with his classic The Lure and Lore of Trout Fishing. *Sam Slaymaker's series of "Little Trout" streamer flies have perhaps made him more famous than the lock that bears his family name. Intense fishermen who are just as intense about preserving the sport of trout fishing, these two write with great knowledge and affection of the sport to which they are both devoted. I'll admit I sound like a reviewer, but this chapter is worth the price of admission for the trout fly-rodder.*

CHAPTER 14

Trout Angling

SAM SLAYMAKER II and
DR. ALVIN R. GROVE, JR.

Where It All Began

Five will get you ten that most trout fishermen spend as much time dreaming about wilderness lakes and rivers as they do fishing more-civilized waters nearer home. The lure of the Arctic char, grayling, and trout of Baffin Island, Labrador, and Alaska renders more familiar locales as mundane as a month-old newspaper. More's the pity that the average devotee of trout fishing, living in populous eatern-strip cities, is unaware that virtual wilderness fishing can be his with minimal expenditures of time and money.

The greatest number of trout in the East are caught on spinning rods and live bait. Waters bordering major population centers are stocked from hatcheries with the three predominating species of trout: brooks, browns, and rainbows.

Opening day in April brings out droves of fishermen in quest of their limits.

Now, it is not for us to find fault with this very common approach, for the fishing of worms and minnows can be raised to an art. But the fact remains that increasing numbers of trout enthusiasts are becoming dissatisfied with live-bait methods. Each year the ranks of fly fishermen increase, mostly because the gamy trout is more fun to catch on light, whiplike fly rods. And flies assure breath-taking strikes rather than slower-paced bites. Not to mention the fact that feathered creations, unlike live bait, are rarely swallowed by fish. Thus fly-fishing becomes a form of trout conservation, for a fish taken on a fly can be safely returned to the water to be caught again. "A trout," as Lee Wulff says, "is too valuable to be caught only once!" Fly-fishing is growing in popularity to the extent that increasing amounts of public water are being restricted to fly-fishing-only regulations, and many bait fishermen are switching to flies in self-defense in order to be able to fish on all available waters. For these reasons (and because, contrary to popular opinion, fly-fishing basics are so easy to learn), we will concern ourselves here with information relative to fly-fishing for trout.

Instructions on fly-fishing are readily available in pamphlet and book form in many tackle stores. But anyone who has any fishing experience at all will be able to master the rudiments from the following suggested approaches to the use of streamers, wet flies, nymphs, and dry flies. Because it is meant to propel the lighter fly when it is cast, the fly line is heavier than the monofilament line used for spinning or the silk line used for bait-casting. A serviceable fly rod that will meet all situations covered here is a seven and a half or eight footer of fiberglass fitted with a single-action fly-rod reel. The line should be matched to the rod. Tackle dealers should be able to give sound advice about the various lines and leaders needed to meet the differing conditions encountered on rivers, streams, and lakes. They are also helpful in providing information on such miscellaneous equipment as boots (for shallow streams) and waders (for deeper ones). The aforementioned booklets (provided free by tackle manufacturers and dealers) will describe the knots that are used for tying line to leader and leader to fly. These booklets usually contain easy-to-follow fly-casting instructions. After a little backyard practice, the beginning fly angler is ready to go.

Streamers are meant to imitate small food fish, such as the minnows and young fry, that are often eaten by trout, particularly larger ones. When a streamer or bucktail is manipulated in the current and retrieved against it, it gives trout the impression of a minnow darting upstream. We refer to an impression because the current's turbulence robs fish of too close a look. Thus, he cannot see the streamer for what it really is: fuzz and feathers. Since streamers are more effectively fished in strong currents, they are usually used in the high, roily waters of early spring. And under these conditions, streamers are excellent fish finders because they are usually large and colorful, and fish can see them from a greater distance than they can smaller flies. In the lower waters of summer, small streamers—streamerettes—are often very effective.

The traditional method of presenting streamers is known as quartering. The angler faces downstream and casts to either bank. He permits the lure to drift along the bank, thus simulating a minnow drifting downstream. When the desired amount of slack is paid out, the streamer is drawn in a curve to midstream. During this sweep the current, periodic twitches of the rod tip provide a darting, minnowlike action. This is continued at intervals until the streamer is fully retrieved. After moving a few feet downstream, the angler casts again—to the opposite bank, this time—and the same procedure is followed. Thus, water is systematically covered and the maximum number of fish see the fly.

A trout's strike at a streamer is usually vicious, probably because he fears his dodging quarry will escape, and trout often hook themselves when striking them. Still, it is wise to strike back with a smart but not powerful lift for the rod tip. After the trout is hooked, the angler should get below him. If the fish is not big enough to run line from the reel, it can be drawn with the current toward the angler by stripping in the line with the free hand. Fish big enough to run a reel should be played.

A fish is played by simply giving him his head. Permit him to run until he stops. Then retrieve him. When he begins to run again, surrender line, always evenly so as to avoid a belly of slack line, which will cause you to lose control of the fish. When he is worn down, he will show his belly. He is then ready for netting. If you intend to release your trout—a recommended procedure—it is better to bring him to within releasing distance as quickly as is practicable. A trout that has turned belly up with exhaustion has a reduced chance of recovery.

Artificial nymphs imitate the prehatched nymphal stage of aquatic fly life. Nymph imitations are fished upstream by the sink-and-draw method. Since natural nymphs generally inhab-

it stream bottoms, artificials should be presented as deeply as possible. Cast upstream and allow the nymph to dead drift back to you. It will wash along the bottom or slightly above it as you retrieve slack line with your free hand. Since nymphs move slowly, trout usually take them in a leisurely fashion. During the drift-back, therefore, slack should be carefully controlled, so that you can detect the telltale bump or twitch of the line that marks a trout's pickup of a nymph.

Wet flies represent either nymphs in the act of hatching or sunken adult flies. Some anglers fish wet flies downstream, like streamers. A more realistic method is the one used for nymphs: sink-and-draw, dead-drift. The drifting wet fly, with its flaccid hackle feathers and protruding wings, gives trout the impression of a nymph breaking out of its shuck while floating toward the surface.

Dry flies simulate floating naturals that have hatched on the surface (duns) and are about to fly away, or adult flies (spinners) that have dropped back to the stream to die. Like nymphs, dry flies are presented upstream. On the float-back, care must be exercised to prevent drag. This occurs when line drifts too far ahead of the fly (or behind it), so that the current's pull on the floating line drags the fly unnaturally. Drag is avoided by mending the line (flipping accumulated slack upstream with the rod tip) so that it and the fly and the line float in a generally equidistant relationship.

For dry-fly fishing, floating line is required. Under most stream conditions, it also serves effectively for subsurface fishing, since most trout streams are rarely so deep as to prevent sinking flies from approaching the bottom, During high-water conditions, and when fishing wet flies or nymphs in deep pools, ponds, and lakes, it is wise to switch to a sinking line. There are lines of differing sizes, tapers, and degrees of specific gravity. Care should be taken that they match the rod.

The Appalachian Backbone

Lying inland from the Atlantic seaboard and running in a rough southwesterly-northeasterly direction are the Appalachians. Extending from Newfoundland and the Gaspé Peninsula to the rugged country of Georgia, these mountains are the backbone of the East as well as the backbone of its trout fishing. From this Appalachian backbone flow the great river systems of the East, along with their tributaries, which are the native home of the brook trout and which have been for nearly a century the place of introduction of both the rainbow trout from the West and the European brown trout.

Our immediate concern is with the Appalachians and related mountains in West Virginia, from which flow the Potomac River and tributaries of the Ohio River, such as the Cheat River; the Susquehanna River in Pennsylvania and New York; the Delaware River in the Catskills; and the Hudson River, with its tributary streams, flowing from the Catskills. The Connecticut River, along with its tributaries in New Hampshire and Vermont, the important rivers of Maine, and yet other tributaries originating in the Gaspé and the low hills of Newfoundland flow into either the Saint Lawrence River or the Atlantic Ocean.

Although a part of the Canadian Shield and not a part of the Appalachians, the Adirondacks of New York are an area of important trout waters, too valuable to be overlooked by the trout angler.

The Applachians, estimated to be from 500 to 1100 million years old, are among the oldest of the world's mountains. Much folding of these mountains took place sometime during the end of the Paleozoic era, and since then, much erosion has occurred, mostly caused by water. The coastal plain to the east of the ridge, which has been layered with sediments eroded from the higher lands of Appalachia to the west, offers limited but often excellent trout angling. The line of separation between the deposited coastal-plain soils and the harder rocks of the mountains is called the fall line, and here the steeper gradients of the streams, the numerous falls and cascades, and other geological phenomena produce interesting trout waters. The fall line also represents the upper limit of navigation, and it became the natural area of settlement along the eastern seaboard. Thus, not only have the Appalachians provided the necessary topography for excellent trout streams but also for the establishment of the most heavily populated area of the United States.

The distinctive Appalachian topography is referred to as the ridge-and-valley province, with its steep ridges separated mostly by narrow valleys, which lie in a southwesterly-northeasterly direction and have a trout stream in each valley. Periodically, the water of one valley breaks through to another. These water gaps are characteristic of all the great rivers of the northeastern seaboard. Smaller gaps—now dry—are called wind gaps, and many of these are distributed throughout the length of the Appalachian backbone.

Of some interest to us, and often a matter of particular concern, is the presence of fossil fuels, which were created near the end of the Devonian period of the Paleozoic era. These fossil fuels, both coal and oil, have added much wealth as well as pollution to the Appalachian area. Thousands of miles of trout water have been polluted in Pennsylvania, West Virginia, and Kentucky by hard and soft coal as a result of both deep- and strip-mining practices.

The Appalachian backbone provides the topography and water for trout angling, the fossil-fuel richness that made the industrial East, and a resultant pollution surpassed by no other part of this country. More native American brook trout were spawned in this region than anywhere else on the continent. It is small wonder, therefore, that this was the cradle of American trout fishing—the place where it all began.

Trout angling has produced a greater volume of fine literature than has any other outdoor sport or pastime. The earlier written work on sport fishing dates from 15th-century England. In this country, the preponderant amount of angling literature has come out of the Northeast. It is seldom realized by the occasional trout fisherman that he can still fish some of the waters described in the superb writings of such bygone giants as Theodore Gordon, George E. M. La Branche, and Edward Ringwood Hewitt. To do so is soul-satisfying. It makes for better fishermen—those who will enjoy the pastime the more for it.

New England

No region on the Atlantic seaboard offers more varied fly fishing than New England. In addition to brook, brown, and rainbow trout, anglers can match wits against such spectacular battlers as Atlantic and landlocked salmon and that heavyweight brawler the lake trout. Waters range from majestic, flashing rivers to azure lakes and placid, shellac-colored beaver ponds. And none of these waters is more than a few hours from the area's main population centers. Even New York, New Jersey, and Pennsylvania anglers are little more than a day's drive from some of New England's prime trout waters.

One of the authors of this chapter often relives vivid memories of five glorious spring days in 1955 spent fishing for wily brown trout in Vermont's Battenkill, high-jumping rainbows in some small streams in New Hampshire's White Mountains, scrappy brooks in beaver ponds near Cherryfield, Maine, and landlocked salmon in Lake Mooselookmeguntic in Maine's Rangeley Lakes region. Believe it or not, the trip seemed anything but rushed.

Such diverse waters and species of trout permit a wide range of angling methods. Few areas afford trout in waters other than streams and rivers, but northern New England's cold water enables trout to flourish in ponds and lakes, so that inexperienced stream fishermen (or those who would rather float than wade) can enjoy superb action by that simplest of methods of fly presentation, trolling from canoes and skiffs.

Many daytime hours can be enjoyed lazily rowing in northern Maine's Chain of Ponds, with a fly rod on the lap and a deeply sunken wet fly dragging behind. During the evening, when the brook trout (or squaretails, as they are often called in New England) begin their evening rise to hatching flies, a floating line and a dry fly will take these plump, speckled battlers from the surface.

Lake trout are best taken along the shorelines of the larger northernmost lakes in early spring. In late season they move to depths out of the convenient range of most fly-fishing rigs. Bait fishermen seek them with casting rods and wire line.

The king of sport fish, the Atlantic salmon, is generally sought with heavier fly tackle and distinctive salmon flies. In Maine, in early September when salmon return from the ocean to spawn in certain rivers, the best bet is to ask the advice of natives who know the local guides. A guide's fee will be quickly forgotten after one has tangled with his first Atlantic salmon.

Although we presume landlocked salmon might be caught at any time during the fishing season, either early- or late-season fishing is preferred. During the early season in Maine, landlocks can be taken from the surface of lakes with dry flies, but sometimes a fast-sinking wet fly such as a size-12 hard-bodied ant is better. Early-morning angling can be the most exciting of the day, but the cast must be made to the dimple caused by the fish. Just fishing the water usually is a waste of time. Frequently, the landlocks are in schools and can be followed across the surface of the lake by the dimples they make.

In the fall landlocks move up feeder streams to spawn, and this fishing can be even more exciting than that in the lake itself. The large Wulff flies are excellent for this fishing.

An ideal locale for landlocks is the Rangeley Lakes region of Maine. Mooselookmeguntic, Kennebago, and Little Kennebago lakes offer some good landlocked-salmon fishing early in the season. The Kennebago River has some of the finest fall fishing available.

Fishing for trout in lakes is usually slower than fishing for them in a stream, but when a trout is hooked, the action can be fast and furious. The squaretails of the Maine lakes try to sound when they are hooked; the browns might go down or up, and often they do both. There are periods of no activity, though, when fishing talk at the bar is no less enjoyable than being on the lake. But when the trout are rising, it is important to be fishing. Drop everything, including the martinis, the *filet mignon*, the Maine lobster, and the wife and kids, and get on the water.

The flies fished are most commonly either dry flies or deep-sinking streamers. Faster action may take place on the surface, but the deeply fished streamer usually produces larger, but almost invariably fewer, trout. A sinking line is valuable, and some weight is sometimes also added to the streamer, either tied in as a part of the pattern or added to the leader if regulations permit this. The additional weight helps to sink the streamer, thus providing more productive fishing time. Some of the old-time streamer fishermen on Maine lakes cast their streamer, light a cigarette, and when it is smoked, make the retrieve.

On a lake, the fly should be cast to the rise. If the trout is obviously cruising, it should be cast before the trout. This kind of fishing results in the fly resting on the surface of the water no longer than most flies that are cast to moving water in a stream. There are times, however, when hours are spent fishing the water. Then, there can be some advantage in allowing the fly to rest on the surface for longer periods of time. A poorly tied fly, either one made of water-absorbing materials or one too lightly hackled, will not float long enough. Well-tied, even heavily tied, dry flies will be the most satisfactory. The Wulff flies and similar patterns are satisfactory for fishing the water. But be ready to switch when a specific hatch appears and the fishing turns to the trout rather than to the water.

When, for one reason or another, large numbers of terrestrials or spent aquatic insects fall to the surface of the lake, fishing can be more productive on the leeward rather than the windward shore. The wind apparently drives the floating insects before it, and the trout are not hesitant about following this food supply into water only inches deep along the shore.

New England's fly patterns have been many and distinctive, and for good reason. As was noted, North American fly fishing had its beginnings in the Northeast. Original patterns were imported from England in the mid-nineteenth century.

Most were highly colored, so early New England flies sported bright hues. Evidently the brightly colored flies excited the wild trout of these cold, virgin waters, and excellent results were obtained.

The wet-fly and streamer-fly patterns of New England evolved before the advent of dry-fly fishing in America, which developed around the turn of the century. Perhaps, the best known wet-fly of the region was the Parmacheene Belle, which imitates a brook trout's fin, a common bait for brookies in the early days. The Gray, Black, and Green Ghost streamers were tied to imitate the smelt, a common New England food fish. In the 1930s, the late John Alden Knight popularized the Mickey Finn, a red and yellow bucktail, originally of New England origin.

For subsurface fishing, the above patterns are tried, true, and accepted by Yankee fly fishermen. Of course, there are many more patterns, some more popular than others, depending upon the locale.

Although colorful dry flies are sometimes fished in New England, the duller, natural-looking stand-bys of the mid-Atlantic states are more generally favored because many dry-fly anglers seek realism in order to match specific insects that are on the water—or should be—at given times. In the early season, the Quill Gordon, the Hendrickson, and the Blue Dun are widely used. In mid- and late-season, March Browns, Ginger Quills, Green Drakes, Light Cahills, and Pale Evening Duns are popular.

In New England's larger streams and rivers, where heavy water prevails, larger hard-to-sink dry patterns are often fished. Deer-hair Wulff flies, in sizes 8 to 12, are effective here.

Motel accommodations near top fishing spots are easy to come by over most of New England; so are campsites in state and national parks and forests.

Since boat fishing is widely practiced on the lakes and some rivers of New England, it is the perfect place for family vacations. Not every wife or child is up to wading streams, but anyone can troll on lakes. A New England vacation is the perfect answer for those who must live with the complaints of a fisherman's widow, for no region in the country has more scenic and historical attractions, along with varied recreational facilities for all of the family. The angler can fish full time with an easy conscience while his family is sightseeing, swimming, hiking, or picnicking close by.

New Jersey and New York

Certain good but somewhat artificial trout fishing is available in New Jersey. Most trout streams there are stocked on a regular basis, in some instances on the same day each week. Such information can be secured from the Department of Conservation and Economic Development, Labor and Industry Building, Box 1390, Trenton, New Jersey 18625. However, New Jersey lies within the coastal plain, and most of the East's best trout water is found in the Appalachians.

The most famous of New York's trout water is to be found in the Catskills, with a lesser amount in the Adirondacks. Elsewhere in this chapter, reference was made to the Northeast as being the cradle of trout angling in this country. The statement applies with specific reference to the streams of the Catskills and some of the Delaware Water Gap area of northeastern Pennsylvania.

The Beaverkill, Neversink, Willowemoc, Schoharie, Esopus, and East and West branches of the Delaware can provide some of the most interesting trout fishing in the East. These streams are close enough together to be fished on the same easy trip, and although they are not the same as they were in the days of Theodore Gordon or Edward R. Hewitt, they still provide much good angling. The Beaverkill, Willowemoc, Neversink, and Esopus are the historic streams referred to by Theodore Gordon in a letter printed in the *Fishing Gazette* in 1904.

The Antrim House at Roscoe, New York, is still a haven for anglers, and many well-known fishermen will gather there to participate in the ritual of opening the season on some of the most famous trout streams in the East.

Because of high water and low water temperatures, fishing is more difficult in the early season. The fly fisherman will find it nearly impossible to do much with the trout, but this may matter little. The spin fisherman and the bait fisherman are the heroes of the day, if the number of trout carried away from the stream is one's criterion. But as the water drops, as the flies hatch, and as the stream clears, the fly fisherman comes into his own. Long, fine leaders are needed to do an effective job on the shy trout on such streams as the Willowemoc, but even sloppily cast wet flies will take trout from much of the white water of the Esopus.

Mention should be made of the specialized fishing for rainbows in some small streams in the Finger Lakes area of New York. The most famous of these streams is Catherine Creek, which rises along Route 14 just north of Horseheads and flows into Seneca Lake at Watkins Glen. Early in the spring, migration of the rainbows from Seneca Lake into Catherine Creek provides what might be considered either exciting fishing or no fishing at all. The use of fish foods, and even bare hooks for snagging, is disgusting to many, and anyone who prefers the loneliness of a remote trout stream should not visit this madhouse.

Pennsylvania

For the sake of simplicity, we will assume that Pennsylvania is divided into three parts by three highways running east and west: The southern third can be reached by the Pennsylvania Turnpike; the center of the state by Interstate 80, locally referred to as the Shortway; and the upper third from Route 6 or connecting links.

In a limited presentation of the trout waters of the Commonwealth, the inclusion of any stream or watershed must be a matter of restricted choice. Dozens of different lists of Pennsylvania trout streams could be prepared. Streams of some reputation have been picked for this list, but the local trout fishermen often can find angling in his area which is superior to that found on better-known and more heavily fished streams.

Streams can be found in all parts of the state, but the trout water in the western counties and in the northwestern part of the state, often polluted with acid mine drainage, is much less significant than that of the central and eastern portions. Much of the water in the eastern counties is under the control of private clubs and may not be available to the angler, but this need not be a special hardship, since thousands of miles of water are available for the using.

In most counties in the southern part of the state, an easy trip to the north or to the south of the Pennsylvania Turnpike will provide enough trout angling to satisfy the visiting angler. The Conococheague Creek offers average angling most of the time, and occasionally it can be excellent. The Turnpike crosses the West Branch of the Conococheague near Willow Hill, and many miles of fishable water, both upstream and downstream, are available. The East Branch of the Conococheague is also good and can be reached at Chambersburg. Once again, many miles of water are available. The water is fishable south of Chambersburg as the stream flows toward the Potomac River.

Slightly east of the Conococheague watershed are the West and East Branches of the Antietam Creek; these can be reached in the area of Waynesboro, and both are excellent. A rather short limestone stream of excellent quality is Falling Springs Creek, which flows into the Conococheague at Chambersburg. This small limestone stream includes some fly-fishing-only water, and although it flows only for about six miles, it is one of the finest streams in Pennsylvania.

A short distance to the east, in the part of the Cumberland Valley between Chambersburg and Mechanicsburg, is some of the finest limestone-stream fishing to be found in the eastern United States. In addition to Falling Springs Creek (already mentioned), there are Boiling Springs, the Letort at Carlisle, and Big Spring at Newville.

Boiling Springs is one of the two largest springs in Pennsylvania; unlike other streams, it is, in fact, a spring pond of about eight acres. Generally the fly hatches are good, especially in the early season, but the fishing is tough. Long, fine leaders, the correct fly for the occasion, and good presentation are essential. Trout here are easily put down, and it may take an hour for a fish to resume its feeding.

Big Spring rises from a spring several miles above the town of Newville and flows into the Conodoquinet Creek several miles below the town. It is one of the finest brook-trout streams in the United States. Some degradation of the stream has taken place in recent years because of a commercial hatchery located near its head, but to fish it is still a joy.

If one locates the city of Harrisburg, the capital of Pennsylvania, and follows the Cumberland Valley directly west for a distance of about 30 miles, it will be seen that the Conodoquinet Creek limits the area on the northern side of the Yellow Breeches Creek on the southern edge. These two streams enter the Susquehanna River, one a little to the north of Harrisburg, and the other a little to the south. Limestone streams, fed from springs usually filled with watercress, flow from this valley northward to the Conodonquinet. Most are relatively short and offer excellent but exacting fishing. Many more streams flow into the Conodoquinet from the north, but these are soft-water streams; some are longer than the limestone waters, but most are as small. All offer trout fishing of less desirable quality than that available on the Letort or Big Spring.

The Yellow Breeches can be an excellent trout stream in the early season, but it must be clear for fly fishing. Fly hatches are most abundant at the opening, about the middle of April, and get progressively poorer as the season advances.

On the west and east banks of the Susquehanna River, in York, Lebanon, Lancaster, and Adams counties, the Pennsylvania Dutch have, since pioneer days, cleared their lands and tilled the soil. In this Dutch country, there are many small trout streams, each presenting a special problem in angling. None is famous but all can be rewarding. A short list of these waters might include the Hammer in Lebanon County; the Conowingo; the West Branch of the Octororo and Fishing Creek in Lancaster County; and the Muddy and Otter creeks, both tributaries of the Susquehanna River, in York County.

A trip from west to east on Route 6 covers many miles of

trout water. All of the streams can be classified as soft, or freestone, and most have limited food for trout. Most, but not all, are stocked at least for the opening of the season about the middle of April, and many receive a second stocking approximately a month later. Most of the trout water also produces a stream-bred population of trout, and it is entirely possible that this native stock contributes more to the catch than the stocked fish do. All the baits known to anglers are effective at one time or another. Not only are earthworms and natural insects such as stoneflies and caddisflies productive, but cheese and salted minnows are also sometimes effective. The hardware of the spin fisherman may be too much for many of the smaller streams, but such waters as Big Pine Creek, the Allegheny River, the First Fork of Sinnemahoning Creek, and parts of Tionesta Creek can handle it. Smaller spoons cast with a fly rod may do better in many instances.

Many of the anglers who fish these waters prefer fly fishing. They can work into small areas, using a variety of lures, and any trout caught that is not wanted can be returned to the water with reasonable certainty that it will live to fight another day.

Caldwell Creek, northeast of Titusville, is considered by many to be an excellent fly stream. Part of it has been declared fly-fishing-only water, and one section, under the management of the Northeast Pennsylvania Chapter of Trout Unlimited, is a trophy trout stream from which trout of 20 inches or longer are removed. It has been said of the Caldwell, "I don't know of a fisherman who has fished this sterling stream without becoming completely enamored of it. Select the best feature from a dozen favorite streams, and the chances are you'll find them duplicated on the Caldwell."

Tionesta Creek, above the dam and in the area of Kellettville, offers good trouting. Many feeder streams are excellent for native brook trout, and a week's vacation would be too short a time to reach all the waters available within several miles of headquarters. Summer temperatures of above 70°F may force the trout fisherman to hunt for the spring holes where the trout will concentrate, but in general: "It is one of the best, yet one of the most underrated trout streams in Pennsylvania."

Certainly, no trout fisherman would travel Route 6 through Coudersport without fishing the upper reaches of the Allegheny River. Here, the river flows north to circle through New York, only to return to Kinzua Dam in Warren County to the west. In the past several years, a new tailrace fishery has developed below the gates of this new concrete monster, and three-to-five-pound trout are the rule rather than the exception. Oswayo Creek, an excellent trout stream, can be reached at Shinglehouse, which is slightly northwest of Coudersport.

Cameron County offers the Sinnemahoning watershed—one of the largest subdrainage systems in the state—which empties into the West Branch of the Susquehanna River at Keating. The First Fork of the Sinnemahoning, upstream from the town of the same name, was once considered one of the outstanding stretches of trout water in the United States. The dam builders, highway builders, and stream straighteners have ruined much of this water, but parts of it are still worth fishing. We prefer the area upstream and downstream from the town of Wharton. The East Fork of the Sinnemahoning, which flows into the First Fork at Wharton, is good, but there are times when the horny chubs will drive the normally insane trout angler berserk.

There are hundreds of miles of fishable water in Potter County, but we have room to mention only a few streams. The Kettle Creek watershed, lying east of the Sinnemahoning and flowing into the Susquehanna River at Renovo, offers excellent fishing upstream from the town of Cross Fork. Early-season angling below the town with spinning tackle can be most rewarding, but as the stream temperatures increase, this area becomes better bass and chub water than trout water. Cross Fork Creek, which flows into Kettle Creek at Cross Fork Town, is also excellent, and several miles of it have been established as fly-fishing-only water.

From the mountains of Potter County flows one of the truly outstanding trout streams of Pennsylvania—Big Pine Creek. Part of its claim to fame is its scenery. Although the fishing can be superb, this is not to be taken as any assurance that a visit will fill the creel. Flowing east from the general area of Galeton, on Route 6, it makes a sudden southerly bend at Ansonia and flows through the Grand Canyon of Pennsylvania. Hardy souls walk this long ten-mile stretch; others approach it from the rim at several places, hiking down into its depths hundreds of feet below. It is wild country, and frequently the sight of wild turkey, black bear, and white-tailed deer provides an extra bonus. Some outfitters in the Ansonia area provide rubber-raft trips through the canyon, and local inquiries should produce results.

The trout fishing probably is better early in the season, when the trout are located at almost every site. In midsummer, when water temperatures exceed 70°F and trout tend to accumulate at spring holes or the mouths of cold-water runs, they may be difficult to approach and harder to catch during the daylight hours. At night, as the water temperature drops, the trout frequently leave the protection of their daytime rest and spread out into a larger area, offering excellent angling to the night fisherman. Wet flies as small as size 10 and as large as size 2/0 are used by local anglers. There are those who feel that a larger, woolly-type fly is the thing to use, on the assumption that it serves as an attractor, but many fish the smaller flies with the average amount of dressing. The local fishermen, even those of average ability, are the experts here rather than the visiting firemen. If possible, go fishing with a local and talk him into supplying some of the flies he uses. They work!

There are many tributaries, all of which provide fishing, but two are of special interest: Slate Run, which flows into Big Pine Creek opposite the town of Slate Run, and Cedar Run, which flows into Big Pine Creek opposite the town of Cedar Run. Slate Run is under special regulations and offers the fly fisherman his best angling in some of the most rugged country in Pennsylvania. Cedar Run is equally good if one is there at the right time. About 25 years ago, the no-night-fishing regulation was removed from Cedar Run, and although many catches have been made since by the daylight fly fisherman, he has fared less well than the night bait fisherman. Excellent accommodations are available at the Manor Hotel at Slate Run or the Cedar Run Hotel. A third tributary is Little Pine Creek, which flows into Big Pine Creek at Waterville. All of Little Pine Creek upstream to the village of English Center is worth exploring, and several smaller branches produce native brook trout.

In Clinton County, Young Woman's Creek flows into the West Branch of the Susquehanna River at Great Bend. The East Branch of the creek offers outstanding trout water, and a short section is limited to fly-fishing-only.

The Loyalsock Creek in Sullivan and Lycoming counties is truly one of the great trout streams in the East. It flows in a southerly direction from Dushore, emptying into the West Branch of the Susquehanna River four miles downstream from Williamsport. The Loyalsock has many tributaries contributing to an all-season fishery. Throughout most of its length it is a brawly stream, having long pools with fast-flowing water between. Much of it is deep, and although a boat is not a necessity, there are places where one might be helpful when the angler hooks into a large brownie. Fly fishing is best from about mid-May through June. Night fishing is practiced by a few fishermen, and wet flies take some large trout; three to five pounds is not considered exceptional. Some of the fishable tributaries are Wallins Run, Little Bear Creek, Big Bear Creek, Plunketts Creek, and Elk Creek.

A trout fisherman housed at Millheim in Centre County, only a few miles from Interstate 80, could, from the opening of the season until its dying hours, have some of the finest limestone trout fishing available in the East. Big Fishing Creek, Little Fishing Creek, Bald Eagle Creek (really a mixed soft- and hard-water stream), Penns Creek, Pine Creek, Elk Creek, Upper Spring Creek, and a small section of Spruce Creek would add up to a little less than one hundred miles.

It is, indeed, difficult to determine which of these streams is to be preferred. But if we eliminate, for the moment, Upper Spring Creek (limited length) and Spruce Creek (most of which is devoted to private-club water), we might arrange the streams in the following order of merits: Penns Creek, Big

Fishing Creek, Bald Eagle Creek, Elk Creek. The angler should feel free to move from one to the other because the fly hatches develop successively on these waters, and the trout fisherman should move with them. The main streams offer big water, and in some places they are difficult, if not impossible, to fish properly without waders. On the other hand, most of the water can be reached with fly tackle, although spinning tackle might be advisable on some sections of the Bald Eagle and Penns Creek. Many anglers claim that the Bald Eagle is a most challenging stream, not easy to fish but always unpredictable. Trout to eight pounds, and perhaps more, are regularly reported, and in the stream's lower reaches the recent introduction of muskies has put a thrilling unknown into the equation of angling.

Unfortunately, the dam builders have also been busy on the Bald Eagle, and much trout water will be lost. However, there still will be some good stretches available for the angler, and it is possible that large trout will share the dammed-up waters of the stream with warm-water species when the newly completed Sayer's Dam is filled.

Penns and Fishing creeks, including their tributaries, are rich in aquatic insects and other natural trout foods. Unless the fish are rising, they are not easy—some say impossible—to take on dry flies. Hours can be spent waiting for the visible rise, but when everything goes as it should, dozens of working fish can be seen within casting distance during the evening rise. It would be a mistake to guarantee a catch of trout, even in these splendid streams, and the ratio of success cannot be compared with that on the large limestone waters of the western United States. They are, however, the finest of the East, though they may be tough to fish.

We suggest Big Fishing Creek in the area of Lamar and Penns Creek from Spring Mills downstream. Between what is called Poe Paddy Run and Cherry Run, there is a fly-fishing-only area of approximately three miles, which has some of the most attractive trout water in Pennsylvania.

Fisherman's Paradise on Spring Creek in Centre County was at one time world famous. Much of its former glory is now gone because of pollution in Spring Creek, but the so-called Project is still of considerable interest because it offers year-round fly-fishing on a catch-and-release basis. As a result of pollution, most of the fly hatches have been destroyed. Some Diptera are still in evidence, and trout will surface feed on these minutae and on terrestrials falling into the water. Streamers are still fished by many anglers, and in spite of the lack of fly life, there is always the trout that takes a Green Drake or some other dry fly or a wet fly, out of either curiosity or annoyance. Except in the coldest weather, the stream is fished every day of the week, with weekends in early spring and late fall finding the stream almost crowded. No. 28s are not too small. They should be tied to be fished in the surface film. On occasion, a trout will take a larger fly, but anything much larger than No. 16 will probably be worthless except for casting practice.

West Virginia

Go fish a West Virginia stream
Where fighting trout leap high;
Go share an angler's fondest dream
And watch your troubles die.

Well might the Poet Laureate of West Virginia, Roy Lee Harmon, extol trout angling in the Mountain State. For no eastern area can boast of wilder, less-trafficked streams interlacing scenic grandeur that well deserves of its appellation, "The Switzerland of America."

As noted earlier, some West Virginia waters cannot support trout because they contain acids from coal-mine drainage. New regulations and some innovative engineering projects of the state's Department of Natural Resources bode well for the future of such waters. Large amounts of pure trout water remain, particularly in the Monongahela National Forest, which extends southwesterly along more than half of West Virginia's eastern border. This vast corridor of panoramic splendor parallels Interstate Highway 81, which enters Western Maryland from central Pennsylvania and continues along Virginia's beautiful historic Shenandoa Valley and the Blue Ridge. Thanks to this highway and its east-west offshoots, large population centers such as Richmond, Baltimore-Washington, Philadelphia, and eastern New Jersey are only two to five hours driving time from top-notch wilderness trout fishing.

During one long week end, inhabitants of these strip cities can experience stream fishing in some of the most productive waters of the Monongahela Forest. Enter the forest just below its northeastern extremity at Petersburg, West Virginia, and you can begin on the south branch of the Potomac River at the scenic Smoke Hole caverns. Excellent dry-fly water abounds here. As you move upriver the stream narrows, its current becomes swifter, and there is much white water.

Pockets and slicks are made to order for dry flies; rougher water provides streamer devotees splendid action with husky rainbows. As a bonus there is always the chance of tying into a hard-fighting smallmouth bass. If you begin north of Petersburg, at Romney, where the river is generally wider and more sluggish, you can enjoy excellent smallmouth fishing on the same tackle you use for trout. Streamers are favored. But a few large deer-hair dry flies are in order for the South Branch, no matter where you fish it. Large "floaters" can work as well for large trout as for smallmouth bass.

After an afternoon and evening on the South Branch, you can spend the night in a motel in the area of Mouth of Seneca. A morning on beautiful Seneca Creek—prime brook-trout water—is almost always rewarding. A short drive north brings you to Dry Fork (a fine stream) near Black Water State Park. Here the famous Black Water stream provides excellent trout fishing.

The second night can be spent in Elkins. You will be well advised to fish on the following day on nearby Shaver's Fork of the Cheat River, one of the most beautiful and productive trout streams in the Mountain State. Big water this. You can easily spend the rest of your week end here. And if you stay another night in the Elkins area, the last day will be well spent on the Back Fork of the Elk River. It contains one of the state's prime "catch and release" stretches, full of lunker-size trout.

Several factors are making West Virginia the East's new trout frontier. Much of the wilderness is virtually pristine. Ever mindful of the destruction wrought to trout habitat in seaboard states by road and dam builders, pesticides, lumbermen, and fishing pressure, officials of the Department of Natural Resources have taken far-seeing steps to preserve quality trout fishing. There had been sparse use of pesticides in the mountain fastnesses of the state prior to the national scare which indiscriminate use of these chemicals occasioned in the late 1950s, so many streams still breed clouds of mayflies, which afford hatch-matching dry-fly anglers a veritable paradise. Department officials intend to keep the public well aware of the threat posed to wildlife by careless use of pesticides.

The problem of stream crowding has been attacked by the introduction of a year-round open trout season and all-year nonpublicized stocking. Thus, fishing pressure has been spread out, and stocked trout are afforded enough time to become stream-wise, not patsies for anything thrown to them on "opening day."

Some General Notes on Flies

The reader can explore the fishing books written by the anglers of the Northeast and come up with a set of patterns that would be most valuable. Standard patterns of wets, such as the Gold Ribbed Hare's Ear, soft- and hard-bodied ants, nymphs tied in the humpbacked style of Skues (especially in grays, olives, and browns), the Black and Brown Sedge, the Orange Fish Hawk, the quill-bodied wet flies that imitate immature stages of such well-known flies as the Hendrickson and March Brown, along with individual favorites, should do the job. All sizes might be necessary but a No. 8 would be large and a No. 18 might be as small as necessary.

The usual assortment of dry flies in sizes from 12 to 22 (some size 28s) is needed. Pale Watery Dun, Sulphur Dun, Green Drake, Hendrickson, Quill Gordon, Mosquito, Adams, Blue Dun, Cahill, Red-Legged March Fly—all are good. Imitations of terrestrials, including a Jassid, a grasshopper, a beetle, and an inchworm, may make productive a day that otherwise would have drawn a blank. On many freestone streams, nearly any pattern one can invent will catch fish at some time. Some anglers have speculated that the low food

NED
SMITH

content per acre of freestone water leaves most trout hungry most of the time, and they are not likely to pass up a suitably presented morsel to fill out their daily diet. On the limestone streams, no such nonsense is tolerated by the trout, and here imitations of the naturals, presented in a way that the trout find convincing, will work much better.

Ditching, drainage, pollution, dams, road construction, and siltation have all contributed to a gradual but steady decrease of hatches of aquatic insects. In some instances, pollution has resulted in the near disappearance of mayflies, but a sizable increase in the numbers of Diptera flies, such as midges and other Chironomids, has occurred in many streams. Terrestrials have also grown in importance to the trout angler.

About 90 miles of trout water, all stocked, have been set aside in Pennsylvania as fly-fishing-only areas. Individual stretches of water rarely exceed five miles, and most are shorter than this. A complete list, which changes somewhat from year to year, is available from the Pennsylvania Fish Commission in Harrisburg. Such information is normally provided when a license is purchased.

Pennsylvania probably stocks as many trout per mile of accessible water as any state in the nation. Wild trout can be found in many streams, and late-season fishing is probably over native, or stream-bred, fish. Some lakes are open for fishing into September and, in some instances, for ice fishing during the winter. These lakes are frequently restocked at this time.

Fishing pressure is greatest at the opening of the season, reflecting not only a widespread desire to fish but also the artificial pressure developed by a well-advertised stocking program. After the end of May, trout streams are available for the trout fishermen, and fishermen who merely fish for trout have gone elsewhere.

Random Facts about Fish and Water

Although it is not necessary to know anything about trout to be able to fish for them and only a little knowledge is needed to catch them, it is nevertheless, true that knowing something about fish makes the sport of angling more interesting.

Fish are cold-blooded animals and as such assume the temperature of the water in which they live. Trout, and other fish, are able to live only in a certain range of temperature extremes. It is often stated that the maximum temperature at which a trout can live is 75°F, and this accounts for the fact that late-season trout anglers often carry a thermometer as well as a fishing rod. As a matter of practical application of temperature to trout fishing, 70°F is about the top limit a trout will tolerate. At this point, it will move, if possible, to a cooler place. This may be upstream into smaller, often spring-fed feeder streams or to locations where spring water seeps into the stream bed or from the stream bank. We need not emphasize the fact that trout cannot be caught in water where there are none.

A trout has about the same specific gravity as water and therefore needs no elaborate system of bones to hold its shape. Some strength, however, is needed because the water in which a trout lives is incompressible. This means that there cannot be water where a trout is. When a trout swims, it must displace water. Consequently, the bony system of the fish must supply the support necessary to accomplish this. The shape of the trout is also an important consideration, and we might take a moment to examine it.

The trout has a heavy shoulder area. As a trout moves forward, the closing of the water behind the shoulder helps in its forward motion. Actually, the apparent ease with which a trout moves in the water requires considerable coordination between the fins to provide power and stability, as well as certain internal organs to provide a sense of balance.

The paired pectoral fins, located behind the gills on the side of the head, the pelvic fins located a little farther back, the anal fin behind the vent, and the dorsal fin on the back of the trout provide the means of steering, balancing, and turning. The dorsal fin would seem also to prevent roll. The tail, or caudal fin, provides the power to swim.

Trout fishermen may be more interested in the senses of smell and sight than in balance and mobility. We might guess that the bait fisherman hopes that the trout will smell his offering, and the fly fisherman must, of necessity, depend on the trout's vision. Flies fished in muddy water are probably worthless, except for an occasional accident. But when the water is clear and the trout are feeding by sight as they rise to duns on the water's surface, the taking of the fly is deliberate.

The sense of smell is well developed in fish, and many anglers and authors have suggested that trout feed more by smell than sight. It is just possible that wet-fly fishermen who find it profitable to attach a bit of earthworm to their wet fly would agree with this observation.

The sense of sight of fish is judged to be not significantly different from that of humans, though there are differences in eye structure and eye location.

The ability of trout to see and distinguish color is a fascinating topic, and fly fishermen and fly tiers have spent many hours discussing it. It is a fact that the visual cones of a trout's eye should provide the mechanism to differentiate color. Apparently, it is this ability that provides the basis of selectivity that the trout shows for flies, certain spoons and other hardware, and colored plastic worms. The eye of the trout differs from that of a human in that there is no eyelid, nor is there any need for one, because of the watery environment bathing the eye. The iris of the trout's eye is relatively immobile. Its contractile capacity is limited. A trout can see objects only at relatively close distances.

To all intents and purposes, the vision of a trout is monocular, each eye seeing its own side. There is some evidence of a small area of overlap directly in front of the trout where the vision would presumably be binocular. Some observers of the behavior of trout have suggested that the rather close inspection of an object by a fish, as it slowly moves around it, is to get the object into the small area of binocular vision. Those who study and write about rise forms might find it valuable to examine the rise form in light of the trout's search for a binocular look at the fly. The bending of the rays of light as they enter the surface of the water has been exhaustively discussed, but not always correctly, by several authors. This phenomenon of refraction obviously interferes with the feeding of a trout at the surface of the water, and the fish must rise ahead of the target it sees. No such adjustment is necessary when a trout takes a lure under the surface of the water.

A trout is endowed with all five senses: sight, hearing, smell, taste, and touch. To a fisherman, one sense may be more important at one time than at another, but all are used by the trout. They might also be used to advantage by the trout angler.

Selected Bibliography

Bates, Joseph D., Jr. *Streamer Fly Tying and Fishing*. The Stackpole Company, 1950 and 1966.

Bergman, Ray. *Trout*. sec. ed. Alfred A. Knopf, 1969.

Du Bois, Donald. *The Fisherman's Handbook of Trout Flies*. A. S. Barnes and Company, 1960.

Flick, Art. *New Streamside Guide to Naturals and Their Imitations*. Crown Publishers, Inc. 1969.

Grove, Alvin R., Jr. *The Lure and Lore of Trout Fishing*. Freshet Press, 1971.

Jennings, Preston J. *A Book of Trout Flies*. Crown Publishers, Inc. 1970.

Leisenring, James E. *The Art of Tying the Wet Fly*. Crown Publishers, Inc. 1971.

Marbury, Mary Orvis. *Favorite Flies and Their Histories*. Houghton Mifflin Company, 1892.

Noll, H. J. *Guide to Trout Flies*. 1954.

Quick, Jim. *Fishing the Nymph*. The Ronald Press Company, 1960.

Schwiebert, Ernest G., Jr. *Matching the Hatch*. The Macmillan Company, 1955.

Slaymaker, S.R., II. *Simplified Fly Fishing*. Harper and Row, 1969.

West, Leonard. *The Natural Trout Fly and Its Imitation*. 1912.

Wetzel, Charles M. *Practical Fly Fishing*. Christopher Publishing, Inc. 1935.

———. *Trout Flies, Naturals, and Imitations*. The Stackpole Company, 1955.

*To have Charlie Fox and Don Neal write about muskies, bass, and pan fish is an apparent contradiction. Fox wore out his first pair of waders on the limestone trout streams of southcentral Pennsylvania and has written eloquently about it (*This Wonderful World of Trout *and* Rising Trout*). Unknown to some of his readers, Fox has also spent hundreds of hours pursuing bass and muskellunge and, with his usual thoroughness, has racked up an amazing storehouse of information about them.*

CHAPTER 15

Musky Fishing Around the Calendar and Around the Clock

CHARLES K. FOX

These days they are talking about "getting in on a piece of the action." As one fisherman to another, I want to tell you how I believe such a statement might apply to you. As time goes by, more and more anglers will be catching more and more muskies, thanks to a substantial number of extensive musky programs and to many new man-made bodies of water. This is the one great shining light in the entire fishing conservation picture, a picture that is not in a general way a pretty one.

Fish culturists have learned how to trap muskies, strip them of eggs and milt when they are ripe, hatch the eggs in large glass jars, feed the babies, first with water fleas then with tiny minnows, and finally to stock them in the late summer or fall as exciting little torpedoes of a size too big to be handled by the bluegills of the lakes and the rock bass of the rivers.

They are destined to grow rapidly, yet disappear so far as fishermen are concerned, for two or three years, then show up as two-footers or better. Take one look at a musky's awesome dental arrangement and you'll have no doubt that he is a fish eater. In this day and age, however, this is very much to the good. It is to the good because man, with his system of sewage effluents and his washings of commercial fertilizers into the streams and lakes, is changing the ecology of waters. The results of this overfertilization are a superabundance of bluegills in the too-rich lakes and a superabundance of rock bass in the too-rich rivers, the adult populations of which prey on the young crop of game fish. To this environment should be added a predator of large capacity, a fish eater capable of balancing the populations that man has upset. The voracious musky is just what the doctor ordered.

The survival rate of the planted fingerling muskies is high. For example, a Wisconsin study revealed that 45 per cent of the fingerling muskies stocked in Green Lake survived to become legal game for the angler. Always, in one way or another, a few escape fishing efforts and grow into whoppers—four-footers, 30-pounders, or even larger fish.

This sort of build-up of battle wagons is taking place in many waters in various states and provinces, not only where stockings supplement nature's supply but also where heretofore there were no muskies and even where there had been no waters. The federal government, state governments, private water companies, and water authorities are building new impoundments, many of which will be stocked with muskies. That is why, as time goes on, more fishermen will be catching more and more muskies, increased fishing pressures to the contrary.

This amazing fish is no pushover. As is always the case in angling, the resourceful, analytical, observant fellow does considerably better then the less-dedicated angler. In this instance we are dealing not only with a tackle buster but also with a moody, mysterious, and crafty customer. He has a pattern to his living, though, and that is what makes for angling opportunity. The biggest job is to impale him on a hook; playing and landing him will have to take care of themselves. So if you have become interested in connecting with a musky now and then, consider the following:

All who have to make decisions, be they directors, demagogues, doctors, or developers, study the percentages, then follow them. The purpose of this chapter is to examine percentage musky fishing as I see it. Let's start with the cream of it, then go around the calendar and around the clock.

What Mr. Musky does to a lure when he decides to do it is almost too good to be true, but to enjoy such a fish reaction, the angler must show him the right thing and show it in the right way.

There is nothing in all fresh-water fishing comparable to the strike of a musky to a surface lure. The sight and the sound are terrific, and the feel of the fish is electrifying. There are times when they explode out of water, there are times when they plow into the plug, and there are times when they plow up a great wake as they follow or approach the lure.

Each fall, for a period of weeks, possibly as many as eight, they like their lures on the top. In southern Pennsylvania, Columbus Day is about the start of that time. Further north, this period begins in September, but there it ceases sooner. In a general way, this time is from the first frosts to the beginning of ice. That fierce explosion may happen any hour of the day during this period, the truly fantastic weeks of musky fishing.

To me this is the greatest and the grandest opportunity of the year. Once I'd sampled it, it cut into my bird hunting and deer hunting; then after I'd become experienced in it, it pushed them well back in the schedule of outdoor things. An old bird-hunting companion, with disgust and scorn in his voice, calls me "the musky hound."

Because in one direction seven miles from home there is lake musky fishing and 17 miles away in the opposite direction there is river fishing, I manage to indulge in a considerable amount of casting for them.

At many of the resorts and for many adherents, trolling is

NED SMITH

the accepted system. This is a restful pursuit, and it covers much water. On the other hand, casting makes possible a careful, methodical, and thorough fishing of a given area. I think that good casting will outfish good trolling by a considerable margin. Such a statement demands an explanation.

A case in point is pop-casting. This is done with a floating plug that can be made to act in an enticing manner on the surface and that can also be made to swim under water with a wabbling action. Thus, on the same cast one can fish with two different actions and on two different levels. Consider also the thorough way one can "comb a bay" or "work a field of pads" from a strategically anchored or slow-moving boat. And there are situations in which either a boat is not available or it is such a joy to fish from the shoreline that casting is a logical choice.

In November, 1968, while fishing from a gently sloping bank, I stirred up five fine muskies to a pop-casting lure while it was being manipulated on the surface with rod-tip action before one struck the same lure on the submerged swimming retrieve. There are those of us who prefer a lure that is traveling into shallow water and toward the shore to one that is swimming in the opposite direction. And casting from the bank makes for cautious and thorough fishing.

It is not an unusual experience to have a musky follow the lure almost to the rod, then make a turn, as he comes to the shoreline, that throws water at the angler. Such fish are apparently so engrossed with the lure that they do not notice the caster. Often they follow or strike on a succeeding retrieve.

Working together, several of us have conducted extensive experiments with the various surface actions. We used both lures available on the market and others made at home.

Our first disappointment was with the popper type, either with V mouth or concave face. These turned out to be less than enchanting to the muskies to which they were shown, yet over the years the plunking lures fished with a stop-and-start retrieve have been attractive to both lake largemouth bass and river smallmouths.

The gurgling-splatter type moved some fish, but it seemed

to us that a high percentage would not touch the lure, although they showed to it. It appeared that there was frequently a last-split-second refusal.

After some trial and error we were not sold on the injured-minnow type, those with the propellers fore and aft, until one day two of us tried the old bass-fishing trick of removing the front prop. The result is an entirely different surface action, in effect, the creation of a new lure. Without the drag caused by the propeller on the front end, the nose is free to angle, resulting in weaving and rocking action, rather than a straight start and stop. This continuous drunken movement—a sort of irregularity of course combined with weaving and rocking—we believe to be the most effective of all surface actions for muskies. They snatch lures with this action violently and with fair regularity, always, it seems, coming at the plug from the side, so that it is positioned crosswise in the mouth. There are various floating propeller lures on the market, any one of which can be altered in this manner. In due course this became our choppy-water lure for fall casting.

The greatest refinement, so far as I am concerned, came when I made up two floating lures that can be given bobbing and weaving surface action with rod-tip manipulations and that have a side-to-side swimming action on a fast underwater retrieve. One I call the "Sick Sucker," the other "Whirligig." Promptly each proved its worth and won our hearts too. But they have a weakness: a wind-chopped surface ruins their action. Thus they are basically calm-water lures. Both lures swim submerged about eight inches on a fast retrieve, with the result that now and then there is an awesome wake back of the plug, a situation that makes for anticipation of the butterflies-in-stomach variety.

Thus it was that for fall musky fishing we developed three indispensable plugs. Naturally we try others too, because it is fun to experiment, particularly after a musky has just been caught. But these are our staples for fall fishing.

Something unexpected cropped up in our group relative to surface fishing. It so happens that by preference Norm Lightner spins with an open-face reel and ten-pound-test monofilament line, John Rex spin casts with an encased reel, sturdy rod, and 15-pound monofilament, and I bait-cast with a 20-pound braided casting line, which floats, to one end of which is added a five- to six-foot 15-pound monofilament trace. The slick trace assists casting and adds camouflage. Monofilament, of course, sinks. Side-by-side comparison revealed that the identical pop casters, when fished with rod-tip manipulation, give different action when the line floats than when it sinks. The sinking monofilament pulls the nose of the floater downward, giving it a decided bobbing action, whereas the floating line causes the lure to angle, first from one side then to the other, a decided weaving motion. With the muskies being the jury of lure action, the verdict was in favor of weaving and against bobbing. Now John is experimenting with a 35-foot strip of floating bait-casting line between the monofilament and a relatively short casting trace in the expectation that the lure can be made to perform in a more-effective manner.

Personally, I like to fit the lure to the equipment. Experience demonstrates that muskies will hit tiny lures, medium-size lures, and large ones. I have caught seven and lost a greater number that hit a quarter-ounce two-inch bass lure, but none of these were large fish. The tackle I normally use for muskies handles half-ounce lures best, so that is what I like. John Rex, on the other hand, prefers lures that weigh in at three-quarters of an ounce or slightly more, so that is what he employs, along with his "brute stick."

Color to muskies may be like ice cream flavors to humans. I like metallic green with gold scale and orange with gold scale, but one man I know concentrates on black and another on white with a red head. Maybe the younger generation would not understand, but in the older days when all students had to be exposed to Latin, this situation would have been expressed thus: *de gustibus non est disputandum.* Whether or not you can translate this literally is academic; we know that you get the idea.

It is interesting to study the underwater action of such stalwarts as Pikie Minnow, Heddon Vamp, Flat Fish, Lazy Ike, Rebel, and Rapala, to name some of the popular favorites. They all swim well, but they don't all swim exactly alike. Some cast much better than others, and muskies hit them all.

The action of surface lures is much more varied. Is there any similarity between Jitter Bug, Crazy Crawler, Injured Minnow, Plunker Duck, and Mud Puppy? Only that they all stay on top.

The more I am able to study muskies, the more firmly convinced I am that outside of the time for their heing and sheing, he wants to be alone and so does she. Twice I have had the experience, while shoreline casting, of placing a lure diagonally to one side and raising a musky, then while resting that fish, of casting diagonally to the other side only to raise another fish. That would put them somewhere between 150 and 200 feet apart. That seems to be as close as they will live to one another. I believe there exists a spirit of territorial integrity among them.

In a scientific report a fish culturist wrote about how the little ones would only eat clean kills. When a baby musky struck at a tiny minnow but did not grasp it for keeps, the musky would not follow up the cripple but would invariably attack a fresh one. To confound the angler, it appears that there is a carryover of this trait into legal-size fish, for when a strike is felt but the fish is not hooked, there is no follow up. The best practice when this happens seems to be to quickly change to a new and different lure.

I think that the way a plug hits the surface, be it surface lure or pop caster, is important. There is a casting trick, easily performed with a bait-casting outfit, more difficult with the fixed-spool reel, which allows one to control this. The lure is cast in a low trajectory, with rod and arm extended. Just as the lure touches down, it is swooshed across the surface in a skimming lifelike action. This makes muskies take notice. Incidentally, the same thing is true of bass.

Generally speaking, a fast underwater retrieve with broken action will outfish the slow-going methodical lure.

There comes a time in the fall when chilly water stiffens many fish and curtails their disgestive processes, so they no longer desire to feed and are ready to hide for the winter.

This corresponds pretty much with the first tinge of frost. The musky, however, has a different metabolism than bluegills, crappies, and bass. Instead of slackening off, his digestive process speeds up in 50- to 60-degree water, even as a brook trout. Thus, he wishes to eat more and to eat more frequently at the very time when the available food supply is disappearing. Now by necessity he becomes a prowler in order to enjoy a good stomachfull. During the summer he would wait in hiding, ready to charge an unsuspecting victim, but now he is a hunter on the move.

It has been said and written that 200 hours of fishing are required to catch a legal musky. Fall pop-casting in decent musky water should do better than to remove one zero from that figure. In fact, the chances are excellent that more than one fish will be moved in a single session.

When ice forms in the lakes and the slush ice flows in the rivers, the fantastic fall musky season is over for another ten months, but the fishing isn't over, not if you can get to a musky river. The story is interesting.

Gar Archer had to fish from a sitting position because of an injury, yet he preferred casting with artificials to still fishing. So it was that he started pitching expensive lures into the Allegheny River near his home of Pleasantville. To save the cost of lures, he began to make his own. As things developed they became jigs, and jigs only.

This was the beginning both of the winter jig-fishing up and down the Allegheny River and of the making of jigs on a commercial basis by Gar Archer.

Where and when this fishing is done came as a revelation to me. The river was high and cloudy, too high and too cloudy, I thought, until I heard Tid Sheldon say to Howard Levy, "I had hoped the river would be up another couple of feet and there would be slush ice flowing." And Howard agreed, "Yes, too bad." Then Gar explained to me, "Tough conditions in the river drive the fish into the eddies and the mouths of feeder streams, and that is where they are caught.

"The trick is to cast out, let the lure sink to the bottom, then bottom hop it back," he went on. "If you hook up, grab the line and try to upset the rock that's causing the trouble.

You lose lots of jigs, maybe a dozen a day, but that is part of this game. When the river is frozen over, we go to the warm-water discharge below the power plant at Warren. White jigs with a red head are our favorites for muskies and blue ones for walleyes." In December, 1967, Tid Sheldon caught a 47½-inch musky which won the annual Allegheny River contest, and in January, 1969, he broke the Pennsylvania record for walleye pike with a 14-pound, 5-ounce fish, both succumbing to bottom-hopped jigs.

In most states and provinces there is a closed period encompassing the musky breeding season. At this time the adults have paired up. Nests are not made, as is the case with bass, nor is gravel worked as trout and salmon do it, nor are ribbons of spawn draped over weeds, perch style. Rather in pairs they cruise about, mainly near the shoreline, the hen dropping some eggs now and then which the cock fish promptly fertilizes. The eggs that land on silt and weed are probably doomed to decay, whereas the small percentage that drops in clean gravel or among stones has a chance to hatch.

This means that continuity of the supply in some waters is dependent upon an annual planting of fingerlings. The same treatment for the natural-reproducing waters will supplement the normal supply. It boils down to this: a state or province can develop and maintain improved musky fishing even when and where nature falters. Thus the musky man is not so dependent upon the natural output as he once was.

In May, June, or July, depending upon where you fish, another musky season opens. It starts before the rapid buildup of the food supply. The muskies are not as yet ready to hit on the surface, but they will strike a spoon, a spinner with hair or feathers tied to the hook, or a wabbling plug that travels at least two feet under the water.

Water temperatures fluctuate more in spring and early summer than in the fall, or to put it another way, water warms up faster in the spring than it cools off in the fall, because mild fall days are not as hot as spring days and balance better with cool nights. Spring, nevertheless, has some of that charmed 55-degree water and with it improved fishing, even though the food supply is not in hiding. For the second time during the calendar year musky digestion is in high gear, for again they eat a lot and eat frequently. For a period of a week or two, the lure caster and the troller have a time reminiscent of fall fishing. In Pennsylvania this occurs the last week of May and the first week of June.

Once the water temperature climbs into the 60s and 70s, muskies become lethargic, eating but little and mostly in the early morning and late evening. The end of the hot summer does not enjoy a favorable musky-fishing reputation, but it has its big inning too. The late Robert Page Lincoln dearly loved to fish the fields of pads with a surface plug at dawn and for an hour or so thereafter. Evening and night fishing in summer heat can produce fish. It is believed that northern pike and chain pickerel are not capable of seeing in the dark, but this is not true of their relative the musky.

At the time of year when the water temperature is at its maximum, it is more difficult to induce the muskies of the lakes to strike than it is to tempt river fish. Lake fishing in the northern extremity of the range holds up fairly well because water temperature is not effected to such a high degree. The further one goes northward within the belt for summer musky fishing, the cooler the water and the better one's chances. The water temperature situation in Ontario, where the nights are not stifling, is by comparison relatively good.

Now we are back to the starting point, the wonderful fall days when the musky strikes the most and the hardest, the time of day being of little consequence. So to the one who has an urge to indulge in something engrossing and thrilling, such as showing a musky the right lure at the right time, I say, study the percentages, then play them, bearing in mind that one cast can do a big job.

CHAPTER 16

Bass and Bass Craft

CHARLES K. FOX

The greatest of the recognized authorities on bass, Dr. James Alexander Henshall, considering the fighting abilities of hooked fish, penned the following oft-quoted dictum for his tome, *The Book of the Black Bass,* published in 1881: "Inch for inch and pound for pound the bass is the gamest fish that swims."

It is not my place or intent to challenge the judgment of Dr. Henshall, a man for whom I have great admiration, but maybe this fish has something going for him as wonderful as, or even more wonderful than, his ability to buck angling tackle. He is the greatest striker of them all, whether sought after with bug, plug, fly, spoon, spinner, or bait. In addition to the fact that he hits for keeps, he thrives and propagates his kind anywhere from a soupy farm pond to a large trout stream, and this includes practically all rivers and lakes.

In view of his free-striking trait, fighting ability, and wide range, the bass is the most sought-after game fish in America, and as such the popular favorite. His legion of avid anglers have a strong tendency to specialize in their attempts to meet with success. There are specialists in the following fields: bass-bugging, fly-fishing, plug-casting, spinning, spin-casting, and bait fishing. Each method accounts for a fair share of fish. Let's run the gamut of angling for bass with the artificial, being guided by avid specialists.

Keith Schuyler says, "I'm bugs about bass." This is the same Keith Schuyler who was shot down over Germany in World War II and who negotiated an escape from a *Stalag*. This is also the same Keith Schuyler who for years has conducted the outdoor column for the *V.F.W. Magazine* and has authored several books. He insists upon two things in conjunction with his bass fishing. The first requisite is to see the strike on rise; the second is to play the fish on a fly rod. So it is that he bugs for bass. His favorites are cork floaters in different sizes, which he fabricates himself.

In back of his house is a pond that was made to be the habitat of largemouth bass, and about a mile from his home is the North Branch of the Susquehanna River, which features smallmouth bass and lends itself to fly-rod fishing by wading.

Balanced equipment for bugging is an eight- to nine-foot rod, fitted up with a torpedo-head floating line, a good reel that will accommodate some small-diameter backing under the fly line, and a tapered leader of about the length of the rod and pointed out to six- or eight-pound test. Because a bug offers more air resistance than a fly and because of the slightly burdensome pickup from the water, casting timing may seem odd at first to the experienced trout fisherman, but that does not make it difficult to master. Keith Schuyler says, "I like to fish my bugs slowly with a rather gentle stop and start action."

The late Sol Rupp, Esq., was the pioneer dry-fly fisherman for trout in his section of Pennsylvania, so it was only natural that he experimented with bass when trout were out of season. He cast his flies in the era when smallmouth bass in the Susquehanna River watershed were called "the new fish."

Before and after World War I, Sol used three streams as his playgrounds and testing grounds: Marsh Creek, a feeder of the Potomac River, and the Conodoguinet Creek and Shermans Creek, tributaries of the Susquehanna. Incidentally, anywhere but in Pennsylvania these creeks would be known as rivers. Once a stream in its headwaters narrows to less than 30 feet in width, bass, unlike trout, become disenchanted with it.

After considerable trial and error, he developed a favorite fly. The Sol Rupp pet was a No. 8 long-shank hair-wing fly with a tiny built-in propeller between the eye of the hook and the tying silk. This fly both casts and lifts from the water in a better manner than the usual spinner on a shaft followed by a fly, and the bass seem to think it looks better too. Time has not been good to the propellered hook, for it has all but disappeared (I still have two); but that may be because it received little or no publicity. The fly deserves a better fate than that of an antique; a revival for both bass and trout fishing is in order.

Bill Pfeiffer is of the George Harvey school of night fly-fishing for very big trout. This group employs a big juicy-bodied hair-wing wet fly fished after dusk, ever so slowly. It was Bill who discovered that the same thing works well for river smallmouth during the daylight hours as well as after nightfall. His main bass-fishing area is the bass-laden Potomac River in the vicinity of Williamsport, Maryland, not Williamsport, Pennsylvania (on the West Branch of the Susquehanna), where he spent the days of his youth. Good old dependable bass, they like the night fly too, and at any time. Thus it is that Bill Pfeiffer wrote a new chapter to the story of bass craft.

Ken Reid was one of the amazingly few ardent and skilled anglers who, over the years, have been appointed by a Pennsylvania Governor to the Board of the Fish Commissioners. In fact, now and then His Excellency comes up with a nonfisherman to represent fishermen. Later Reid became the Executive Director of the Izaak Walton League of America. He and Joe Messinger of Morgantown, West Virginia, were friends. Messinger amazed the fly-tying world with a new style of tie in the form of a realistic-looking frog. The tying material was moose mane. After being tied, it was clipped and painted. Here was the forerunner of the present-day clipped-deer-hair flies. Little did he suspect, on the day that he gave Ken Reid one of his hair frogs, that henceforth he would be primarily a fly-tier instead of primarily an angler.

Reid, who got around with his fishing, used the hair frog successfully on many bass waters, and he wrote glowingly about it, particularly in the fine magazine *Hunting and Fishing*, which in the roaring twenties and early Depression years before it was absorbed sold for five cents a copy. This imitation in the hands of Reid did much to promote bass-bugging, and it helped the cause of a special fly-tying technique too. Reid designed the first chest kit to accommodate trout flies or bass bugs. There are still a few of the fine old Ken Kits around.

About four decades later Paul Failor of the Pennsylvania Game Commission put on the market a comparable creation of his own, but the Failor clipped-deer-hair fly is an attractor, not imitating anything in particular, whereas the Messinger hair frog is a deceiver. Failor believes in a generous amount of natural float between manipulations. The bass, the great striker, is well satisfied with this hair bug and the way its adherents fish it.

Those who seek their bass with a fly rod have a tendency to shower attention on one particular fly or bug. A look into the box usually reveals that there is a lot of one thing and a limited variety. The lure man is different. No matter whether he delivers his wares by bait-casting, spinning or spin-casting, he plays around with swimmers and divers, gurglers and plunkers, plastic worms and propeller lures—anything and everything. The history of the bass lure is interesting. Actually, the bait-casting reel had to be developed before casting lures could evolve.

The feeding habits of bass made the invention of the multiplying reel inevitable. However, the fact that George Snyder moved from Bucks County, Pennsylvania, to Paris, Kentucky, hastened the event. In 1803, when he pushed westward, there were no bass in eastern watersheds around his home, for they had not as yet been introduced, but both large and smallmouth bass were native to the waters of the Midwest. Snyder, a watchmaker, fished for them around his new home with minnows and frogs. He recognized the fact that the single-action fly reel was too slow to permit the lofting of the bait to desired spots. The demands of fly-fishing, in which the line is not cast directly from the reel, are entirely different.

In 1805 bait-casting was born in the bluegrass section of Kentucky when George Snyder applied the knowledge of his craft to produce an efficient implement to toss his bait to a fish that was new and strange to him. His stepped-up winch, a quadruple multiplier, made it possible for him to cover great expanses of water that were formerly untouchable. The father of bait-casting presented multiplying reels to friends. Other local metal craftsmen who loved bass fishing produced similar reels as the demand intensified.

The sporting blood of the old Kentucky gentry was intrigued. Horses, birds, and bass furnished recreation, and proprietors of broad, verdant domains became anglers of renown. The multiplying reel became standard equipment for a sport they chose to give the appropriate name, bait-casting.

It should have been an easy, natural step for intelligent and ardent anglers to substitute an artificial representation for the natural bass food for bait, yet strangely enough, the move was slow in coming, requiring a full century. Once the lure was established in the Midwest and commercialized by James Heddon, development was rapid. Quickly the substitute was recognized as being effective, convenient, and less cruel, but both types of fishing were known as bait-casting. The quadruple-multiplying reel was originally designed to cast live or dead bait; however, progress has practically eliminated this practice, and the fisherman has become a caster of artificials. In the years that followed the tackle and technique developed, but the old name, bait-casting, held, misleading as it is. This refinement, the casting of the lure, a sport in its own right, could and should have received a more descriptive title, but the old and established clings tenaciously. We cannot speak or write of lure-casting and be understood, and the uncouth and meaningless word "plugging" can only be regarded as slang.

The refinement of the reel was vastly more rapid than the development of any of the other elements of bait-casting equipment. The light lure, the small-diameter line, and the long, slender rod possessing backbone are all developments of the present generation. Yet the answer is logical. The history of all sports shows that specialization marches on; the keener the competition, the more science plays a part. It is natural that the greatest progress in technique, finesse, and refinement of equipment should stem from the hard-fished areas where fish have become shy and limited in numbers. There were few such areas early in the century; now, because of the car and the plane, this condition prevails generally. Improved angling is the only approach for a fair quota of action. Strange it is that quadruple helical gearing, the level wind, the free spool, and take-down features preceded all other bait-casting refinements. The Kentucky reel makers were in advance of their time.

To these early developments of the reel have been added recently such features as light spools, arbors, shallow gears, nylon gears, live axles, ball bearings, direct drive, and light-weight handles. The demand has come from the light-lure men and the tournament casters. Today, thanks to excellent manufacturers, one is unlikely to go wrong in the purchase of a reel. The main choices for the angler are between a fixed-handle reel as opposed to a free spool, and a level-wind reel as opposed to an open one. This is purely a matter of individual taste, for efficient casting of the midget lure can be accomplished with any combination of the above.

Big bass have one great weakness in an otherwise strong resistance to angling tactics. Frequently they react quickly and surely to a light splash in their proximity. The plug hits the surface, and the bass without deliberation, without hesitation, turns on it and avidly seizes it. Often he strikes the lure before it has been on the water two seconds. Sometimes he seems to meet it at the surface, indicating that part of the attraction is the sight of the small plug in the air. I am convinced that color, shape, and action have nothing whatever to do with deceiving these fast-reacting fish. The splash is everything, and this is dependent on the size of the lure and the way in which it is cast.

There is a fine line between the amount of commotion that attracts bass and that which makes them suspicious. In shallow, clear water this line is drawn at a lure weighing approximately three-eighths of an ounce in weight. If a lure weighing more than three-eighths of an ounce strikes shallow, clear water within a few feet of a bass, it will usually scare the fish beyond any hope of its being taken on that cast or any other for some time to come. A suspicious or startled bass makes for deeper water if it is readily available. A lure less than three-eighths of an ounce makes a light splash, which we prefer to call a spat. A heavy lure either crashes into the water, or, if it is compact, makes a plunking noise like a stone. So much commotion is a danger signal, not a call to dinner. It is the spat we want, particularly for the biggest and best fish of the water. It is perfectly evident that wise old bass know something about noisy casts, and they live on. I wish to operate with a safe margin of error, therefore I choose the quarter-ounce lure, which lights right and which can be cast well.

The angler should make a study of lures, determine which ones are best for given circumstances, and learn how each should be retrieved. A lure handled by one man may be highly effective but in the hands of another may not be nearly so attractive to game fish.

During the days of the Depression, Bache Brown brought from Europe the Luxor outfit, which was the first spinning equipment placed on the American market. There followed about a decade of promotion and some sales, which nudged resourceful U. S. manufacturers into the field. It was in the 50s that spinning suffered its most severe growing pains; thereafter it came of age.

The progress and success of the open reel with the bail and its kindred rival, the encased reel with the push-button release, paralleled each other. Each of the two reel types is built around the same principle, a fixed conical spool from which the line peels upon release. There followed an amazing array of bass lures in the quarter-ounce class, some of which are midget models of old standards.

The choice of a rod is critical. Many are too long and too willowy for the lures employed. When this is the case, all one can do is wave the rod, with resulting high, weak casts. On the other hand, a rod with sufficient backbone for the lures employed can be worked harder, assuring a lower trajectory and a greater range.

The two best spinning enthusiasts I have watched perform prefer stiff six-foot rods. Both Ziggy Plater and Norm Lightner can reach far and wide and still be ready for a strike at the end of the cast. Ziggy is basically a bass fisherman, but Norm showers his attention on muskies. Ziggy uses lures in quarter-to-half-ounce range. whereas Norm steps his up to the one-half- to three-quarter-ounce category.

Tid Sheldon, Western Pennsylvania's great musky authority, induced the Heddon people to produce a special, powerful, fiberglass rod with an offset reel seat to accommodate a large-size encased reel. The rod is now known as "the brute stick," and it is a favorite of big-river fishermen who fish for bass, walleyes, and muskies at the same time. It is pretty much standard for winter jigging too.

The European-designed spinning equipment has two advantages over the American invention. The fixed spool is capable of handling a wide variety of casting weights, including lures of an eighth of an ounce and even less, whereas a quarter ounce is light for the geared reel. The equipment's ability to operate with small metal lures has been responsible for the application of spinning gear to trout fishing. The second advantage is the ease with which one can learn to cast. A requisite of bait-casting is an educated thumb on the reel spool as the cast is in progress. To balance the ledger, though, the American innovation features control of accuracy, trajectory, and the handling of hooked fish. Thus it is that spinning with the open reel and spin-casting with the encased reel constitute a boon to the beginner and those who cast only when on a fishing vacation.

It is claimed by some that large bass do not put up so spectacular and strong a fight as the two and three pounders. My experience, with but one exception, has been that the bigger they are the rougher and stronger they are. I have had two big bass jump completely out of water ten or more times and two other big ones that ran deep into the backing. These four bass were river smallmouths from four to five and a quarter pounds. No two or three pounders have approached these performances. That first jump and that first run of a big bass are two of the greatest thrills a fresh-water angler can experience.

The large bass furnish the cream of the fishing. All fish, like reptiles but unlike mammals, grow until death, therefore the big ones are the old, shy specimens. The very existence of such fish is one of the great appeals of the waters we fish. To many, large bass constitute the essence of angling, and so long as some can be interested occasionally in lures, nothing else matters too much.

The question of whether certain creatures of nature hibernate is contingent upon one's definition of hibernation. In the case of certain animals, such as the groundhog, body temperature drops, respiration slows almost to a stop, heart beat decreases, and there is deep sleep. In the case of bass of the north hibernation is not that extreme. My personal experience with hibernating bass has been limited to two odd instances.

I was wearing my fishing waders while duck hunting along the Conodoguinet a number of years ago when the season in our belt ran through January 1. It was late in the season and the weather had turned cold, but the creek was not frozen over.

As I crossed the stream I noticed a piece of stove pipe on the bottom. For some reason I lifted it with my foot, then pulled it out of the water. Two bass, each about 15 inches long, slipped out of the pipe. They could not swim away, but they could hold their upright position. With my booted foot I eased one to the surface, so I could get my hand under it, whereupon I put it back in the pipe and placed the pipe on the bottom. Apparently the other was not able to re-enter the pipe.

The second incident was incredible. In the days when it was legal to trap and sell bass in Maryland, a group of us in Pennsylvania contracted to purchase some for redistribution in local waters. They told us that these bass were netted on stormy nights at the site of weed beds that were breaking down; then they were held in live boxes. The common practice was to ship them to the Baltimore fish markets. The sales price was 16 cents a pound, two cents of which was the middle man's share.

Our bass were transported in a tank truck a distance of 150 miles. There was no trouble with sick or dying fish, so with each succeeding load the number of bass was increased until a load consisted of about half water and half fish. Included were both largemouth and smallmouth bass.

On one of the trips Russell Melton of Harrisburg purchased a four pounder to take home for the table. The fish was wrapped in wet newspaper and placed under the front seat in the cab of the truck. About seven hours later, after the stocking was completed, he took the fish home. Much to his surprise, it was still alive, so he put it in a tub of water, where it swam.

The point has been made, but the rest of the story is interesting too. Later this live fish was placed on display in an aquarium in a store window in the square of Harrisburg as a promotion to raise more money to buy more bass.

Many fishermen figure that a bass is a bass, but actually the largemouth and the smallmouth are very different. So far as looks are concerned, someone observed that if you can stick your fist in its mouth, it's a smallmouth; if you can jump down its throat, it's a bigmouth. One can see at a glance that a largemouth has a prominent, dark lateral line. The smallmouth's lateral line is much less noticeable. The bigmouth also has larger scales. The largemouth loves quiet water where there are fields of pads and dense weedbeds, whereas the smallmouth insists upon a rocky bottom. The meat and potatoes of the latter are crayfish, whereas the former thrives on minnows.

There is a wide difference in their homemaking too, for the nests are dissimilar. The smallmouth collects stones about the size of Indian darts and piles them in a low mound where the water is about two feet deep. The largemouth simply clears a place among the weeds in about five feet of water. Both fan the nests periodically to remove silt.

After the eggs are deposited on the nests and fertilized, they are guarded by a parent. Nature's scheme of things seems to be that the female makes the nest, then the male guards it.

The eggs hatch out in about 10 days, and for several days the little ones lie in a dark mass on the nest. They then scatter and range and feed in the shallows and safety of the shoreline.

Neither largemouth or smallmouth bass were native to New England, the waters west of the Rockies, or to the Middle Atlantic States east of the Allegheny Mountains. The redistribution of them was fantastic, much of the story being told years ago by Dr. Henshall. The introductory timetable was as follows:

Fox Lake, Massachusetts	1850
Many lakes in Connecticut	1852
Potomac River in Maryland	1854
New Hampshire	1867
Six lakes in Maine	1869
Thirty lakes in Rhode Island	1870
Susquehanna River in Pennsylvania	1873

It is interesting to note that Maine secured its bass from New York State. Pennsylvania was first stocked with Maryland bass. In these plantings differentiation was not usually made between smallmouths and largemouths.

Dr. Henshall's report of the initial Maryland stocking was well documented. John Eoff of Wheeling, West Virginia, entered the following into the 1854 report of the Smithsonian Institution: "Mr. William Shriver, a gentleman of this place, and son of the late David Shriver, Esquire, of Cumberland, Maryland, thinking the Potomac River admirably suited to the cultivation of the bass, has commenced the laudable undertaking of stocking that river with them; he has already taken, this last season, some twenty or more in a live-box, in the water tank on the locomotive, and placed them in the canal basin at Cumberland, where we are in hopes they will expand and do well, and be a nucleus from which the stock will soon spread." General Shriver, reports Dr. Henshall, in a letter to Philip T. Tyson, of Baltimore, Agricultural Chemist of Maryland, in September, 1860, says: "The enterprise or experiment was contemplated by me long before the completion of the Baltimore and Ohio Railroad to the Ohio River at Wheeling, but no satisfactory mode of transportation presented itself to my mind until after the completion of the great work (in, I believe, the year 1853), and in the following year I made my first trip (although I made several afterwards in the same year), carrying with me my first lot of fish in a large tin bucket, perforated, and which I made to fit the opening in the water tank attached to the locomotive, which was supplied with fresh water at the regular water stations along the line of the road, and thereby succeeded well in keeping the fish (which were young and small, having been selected for the purpose) alive, fresh, and sound.

"This lot of fish, as well as every subsequent one, on my arrival at Cumberland were put into the basin of the Chesapeake and Ohio Canal, from which they had free egress and ingress to the Potomac River and its tributaries, both above and below the dam."

General Shriver also states in a subsequent letter to Dr. Asa Wall, of Winchester, Virginia, dated September 17, 1867: "The number of these black bass taken to the Potomac River by me, as well as I can now recollect, was about thirty."

Henshall further advised: "Private citizens of Pennsylvania introduced the black bass (smallmouth) into the Susquehanna about 1869, at Harrisburg. In 1873 the tributaries of the Susquehanna, the Potomac, and Delaware Rivers were supplied with black bass by the Commissioners at thirty-five different points."

By the turn of the century there was a vast native population in many waters of various states. Everywhere it seemed to be the case of a little going a long long way. Early in the twentieth century the Pennsylvania fishermen called them, "the new fish."

Judging by recreational and economic values, the introduction of both largemouth and smallmouth bass into new waters is conservation's brightest success story, not only of that age but for all ages. When the angler counts his blessings, he can thank his lucky stars for the foresight, energy, and activity of some fishermen who preceded him.

In the northern brooks of Pennsylvania and across the southern tier of New York State counties, Don Neal also sweated up the grip of his fly rod with a million casts for the native brookies that still delight the eastern angler. As his newspaper readers know, Don is also an expert on pan fish and walleyes and has spent half a lifetime catching them. Between them this duo, Fox and Neal, have nearly 100 years of fishing savvy.

CHAPTER 17

Pan Fish

DON NEAL

When I come to think of it, I was introduced to pan-fish pleasures by a five-year-old boy, my son. Being an ardent fisherman myself, I wanted him to follow in my boot prints and from the day he was born could hardly wait for the time when he could accompany me to the stream. When he was five I decided he was ready. I wasn't about to take him to the mountainous areas for trout or to the rivers for bass. Instead I settled for a small lake where I had been told the bluegills were plentiful.

And plentiful they were! In fact he kept me so busy baiting his hook that by the time he had tired of catching these willing fish he had caught more than I, something he hasn't let me forget to this day and something I wouldn't have forgotten anyhow, for till then I had never known the fun that could be had fishing for pan fish.

It wasn't too long after this first trip to the lake that I

started to fish for pan fish with flies, both wet and dry. Then in due course my son gave up bait and turned to artificials, so that by the time he was ten I was taking him with me on all of my trouting trips and swelling with fatherly pride at his ability to handle a fly line and catch fish, and all because he had learned his lessons well at the bluegill lake.

From that time on we were constant fishing companions, and neither of us ever lost interest in pan fish. Quite often, on returning from some distant trout or bass stream, we would drive miles out of our way to try a lake where pan fish of one kind or another were said to be plentiful. There was something just different enough about pan fishing to hold our interest and excite our piscatorial desires.

I play no favorites when it comes to the various pan fish, for I find one species as willing as the other, though each has a particular sort of "personality."

The two species that come closest to being brothers under the fin are the bluegill and the crappie. Both like to live in clear, cool lakes and can often be found hanging around sunken treetops, logs, under boats and docks along the shoreline, or traveling in schools in the deep water.

Both species are readily taken on wet and dry flies and spinner-fly combinations, but while the bluegill will take worms or nightcrawler bits eagerly, the crappie seldom will. His preference is for small minnows. Small spinner lures are highly effective in taking both species, too.

Another excellent pan fish, either for sport or eating, is the yellow perch. Though he may be guilty of stealing far too many baits from the bass fisherman on occasion, he puts up enough of a fight when hooked to pay for his prank. And when you have caught the first one, you can usually fill your stringer from the school without moving from the spot.

I find it something of a tossup whether to use bait or artificial lures when fishing for perch. Though perch will readily hit either, there are times when the fastest action can be had with one or the other. In the course of fishing for this species I have used streamers, spinner-fly combinations, small spoons, small jigs, shad darts, bright-colored wet flies, and even bass bugs as lures, and worms, nightcrawlers, minnows, grasshoppers, crawfish, and dobsons as bait. However, I lean to a white maribou streamer as a lure and worms as bait for a starter, then a spinner-fly or minnows as second choices.

Although there are times when the perch school will come to the surface to feed, they are much more likely to be in deeper water. The best luck will usually be had by letting the bait or lure sink to or below their feeding level, then raising it very slowly. Good catches can also be made by jigging the lure or bait within the feeding zone. As this fish is similar in habits to the walleye, I try my favorite locations first, but when these fail me I turn to drift-fishing or very slow trolling until I locate a school.

The rock bass, or old goggle-eye, is a willing taker of both bait and lures, but I have never developed a real affection for his kind. There are far too many times right at dark when a hungry walleye could be searching for my minnow that this rascal makes off with it and takes it beneath a rock. If I can drag him out of his hiding hole I get an excellent scrap, of course, but I'm always convinced that he has robbed me of a chance at a trophy walleye.

Old goggle-eyes will hit anything that swims, flys or crawls, or resembles in any way anything that does. He is an exceptionally heavy night-feeder and often will furnish sport for the fellow who has spent a fruitless evening fishing for bass or walleyes. He is especially fond of the shorelines of lakes and rocky shelves out from the shore. In streams he'll be found almost anywhere, but he'll be most plentiful in areas where sunken logs or scattered rocks are plentiful.

There seems to be no best bait or lure for this pugnacious performer. I have had him hit plugs as long as his own body, then fight like a smallmouth when he did. I can't recall a single bait or lure which I have fished that hasn't brought me one or more rock bass at one time or another. If he has any preference at all, it must be for a three-inch minnow just as twilight fades into darkness.

Other night prowlers that will give the pan-fisherman plenty of action are catfish and bullheads. You can get plenty of daylight action too if it's raining and a stiff wind is blowing, and double the action if it's dark and raining and a stiff wind is blowing.

When this species is on the feed little technique and less know-how is needed to get the makings of a fine meal, but when he's not feeding he can hang tough. However, a good gob of garden worms or all kinds of smelly concoctions whipped up into doughballs will generally tempt him during his most reluctant moods. While I don't go for the real smelly stuff some do, I get pretty close to the real thing the easy way.

Placing three slices of baker's bread in a bowl, I add one tablespoon of condensed milk for each slice of bread. To this I add a fair-sized chunk of soft cheese and some chips of luncheon meat if it's available. By kneading this in my hands I soon have a doughlike mass close to a consistency that will ball on the hook. If it seems too dry I add more condensed milk; if too wet I add more bread. Then when I have it just right, I give it time to age. The older it gets the better Whiskers likes it.

There are times too when he'll really go for a fat minnow or a soft-shelled crawfish.

No fisherman needs to go fishless so long as there are pan fish around. They are a sociable lot that seldom places a noticeable strain on the fisherman's skill as a price for the many pleasurable hours of recreation they provide. And crisp brown, there's no finer fish.

CHAPTER 18

Walleye Fishing

DON NEAL

In your quest for walleyes you may be fishing for doré in Canada, jack salmon in the southern states, yellow pike in the Midwest, or river trout in Missouri, but in Pennsylvania and some other sections of the East you'll be directing your piscatorial efforts toward netting a Susquehanna salmon. Yet regardless of what moniker you prefer to use in referring to this highly appreciated eatin' fish, you're in for the time of your life when you hook into a really sizeable specimen.

Actually this fish, if properly named, should be called a pike-perch. It is his protruding eyes that have earned him the more common name of walleyed pike, though in fact he isn't a pike at all. He has one too many dorsal fins to be accepted as a member of this notable family of fishes. To simplify matters, I'll just refer to him as a walleye, as I generally do in conversation, and let it go at that.

I had better admit straight off that I am a walleye addict,

which turns out to be rather an odd development after having spent the better part of a lifetime as a fly-fishing purist for trout and a bait-caster for smallmouth bass. Yet I find that the moods and cantankerous ways of this species present a particular challenge I can't resist. Hour after hour, and day and night throughout the season, I find myself plying the walleye with my utmost skill and accumulated know-how, as if his kind constituted the only worthwhile prize in all of fishdom. And though I'll admit that when being played he may not have the spectacular fighting ability of the pike, I'll rush to his defense by stating emphatically that he's no piker, either. A big walleye can give you as many thrilling moments as any fish that swims.

But it's the walleye's moody ways that fascinate me most. I find him comparable to the brown trout in this respect. Like the brownie, he'll go for considerable periods of time when no bait or lure will bring a strike, then as if someone turned a switch he'll be hitting everything in sight. There have been many times when I have fished three or four hours without a single strike, only to take my limit within an hour of my first netted fish.

Sometimes such an experience is due to the fish's moody ways, at other times it isn't. I have learned in the course of my walleye experience that there seems to be no time when you can point to a particular spot in a lake or stream and say that is where the walleyes will be feeding if they are feeding at all. With some species of fish you can be fairly precise in doing this, but not with the walleye. He moves with the school, and the school will be feeding wherever they find an abundance of the type of food they are feeding on.

This is a fact that came to light quite early in my experience with walleyes. In a large pool on the Allegheny River, actually alive with sizeable walleyes at the time, I wasted several valuable hours of fishing time concentrating on the area near the head of the riffle where just the evening before I had had considerable success. When I finally became discouraged, I started to fish other likely locations. Sometime later, and not more than 20 yards from the spot I had first whipped to a lather, I found the feeding school.

In those early days of walleye fishing, I reasoned that my failures were due to the fact that the fish just weren't feeding at the time I worked the likely looking spots. But later I learned that this was far from a fact. There were times, I soon discovered, when the lure or bait had to be cast precisely to the school's position or no action would be forthcoming. Sometimes this position would be well up at the head of the riffle, at other times it would be as far down as where the riffle flowed into the pool below. And of course there were times when I located the school at points in between, and in the pool itself. One of the most elementary requirements for success, I learned, was to locate the school.

If there's a second elementary requirement in fishing for walleyes, it surely must be fishing for them at the proper time. For though the walleye will strike and can be caught at any hour of the day or night, there are times when he seems to be far more gullible, and therefore more easily caught. My personal preference runs to the two hours just before dark, the hours between midnight and dawn, and the two hours following full daybreak. During these hours I seem to have the most luck fishing on or near the bottom.

However, there are times when I fish the hours between full darkness and midnight. On these occasions I find surface lures give me the most action, for I hold a firm conviction that these are the hours when the walleye is a habitual surface feeder. At all other hours of the day or night I seem to do best by fishing on or near the bottom. However, I should admit that I have something of a psychological block against fishing for walleyes during the bright hours of the day, so I seldom fish for them at this time. I spend the bright hours fishing for species I find more inclined to give me the kind of action I want. Yet I do occasionally give them a try at this time of the day. By fishing the deeper pools on a stream, or working a lake bottom in the vicinity of a known underground spring, I sometimes have some pretty fair luck. But this isn't to say that I pass up the fast runs on a stream or the channels of the man-made impoundments. I don't. In fact, there are times when I find them to be rather productive during the bright hours, but not as productive as when there is little or no light at all on the water.

In fishing for walleyes during the day, I have come to form some definite opinions which, I suppose, could be either right or wrong so far as any other walleye fisherman is concerned. I like stream fishing rather than lake fishing. I prefer lures to live bait. And I think that the appeal of any lure can be improved by adding a bit of live bait in one way or another.

To improve the appeal of a lure, I'll often add a minnow or nightcrawler to the hook of a spinner or a spoon, and I have often added a nightcrawler to the hook of a jig or a deep-running plug. Averaged out, I think the addition of the live bait pays off. But with some spoons, and especially with plugs, the fisherman has to be certain that the addition of the live bait hasn't interfered with the lure's basic fish-getting action. Whether or not it has can easily be determined by drawing the lure along slightly below the surface before the cast is made and watching to see if the action is unhampered.

Among the lures I find to be most productive while daylight fishing for walleyes are spoons, spinners, jigs, deep-running plugs, weighted streamers, and wooly worms tied on a long-shank No. 4 hook. Some I fish in the conventional manner, but with others I have my own pet ways of presenting them to the finicky walleye. The lures that lend themselves best to these somewhat off-beat presentations are the jig, the weighted streamer, and the wooly worm.

Although I do cast a jig downstream or across and retrieve it with short jerks while manipulating it with the rod tip as most fishermen do, I'll reverse the procedure if the going gets too tough. Instead of downstream or across, my jig is cast directly upstream into the deeper fast-water runs and brought back towards my position bumping along the bottom. This method really gets fish, but it isn't the all-time greatest, owing to the number of jigs lost from getting hung up on the bottom.

Depending on the particular stretch of water, weighted streamers are sometimes the better lure to use while fishing in this way. Their main drawback seems to be that they don't always sink fast enough to be effective, and they are carried along by the current at a faster rate than the heavier jigs—too fast, it seems to me, to get the ultimate attention from a feeding walleye. So my favorite way of fishing the weighted streamer is to cast it across a fast-moving current into quieter water, lower the rod tip to allow the line to be caught by the current, then depend on the belly pulled into the line to pull the streamer head first downstream to where the line straightens out in the fast water. From this point on, I retrieve in a slow, jerky fashion which allows the streamer to work fairly close to the bottom. A larger belly, and therefore a longer downstream course on the part of the streamer, can be had by allowing line to run from the reel as the belly forms in the current. If he carries this to an extreme, however, the fisherman will find himself in trouble when it comes to hooking a striking walleye.

The wooly-worm method has been a proved killer in both fast and smooth water for me. If a riffle is to be fished, I wade out as far as possible at its head or down close to where it breaks into a pool. Then I cast the wooly worm as far downstream as I can. A splitshot pinched to the line about 18 inches ahead of the worm carries it beneath the surface but not so deep as to bump on the bottom before I start the retrieve. The speed with which the worm is returned can best be described as a snail's pace as I turn the reel handle as slowly as possible. In fishing smooth water the same retrieve is employed with the casts being made so that not an inch of likely water is overlooked.

Although these are my favorite methods for fishing for walleyes during the daylight hours, every one of them will work just as effectively at night, with the possible exception of those hours between full darkness and midnight, when, I am convinced, walleyes are working closer to the surface and would likely ignore these deeper-running lures. But during the early evening hours, then again between midnight and dawn, and through the first couple hours of daylight, they're close to unbeatable.

If I have been guilty up to this point of implying that live bait isn't worth a hoot when it comes to fishing for daylight walleyes, it hasn't been intentional. Far from it! Nightcrawlers, garden worms, crayfish, and minnows are all on his menu, and rolled down a riffle or bottom-fished in the deeper pools or in lakes by any knowledgeable fisherman, they'll certainly account for their share of fish.

In fact, I am an almost constant bait fisherman myself except during the daylight hours and those hours between full darkness and midnight when the walleyes are inclined to be surface feeding. My chief reason for not fishing live bait during these hours is that I refuse to use up my supply of choice minnows or chubs, which happen to be my favorite form of live bait, during those hours when lures will do the trick as well or better.

I am often asked why I prefer minnows and chubs over the other acceptable forms of live bait. To be truthful, it's a personal quirk. In using them I can eliminate to a great extent the possibility of various other species, considered to be undesirable when I'm fishing for walleyes, from responding to my bait. It seems to me that nightcrawlers and garden worms appeal to too many varieties of trash fish, and it has been my experience while fishing with suitable soft-shell crayfish to catch more carp than either bass or walleyes. I have very little trouble with these "off" species when fishing with chubs or minnows.

I hesitate to disagree with many of the experts and several widely experienced walleye fishermen as to the size of minnow or chub that should be used in walleye fishing, but I will. I have become completely convinced that there is no specific size that can be recognized as the best. All sizes work at times, all sizes fail at times. If the walleye shows any preference of size at all, it would seem to me from my own experiences that a smaller minnow is the best bet during the warmer months of the year and a larger one of chub proportions during the colder months.

However, I don't even consider this observation myself when I start fishing for walleyes at any time of the year. It is my usual procedure if fishing live bait to use two rods and bait one with a small two and a half to three and a half inch minnow and the other with a larger four to seven inch chub.

From this point on the matter of whether I use large or small bait fish is determined by the results I am having.

Ordinarily I will start off by still fishing. But if I find that I am getting strikes while reeling in to make another cast, or if I see interested fish following the bait as it comes in, I'll turn to casting. If the fish continue to follow my bait without taking, I switch to a spinner-minnow combination, usually with excellent results.

I have caught walleyes on almost every surface plug I have in my tackle box, when the walleyes approach the surface during the hours between darkness and midnight, but I have to admit that the spinner-minnow combination fished without weight so that it stays on or near the surface is probably the best producer I have ever used. But there have been times when my friends, fishing spinner-nightcrawler combinations, have given me some tough competition, as have a few who swear by a spinner-pork-rind combination.

Another popular and highly productive method for taking walleyes at this time of night, but one which I just can't stomach, is skittering live frogs. An exceptionally long pole, as long as 18 feet, and a fixed amount of line about the length of the pole are employed by those who use this method. A frog is impaled on a hook at the end of the line and then swung out as far as possible and retrieved by skipping it over the surface.

So far as plugs for this surface fishing are concerned, I seem to lean to the Jitterbug, Skipjack (crippled minnow), and mouse. I've also found ducking plugs work quite well too, so long as they don't go too deep.

I have tried both wet and dry flies on the surface-feeding walleyes, but my luck in this respect hasn't approached the sensational. I have caught fish, of course, and I have heard others tell of making some fabulous catches with flies, but it seems to me that the walleye prefers something rather closely resembling a minnow, if not quite the real thing. That is why, I suppose, my best results while fishing with a fly rod have come from using streamers.

During the "surface" period of the night and on through the midnight-to-dawn portion of the walleyes' schedule I have tried to determine if moon phases play any important part in their moods and behavior. To date I haven't formed any definite conclusions. I have been told, however, by many of my experienced fishing friends that they do. There's a general belief, it seems, that walleyes are more active during the full-moon periods, especially during the cooler months of the year, and that to some extent the hours when they will be most active are governed by various moon phases. I won't argue against this theory.

It seems more likely to me, though, that success in walleye fishing is more dependent on a school of hungry walleyes being present in the vicinity of the fishing activity than on anything else. I have seen many times, and I suppose other walleye fishermen have too, when one fisherman on a stream or lake wouldn't be getting a strike on any lure or bait he used, while another fisherman not too distant from the luckless spot would be having a heyday. With the walleye being a school fish, and with the school being constantly on the move, such incidents are to be expected, I suppose. But it's hardly logical that the moon was right for one and wrong for the other. It's more likely my friend Jeff, a real river rat when it came to walleye fishing, had a better theory. "Walleyes are where you find 'em," Jeff would say, "and you find 'em 'fore ya catch 'em." That's a theory I can accept.

Jeff was an expert at finding walleyes, too. I've watched him work the deep rapids, the shallow riffles, the pot holes behind large river rocks, the swift-water areas at the heads of pools, and the pools themselves before striking a productive spot. But given time, he always would. And by the time his flashlight would come bobbing along the streamside path that night he would have collected a respectable stringer of fish.

There is also the question of whether there is a best time of the year to fish for walleyes. I have heard some fishermen become jubilant over the prospect of spring fishing, others equally enthusiastic about fall fishing, but from watching the successes and failures of such old-timers as Jeff, I have come to the conclusion that the best time of the year is anytime between the opening of the season in mid-May and the closing of the season in mid-March of the next year. The real walleye fisherman takes fish in the spring, summer, fall, and through the ice with an almost unpardonable consistency.

The big "time factor" in walleye fishing, if there is such a factor, is not the time of year but the time of night. Some of the really expert walleye fishermen I have mentioned show a particular preference for the hours between early twilight and full darkness; others favor fishing from the break of day to the early-morning hours; and a few, like myself, have a decided preference for the hours between midnight and morning. Which of these fishermen are the more successful, there is no way of knowing. Even those who fish the surface, usually between full darkness and midnight, take their share of the walleyes at times, while at other times, like the rest of us, they couldn't catch a fish to save their souls. So I suppose the thing to say here is, taking a leaf from Jeff's book, the best hours to fish for walleyes is when you can catch them.

Such an answer, though, offers little in the way of advice to the beginning walleye fisherman. In offering him a suggestion, I would say that the most pleasurable time to fish with better than average chances of success would be the twilight hours through to full darkness, and the hours between predawn and bright daylight. If these hours fail to produce the desired results, then the hours between midnight and dawn should be given a try, fishing bait on the bottom, or the hours between full darkness and midnight while fishing lures on or near the surface.

The beginning fisherman who has trouble locating a school of feeding walleyes would be well advised to concentrate his attention on pools below waterfalls, the discharge areas of dams, or behind any obstructions in a stream that cause any kind of turbulence. Walleyes show a preference for such places when they are in a feeding mood.

There are times when it seems the techniques of walleye fishing are the all-important requirement for success; then there are times when it seems the walleyes are so willing that techniques are needless knowledge. The one exception to this generality, though, is the art of trolling for walleyes in a lake or in the larger eddies of a river. In trolling, there is no substitute for know-how.

Of first importance is the requirement to keep the bait or lure riding as close to the bottom as possible without its becoming snagged. To accomplish this, a three-way swivel is used. The line is attached to one eye, a short length of line and the bait or lure to a second eye, and about 12 to 18 inches of line with sinker attached is tied in the third eye. The sinker drops down to ride on the bottom, so that the bait or lure follows at a safe distance above the snags. The length of the sinker line can be varied up to as much as four feet to get the bait or lure action the fisherman prefers.

A second requirement is a slow trolling speed. Walleyes are not noted for chasing after their prey as speedily as muskies or northerns do, and they will ignore the bait or lure that demands a spirited chase. Usually, if the boat is moved just fast enough to keep the bait or lure off the bottom, the speed will be right.

The amount of line trailed behind the boat can vary and is usually determined by trolling conditions. However, less than 50 feet is not considered practical in most cases. But, since the length of the trolling line controls to a considerable extent the depth at which the bait or lure rides, this should be taken into consideration.

Personally, I never troll in a straight line. I zigzag my course, as I cover more fishable water by swinging back and forth across a channel or bar, and with each turn of the boat I alter the action of my bait or lure, for as the boat changes course the line slackens to provide a change in the trolling speed. When I am required to run straight on the longer sweeps, I give my bait or lure action by drawing the line back and forth slowly to imitate a minnow's dart. These maneuvers, I find, add appeal to any bait or lure.

Whether stream fishing or trolling, I have one little personal preference I haven't mentioned–I like wind for walleyes. Although some of my fishing friends will go all out for such things as rainy days, higher-than-average water levels, colder weather, and a number of other conditions that are supposed to put the walleye on the prod, I'll settle anytime for a hard-blowing wind. If it comes from the east or north, I'll accept it, but I'll be more pleased if it's southerly or westerly. Rain, high water, and cold weather probably do encourage walleyes to feed, but high winds seem to make them absolutely hoggish.

But whether he is on the prod and feeding vigorously or sulking in his favorite hideaway, the walleye has his mark on me. The challenge he offers provides a fascination I have never experienced in fishing for any other species, and I've about covered the book when it comes to fresh-water game fish. Why? I don't know, unless it's just that I'm too contrary to admit that this is one species that can occasionally send me home talking to myself.

Anyone who spends any considerable amount of time fishing for this unpredictable over-grown member of the perch family will go home talking to himself on occasion, sometimes bubbling over with enthusiasm because of the success he has had, at other times cursing the finicky so-and-sos that outsmarted him. It is then that he will realize, as I have realized many times, that there is no fish more challenging than the walleye.

PART FIVE
Camping

Anyone for camping? I guess so! This is the fastest-growing pastime in America today, and Del Kerr and Day Yeager have some thoughts and advice on the subject that every would-be Lewis and Clark should consider. This pair of writers has experienced all of the pitfalls and calamities that can befall the tyro camper, and they make an effort to lead you away from disaster.

CHAPTER 19

Camping Techniques and Equipment

DAY YEAGER and DEL KERR

With all the modern conveniences of the American home, the plush hotel, the swanky motel, and the posh resort, can there be a sensible reason to go camping? Can a sleeping bag outclass a king-sized trundle, a self-smoking campfire outrank a self-cleaning oven, or a black-capped chickadee outawe a black-tied maître de? In short, are the few days spent alfresco more memorable than the hundreds that are spent just so so?

Well, nearly 20,000,000 American campers, if laid end to end, would all jump to their feet and shout a resounding "Yes" to all the posed questions. And they are putting their time and money where their mouths are. While Joe Small-check is assembling his pots and pans for a week-end jaunt, Courtney Bigbills III is busily cranking up his $18,000 house car for a cruise across the continent. They will share equally the rewards they seek for their efforts: a change in their routine lives, a means of extending their outdoor activities, the pleasures of living close to nature, and, if necessary, an economy in traveling.

Camping has always been a way of life in the continuing adventures of man. Today, it is an essential means of exploring the moon; in years gone, it was the means of exploring America. Without the benefits of route signs, hotels, motels, and credit cards, the early colonists camped as they traveled and built as they camped.

If you are already an accomplished camper, we hope that this chapter will serve to offer you some helpful information to add to your pleasures of the sport. If you have not camped, we hope that you will become intrigued enough to join the ranks of those enjoying the outdoors for more than a day at a time. There are many different types and styles of camping. To enjoy your camping, you should first decide which style you can best afford and most enjoy. The selection of equipment for an overnight stay will not prepare you for a week in the wilderness. On the flip side, you need not spend a bundle or plan for weeks to spend a week end in a state park or at the creek on a friend's farm. It is a good idea to rent or borrow from an accomplished camper the equipment you need for a simple trip not too far from home. You can get by with a tarp or small tent, bed rolls, simple foods, and a few essential items for your comfort. Just remember that you will not enjoy yourself unless you are comfortable. Plan ahead, and that's a good deal of the fun, and you may find that the stars are brighter out there, the tree toad's song is clearer in the night, and you have moved closer to nature than you have been in years.

Most campers take to the trail in order to enjoy a change of routine. The 35- and 40-hour work week has become a bit more hectic with each passing year, but it also offers the time that is needed to break away. Three and four-week vacations provide the opportunity to make extended trips to almost any point one chooses to visit. The hunter can seek that exotic trophy at a remote camp, the fisherman can do battle with the big ones on a faraway lake, the camera bug can snap his shutter along the trail, and the rock hound can chip away on topaz, petrified wood, amethyst, or bloodstone. The entire family can participate in the adventures that wait their arrival, and all can share in the planning, preparation, work, pleasures, and memories that come from camping.

To some, camping is a means of enjoying their week ends and vacations within a limited budget. One family we know has seven children, and all camp regularly. When asked why they camped, the father said, "Have you ever given seven children their choice of restaurant menus three times a day for a weekend? It looks like the national debt. We can go camping for less money than it takes to stay home. They may eat more, but it is honest to goodness food that costs a lot less. Yes, it did cost us a bit to build up our list of camping equipment, but we have had four of the children since we bought our tent, and it is good for years to come. As the children come along, we simply add a pup tent and sleeping bag. They are cheap when compared to the cost of a week end in a motel. Each member of the family has his task to perform and he enjoys it; so much so, that Mother has very little to do. The cost is very low for the benefits received."

Early camping had little to offer in the way of comfort. The tent was heavy, had no floor, and very little means of ventilation. It was difficult to erect, provided very little headroom, and became rather dismal during inclement weather. Beds were made of blankets or bed rolls, placed on a mattress of boughs, leaves, or the bare ground. Cooking was done over an open fire, replete with sparks and smoke and dependent upon the weather. Dry weather permitted a hot meal, wet weather accompanied a cold one. The weather man helped you to plan your diet. Light was generally provided by the sun, the moon, and the remnants of your campfire.

The "camping boom" has grown in direct proportion to the development of modern equipment that makes outdoor living comfortable. Tents have become nearly as comfortable as a home. Sleeping bags, mattresses, cots, and pillows make sleeping a pleasure in itself. Cooking depends on the turn of a valve; lighting on the flip of a switch or the flick of a spark. For the more affluent, the tent has been replaced by campers, trailers, house cars, and recreational vehicles of all types and price ranges. And there is much more to come.

The basic item for camping is still the tent. The best method of determining quality is by price. The best bargain is the higher-priced unit. It will last, with reasonable care, 20 years or more. Very cheap tents are loosely woven and poorly waterproofed. They will not erect symetrically or hold their shape and will require replacement within a few years. If you pay the additional money for a quality product, your trips can be made more comfortably and with confidence. When you pick your tent, it will be necessary to first decide on type, size, and weight for the type camping you will prefer. Your choice will be determined by the type of country you will visit, the number in your party, the climate, and the method of transportation you choose.

The size of your tent can be determined by a simple formula. If you must pack in, figure a minimum of 18 square feet of space for each camper. If you use a pack horse or motor vehicle to arrive at your site, you should allow a minimum of 25 square feet per person. Remember that a little extra space is desirable on the days that keep you indoors. It is usually preferable to place two adults in a tent than to try to squeeze four or five into the confined area. Don't be concerned about the prospects of placing the little ones in their own units; they will love the independence of living away from the older folks.

Since the average camper doesn't wish to own more than one main tent at a time, he should choose the type that has most of the features listed below.

(1) It must be light enough to handle and carry, whether it be a pack trip over mountains or a family trek across the creek. A heavy tent becomes heavier with each step. Pack tents should weigh not over six or seven pounds, canoe units not over 20 pounds, and tents for motor trips not much over 50 or 60 pounds.

(2) The tent must go up with ease and alacrity. Fatigue and confusion reigneth at the end of a long trip if it becomes necessary to go searching for suitable ridge poles, pole shears, or stakes. Your quarters should be erectable by one person while others are assigned to gather wood, cook up the grub,

or unpack and prepare the sleeping gear. It should also involve a minimum of poles, ropes, stakes, and loops.

(3) The tent should be versatile, capable of being used during various seasons and in various terrains. It should provide adequate protection from the weather, insects, and tiny roamers of the animal world while offering the advantage of being opened up to accept the warmth and comfort of a campfire on cool nights. It should be capable of riding out a windstorm, turning away rain or snow, and still allow adequate ventilation on those warm summer nights. Privacy should be available when privacy is desired.

(4) It should have a built-in floor, preferably a vinyl-coated material that is waterproof and easily swept out after everybody has made his numerous entrances and exits. The flooring will also provide a dry foundation for the sleeping bags and clothing that can become uncomfortable when damp.

A word about waterproofing. A tent is not truly waterproof and should not be. Tent materials are designed to be porous to air even after the waterproofing has been applied. The tent must breathe to be viable and safe to live in. The threads in the fabric swell when wet to seal the tiny holes in the fabric enough to permit the water to run off. It is for this reason that Dad must always shout many times during the rainstorms, "Don't touch the tent or it will leak." Although this problem is not as serious with new and modern materials as it was in days gone by, it is still good practice to move items away from the walls during rain and to keep idle fingers from the ceiling or walls. While waterproofed tents may be packed wet for a short time, it is imperative that they be opened and dried as soon as possible upon returning home. This is necessary in order to prevent mildew and rotting of the fabric. A weak solution of lime and water will remove some mildew, if it should occur, but it will not restore the strength lost over a lengthy period of attack. Modern lightweight tents are more susceptible to damage, and care should be taken not to pack them among sharp objects. Remember, also, that they should be erected with a bit of slack in the guy lines. The material will shrink when wet and damage can occur. It is better to have a tent look casual and unconcerned than to suffer undue strain.

If and when your tent begins to lose its waterproof characteristics, there are a variety of excellent materials on the market to renew its protection. These materials can be applied to an erected tent by brush or spray can and are quite efficient. Be sure to pick a quiet day when there is no wind. Small leaks can be repaired in the field by applying candle wax, spruce gum, nail polish, or adhesive tape. Rips and tears should be repaired with patches of tent material either sewn or cemented to both sides of the damaged area.

The lightest and simplest tent is the type referred to as a "tarp." It is merely a rectangular piece of material. It can be made of cotton, silk, sail cloth, canvas, or one of the modern plastic materials. It is best designed if fitted with grommets around the perimeter and at the four corners. It can also be fitted with tie tapes, sewn through the center or top of the "A" to take up slack when the ridge-rope type of suspension is used. When the tarp is used to construct the wedge, or "A," tent, you merely run a ridge pole through the center line of the shortest dimension, tying the sides down with the ropes running through the grommets. Do not nail the ridge poles to adjacent trees, as this can do permanent damage to the trees. If you decide to use a ridge rope instead of a pole, the length of the rope shouldn't be more than 10 or 12 feet to prevent a sag. The rope can be supported by two pole shears, poles tied together to form a pyramid, at each end of the tent supported by guy lines, much in the same manner as the ridge pole is suspended.

Your tarp can also be used as a slant roof reflector. This type of construction is popular with those who travel light in bug-free areas or who wish to stay warm at night by utilizing the reflected heat of a campfire. To get the slant effect, stretch your tarp over a ridge pole or ridge rope, guy out two of the corner grommets to poles or trees in the front and tie down the back to tent stakes. Such a setup is at best an emergency or overnight arrangement, but a good one to remember if you are caught away from a main camp overnight. A fine addition to both the reflector and wedge-type tarp tent is a piece of additional plastic to serve as a ground cloth. It is worth the small expense and slight additional weight. Stakes can be carried or cut from available wood or limbs in the area. Always check the rules of campgrounds and the owners of private land before cutting any living trees or limbs. Both units described can serve as fine back-pack homes or suitable storage tents for the larger camp.

Another basic type of tent is the wall tent. It is one of the oldest, though perhaps fastest-disappearing, designs. There are few modern types that have more to offer for the permanent camp, since it is very sturdy, will ride out the worst of storms, and provide plenty of space, all of which is usable. It is a direct descendent of the wedge tent, with the addition of a break in the sloping side, creating a wall, from which it gets its name. This design allows placing cots against the wall, permitting unused space of the wedge type to be utilized for sleeping while maintaining the same basic floor area. Headroom is provided in the center of the tent where most of the living is done. A wall tent becomes even more practical when it is placed on a permanent wood floor constructed above the ground. With the addition of a camp stove, vented by an asbestos-collared hole in the roof to permit a stovepipe to protrude, winter camping becomes quite comfortable. The newer models provide for some ventilation by the addition of screened windows complete with storm flaps and the screened entry protected from storm and cold by the usual door flaps. Some designs include built-in floors, screened interiors with roll-up side walls for those warm nights, and fly fronts for bad-weather cooking and dining.

Still another basic design is the explorer tent. It is one of the easiest of tents to erect with only one center pole. The outside walls are equipped with loops (often called "parrels") that can be guyed to trees or stakes to form walls that increase the interior area considerably. Properly set up, the explorer tent offers many advantages and much space for the weight. The newer versions have flies that serve as fine protection in inclement weather and double as front awnings when extended. The door openings are screened and they may have sills. Most of the models have sewn-in floors to complete your comfort.

An advanced version of the slant-roof reflector is the Baker tent. It is a three-sided tent with the front normally open. It is often used in the summer months when insects are no problem. In poor weather, the extending fly can be dropped to close the tent, but this practically eliminates air circulation within. It is best used as a second tent in a permanent camp, serving as an area for cooking, dining, campfire sessions, or storage. It requires a bit of extra effort in setting up, since it employs ridge poles, pole shears, ropes, and stakes.

The miner's tent is shaped like a pyramid. The floor is square, with each side sloping up at a steep angle to a sharp peak. The front is open from the ground to the peak with enough material to overlap and form a storm-proof door. There is only one pole used in erection; it is in the center and can often be eliminated by simply throwing a rope over a tree limb and pulling the tent to its full height. A bit of caution is necessary, however, when resorting to this practice. The swaying of a tree or limb can damage a tent if the suspending rope is too tight or should shrink owing to dampness or rain.

The latest thing in versatility is the pop tent. It is provided in the smaller, light-weight sizes and makes an excellent packing tent. It is big enough for two persons and can be set up quicker than the wink of an eye. In fact, it is always amazing to see this tent literally pop out like a kernel of popcorn. All you do is release the fiberglass rods that are secured to the outside of the tent and that serve as the frame. You say, "Pop," it pops, and you crawl in.

We come at last, but perhaps best, to the modern umbrella tent. Most campers today have become highly mobile in their habits and have a means of carrying the extra weight of a tent that provides "poleless" supports, sewn-in flooring, doorway sills to keep out snakes and insects, adequate windows complete with screens and storm flaps, and speedy erection and striking. These tents come in all materials, all sizes, all weights, and with every possible combination of side rooms, canopies, flies, and supporting framework. If you have the room and load-carrying capacity, by all means give very serious consideration to choosing your one main tent from the long list of umbrella types. They offer plenty of floor space, nearly vertical walls, allow a six-footer standing room, and can be set up in a matter of ten or fifteen minutes without cutting, splitting, swearing, or looking for poles, trees, or limbs. They can be erected under a pine tree, in the middle of the back yard, or anywhere your heart desires. But under the pine tree is not the best place for a few good reasons: it rains on your tent a long time after the storm is over; pitch may drop on your equipment; and lightning always looks for a tall tree to zonk. Place your tent so that a tree provides shade when you want it and sunshine when you don't.

Erection is simple. You unroll your tent, spread it to its full floor size, stake the four corners, insert the inside umbrella frame from which the tent gets its name, and then drive the balance of the stakes. Erect the flies and/or canopies, and you are ready for a night or a month of pleasant, carefree living. The newer models have gone to an outside "umbrella" framework to which the parrels are attached, leaving no part of the frame inside the tent.

There are too many versions of the umbrella tent to explain here in detail. There are tents that offer 200 square feet or more of living space, some with separate side rooms, screened-in porches, awnings galore, and all but the kitchen sink, which may have been added since you began reading this chapter. Let it suffice to say that somewhere there is an umbrella tent that will fit your needs, whatever they may be.

For the hardy packer who travels without a tent, or the camper who strays too far away to return, there are ways of using nature's products to construct a shelter. Begin your plan for spending the night while there is yet enough daylight to complete your plans. If you are traveling in mountainous country, the driest and most comfortable shelter will be provided by an overhanging ledge of rock that will offer good protection from rain and a reflective surface for heat from a campfire. Gather enough firewood for the night and conifer boughs or leaves for your bed. If the floor is soft, dig depressions to conform with your shoulders and buttocks and you will rest comfortably. In snow country, dig out or build a snow shelter, line the floor with boughs or leaves, and you will manage to stay warm.

If you are traveling in forests, use the axe you should not be without to construct a tree tent. Pick out a fair-sized evergreen and notch it at eye level on the side you wish to pitch your tent. Then chop the tree opposite the notch, not quite through, and push the tree over. You now have a tree suspended at the stump by the remaining fibers. Cut out the lower or inside limbs and toss them out as you go. You will soon have ample space for your living quarters. Use the branches that have been removed from what is now the inside of the tent and weave them into the remaining foliage on the outside, along with those cut from the top to provide additional protection from snow or rain. In extremely cold weather, an additional smaller version of the tree tent can be built inside, offering twice the protection. Any of these rigs will be less than the best but far better than roaming in the dark or sitting by a fire all night without sleep. If you are lost, build a fire that can be seen by those who might be searching for you.

Mobile camping has developed many aspects. The highways and byways have become busy with RV units that range from station wagons filled to the gills, nondescript homemade rigs on pickup trucks, camper trailers, van campers, travel trailers, and homelike house cars. The conveniences and comforts have no limit except your bank balance. Your authors would be the last to knock comfort in the wilds, but some of the modern campers carry more equipment than exists in the entire arctic village of Kabangamoo, and all this may be for two people. Camping, to us, is still the fun and art of living from and with the land. We take pleasure in facing a wind that doesn't originate from a grill, a sound that isn't taped, a smell that can't be squirted from a can, and a silence that isn't punctuated by tail pipes and auxiliary power units.

For those of you who love the RV expeditions, we shall not try to cover the vast array of equipment in detail. It

NED
SMITH

would be better, perhaps, to offer a few suggestions for your motor travels. Many units require the hookups necessary to enjoy the lighting, water facilities, and disposal that is provided only by established campgrounds. Lately, there has been such a growth in interest that many campgrounds have become jammed with camper vehicles of all types. Efforts to keep up with the crowds have lagged behind the demand. For this reason, it is recommended that you pull off the road in midafternoon in order to prevent that sinking feeling that goes with being turned away from camp after camp. It is also advisable that you have all necessary supplies aboard before you stake out your territory. Although you may have a nearby store, you will often learn that their supplies are limited to essentials and that special item you need is 20 miles away.

Pay special attention to the combination of power and weight of your units. Take the time to inquire and study the problems of handling trucks, trailers, and house cars. Each one is unique and some pose a few problems. Your light engine won't suffice for hauling heavy trailers over steep mountains. Your light spring suspension may suffer damage or present hazards with too heavy a tongue weight. Your light tires may not complete the trip under the grueling abuse of rough roadbeds. Unless you intend to do all the driving, choose a unit that your wife or friend can safely maneuver.

Most RV units can be rented for reasonable rates. It might be wise to try a rental for one or two trips before making a purchase. Your trips should be well planned. If you are going on an extended tour, master the art of parking and backing before you hit the trail. Plan your route beforehand; some bridges, tunnels, and turnpikes will not allow RV travel and many of the scenic roads in the mountains or western states are not suited for such vehicles. Also, check ahead for seasonal and surface conditions that may confront you.

Trailers have become the most popular and varied of the recreational vehicles. The choice is one of hundreds, from the small pop-up trailer to the mobile home. Starting with the smaller end, the pop-up convertibles offer a happy medium between the tents and the travel trailers. They measure about four by seven feet and larger. They have the advantages of stability on the road, low wind resistance, and rear-window vision while traveling. At the campground, four legs are extended to provide a level foundation, the large tent expands upward and outward, and your home is ready for occupancy. Some units have one double bed, others have two, complete with bedding and mattresses. Pop-ups take up little or no more room than a tent and can be rolled into position by hand if necessary. Most of them offer ample storage space for equipment, food, and clothing. As with all trailers, however, you will need a parking space between trips, preferably indoors to protect the canvas. The more expensive designs have covers of aluminum or fiberglass that permit outside storage without harm. Pop-ups, though relatively cheap as trailer units, still require quite a sizable investment over the simple tents.

The modern travel trailer offers all the comforts of home. A fairly large family can live in one of the spacious models for months without complaint. Modern chemical toilets can serve for weeks without attention or outside connections. Water tanks carry ample water for dishwashing, drinking, cooking, and bathing in shower fashion. Bottled gas supplies the energy for the range, refrigerator, heater, lights, appliances, and many units offer the alternate choice of electrical refrigeration. Some models are equipped with small generator plants to supply electrical power for out-of-the-way campsites. Many of these trailers may weigh 2000 pounds or more and require good hitching, adequately welded to the frame of your car or wagon. You will also have to provide for built-in braking and wiring for brake and tail lights.

The pickup-truck camper is a special design of trailer construction that is fitted to the particular bed of the truck used. It must be hoisted on and off if the truck is to be used for other purposes. Most trailer comforts are provided, and usually two beds are installed, three if an over-the-cab design is chosen. Such combinations are quite rugged and can go anywhere a truck can go with its heavy springs, power, and compactness. Price gets pretty salty if you plan to use the truck for camping only.

The newest and most expensive type of camping vehicle is the house car, and that is exactly what it is, a house on wheels. It is a self-contained unit that permits the convenience of the home while rolling along the highway. Practically everything can be done as you go. The children can run around, play their games, or sleep while mother makes lunch. Many need no hookup and can be parked for days or weeks without outside attachment. Disadvantages include the problem of having to move the entire unit to go shopping, only to return and find another house car parked in your spot. They are very expensive and pose the problem of parking between trips; they serve to see the world from a living-room window. They do not serve well as a second car.

Perhaps nothing is more important to a successful camping trip than a good night's sleep. The seasoned camper ends up with the best sleeping equipment he can afford. The sleeping bag should be able to "breathe" and repel water in the same manner as a tent. Some provide rubberized bottoms that are fine for dampness but pose a problem for dry cleaners. If you are going to use an air mattress or some type of floor, stick with the bag that doesn't have a waterproof bottom. Buy a bag with good filling, stitching, and zippers. The filling should be resilient, mildew-proof, and warm without becoming damp. The long-used kapok, taken from the silky fibers investing the seeds of the silk-cotton tree or milkweed plant, is not desirable. Cotton batting is also a poor choice, since both materials will lump, lose shape, and provide little warmth. Medium-priced bags are now filled with long fibers of Dacron or similar material. Three or four pounds of Dacron Fiberfill will suffice for most weather conditions and situations. Eider down, no longer available, and goose down are needed only in the coldest of climates and used only in the most expensive bags.

Linings are generally some type of flannel. If no inner liner is provided, one can be purchased or made from a bed sheet. Tie straps should be provided inside the bag and on the liner, so that easy removal is possible. Zippers should be heavy duty and made of brass to prevent rusting. The bag should be well quilted to prevent movement of the filling, and insulating beads of material should protect you from the conductivity of a cold zipper. Some bags have a single layer of filling on the top and a double layer on the bottom, offering the advantage of using the same bag on warm or cold evenings by the simple process of turning the bag over. Pick a bag that can be opened fully and joined with a matching unit to form a double bed. This arrangement is most popular for the man and wife sleepers and offers the chance to steal more than one's share of the bed.

Backpackers often choose the form-fitting "mummy" bag. It offers maximum warmth for the weight but is more confining until you learn to roll the bag as you turn over. All bags should be opened completely each day, aired out, and remade a short time before retiring. They should be dry cleaned yearly or oftener if used heavily and stored in a cool, dry location for the off season.

Sleeping on the ground appeals to very few people and often brings an abrupt halt to future camping trips for the less than rugged. Cots of the World War I style are available, but they are no more comfortable than they were then. Modern cots are low in profile, light in weight, and compact when folded, but can be cool on your bottom unless you lay on a blanket. Cots will sag and buckle if used as a seat. However, unless you have an aversion to a bed that has no legs, you cannot beat the comfort of the air mattress. They fold compactly and are quite dependable if made of quality materials. The cheap plastic ones are not recommended unless price alone is the object. They are slippery and try to get away, they leak at the slightest insult, and they are usually skimpy in size. Select your air mattress from one of the rubberized materials, either tubular or quilted in design. The quilted style costs more and offers greater comfort. Check for snap fasteners if you intend to use two mattresses in a double sleeping bag.

Air mattresses must be filled with air. Some come equipped with built-in step-on pumps. You might prefer the type that uses a hand pump for inflation but which can also be blown up by mouth. Hide the pump and you can stop arguments, slow up ambitious children, or get an exercise in deep breathing. Never overinflate your mattress or you'll not rest comfortably during the night. Inflate just enough that you can sit on it and your buttocks touch the ground. We do not advocate smoking, but you can check for leaks if you suck on the old pipe before blowing up your mattress. The escaping smoke will reveal the hole. If your mat includes a built-in pillow, make certain that the pillow is blown up with a separate valve. This allows you to choose the pillow hardness and height you like. Make sure that none of the valves are made of plastic, which sooner or later will fail.

Foam mattresses and cotton pads are often used for camping. Unless you can carry them with ease, as in a station wagon or camping trailer, they take up too much room to be practical. When used on the ground, cotton can become damp and uncomfortable.

If you should be without a mattress, don't try to be a sourdough at the expense of a good night's sleep. Make up a bough bed of evergreens, placing stems downward to prevent puncturing yourself, and renew daily. The first night on a bough bed is good, the second night is not worth the price, and the third night has you back on the ground. In some areas, wild hay or long grass can be wrapped in a blanket or stuffed into the mattress pocket to help soften your night.

If there is one thing camping does for a camper, it is to make him hungry. Casper Shortbelt, given a week in the outdoors, will be consuming about the same amount as a ponderous pachyderm. And if he wants to eat regularly, which he will, he will need a stove. For years, the favorite pot warmer has been the pressurized, white (unleaded) gasoline stove. It is dependable, hot, and economical. It will burn about a half-pint an hour per burner at full tilt, which is still a bit less effective than the kitchen range you're trying to forget. It will generally, depending upon the altitude, boil a quart of water in less than five minutes. The standard models are easy to operate, but take the time to read the directions before firing up. You fill them up, pump the pump, turn the little flipper up as it says on the fuel tank, open the valve, light with a match or spark lighter, and you're in the cooking business. Two-burner models will suffice for most camps; the three-burner model is for more people or those who want their peas and carrots separated. They fold into a neat suitcase unit and open to provide a shield with the lid and foldout windscreens. We like to include a stand that can be tucked inside the three-burner model along with a gallon of fuel and the tank. This way, you never end up with a stove and no fuel. It is also advisable to carry an extra valve and generator assembly on extended trips.

If you want to go first class, the bottled-gas or liquid-petroleum units are in the competition. They are similar in size, weight, and price for the stove. Fuel cylinders are disposable, and you save on gasoline pouring. There is no pumping, no generators to foul, and they are virtually trouble free. The only catch is that they cost a lot more to operate. You can figure about two-bits an hour per burner versus pennies for the same heat. Propane and LP are not always readily available at the local hardware emporium, so you had better plan ahead by carrying enough fuel.

For the backpackers, there are several Primus stoves available from Sweden in the one-burner model. They weigh little over a pound and burn alcohol, naphtha, or white gasoline.

Many campers prefer to do their cooking over the old-fashioned, readily available wood fire. The pots get black, the hot dogs get black, the tools get black, but there is something romantic about standing in the smoke and cooking. And the food tastes better than the diner serves back home. Before you start rubbing two sticks together, please check your rules regarding open fires. Many camps do not allow other than charcoal fires, and most do not have any wood available. You are probably No. 1,000,056 camper in an organized campground, and every stick within reach and walking distance was burned long ago. If you are allowed to build a fire, clear the ground for four or five feet from the center of your proposed fire. Scrape down to damp earth to make certain that you aren't building a fire on humus that may break out in flame after you leave. You should outline your fire on three sides with rocks if they are available. This will serve to reflect and maintain heat on cold or wet nights and serve as a support for a grill or fire bars. Experienced campers find that a long, narrow fireplace will do a better job than a round or square one. A small fire can be maintained for a coffee pot or extended to accommodate several pots or pans. Also, you can keep a blazer going at one end and rake the coals to the other for a nice steady heat without all the soot.

Whenever you have an open fire, keep a supply of water or sand near at hand. Watch for flying sparks into the nearby trees or on windy occasions with dry conditions. Nothing is more awe-inspiring than a forest fire that you started, and you won't make friends with any bears wearing Boy Scout hats. Hardwood (hickory, oak, maple, birch, ash, etc.) burns the hottest and lasts the longest. Softwood, however, is more common and easier to come by. If you have a choice, use the hardwood, as it makes for less hauling and chopping. If it has rained, look for a standing dead tree. It will be less water-logged than the fallen logs. To start your fire, use tinder. Tinder is any small twigs, bark, weeds, leaves, or pine cones. Birch bark makes excellent tinder. It will burn wet or dry. Paper, milk cartons, used waxed cups, candle remnants, card-board boxes, etc., will serve your purpose and keep the camp clean. Place kindling in a teepee shape over the tinder and larger split logs or limbs over the kindling. Then one match should get you a merit badge for fire building.

For regular camping trips, nothing beats the nesting cook kits of stainless steel or aluminum. They are cheap in the long run and serve as many as six people. They usually include two- four- and eight-quart pots, lids that serve as skillets, cups, plates, and removable handles for all. We do not care, however, for the cups furnished with these kits. Find a set of nesting enameled cups for your cooking kit. They can be used to serve a cup of hot coffee, tea, soup, or chocolate without burning your lips as the contents get cold. If weight is not a serious problem, get yourself an old cast-iron skillet and a flat grill. A long flat grill will hold the heat and spread it evenly through the pots and pans.

Buy or make a small chest for knives, forks, spoons, various serving, cooking, and handling utensils, can openers, and other small items used in cookery. Stock your chest and issue a warning that anyone who touches it will lose an arm up to the elbow. You will find that if you can make your point, all trips will be replete with the items you started out with. This beats all hollow the practice of running around a kitchen at the last minute to gather up utensils for a week-end camp.

If you intend to do your cooking in the higher altitudes, it is advisable to include a pressure cooker. Higher elevations will cause the water to boil at a lower temperature and thus it will take a longer time to cook your food. The pressure cooker will solve your problem. A lightweight item that serves well under all conditions is the aluminum foil wrap. Many items, even entire meals, can be sealed and placed on the stove or hot coals for serving when required. It also saves dishwashing, but don't toss the used foil about your campsite when you leave; it will remain indefinitely as proof positive that you were there. Pots and pans can be cleaned with water from a nearby stream. In an emergency, sand or hardwood ashes will remove grease and grime from your cookware.

The problem of refrigeration in camp is best solved with one of the well-insulated ice chests, preferably oblong in shape and with inside corners rounded for easy cleaning. The chest should have a drain plug for draining off the water from melting ice. Cool your chest by loading it with ice the day before you leave and your ice will last longer. Chunk ice will last longer than cubes, and the purchased water-filled cans frozen at home do a fine job without the problem of draining water. You can make similar items from empty paint thinner cans or waxed milk cartons, taking care to allow room for expansion of the water when frozen. Load your food into the chest with the most perishable items on top. Use these first in the event you lose your cool. Begin your menu with the frozen steaks and end it with the smoked sausage or bacon.

As is often the case, you might have to make do with the ice you take with you. If this happens, take as large a piece as you can carry in a large cardboard box or covered metal container. When you reach camp, use the container as an ice box. Dig a hole into the ground in a shaded area, punch holes in the bottom of the box or can, place your food around the ice and bury the works in the pit. Then crisscross sticks over the hole and cover with sod or moss. Open your icebox only when necessary and your ice will last a surprisingly long time.

If you have no ice at all, you can make a cooler that works by the principle of water evaporation. Wrap a burlap bag over a box filled with food. Then on top of the box, place a basin or pan of water with the burlap inserted into the water so it soaks up the water by absorption. The water from the bag will seep down the sides continually and by evaporation will keep the food cool. You can help by dousing the cloth with additional water now and then.

A similar principle can be used by digging a hole in the ground and sinking a box in it. A blanket, layer of moss, or grass spread over the box and kept soaked with water will keep the temperature of the box far below the air temperature. This is also a good way to protect your food supply from roving animals. Of course, one of the simplest coolers is a running stream, and this will serve for all foods that can be placed in jars or cans with some means to protect them from floating downstream.

It always adds a cozy atmosphere in camp to have one or two lights burning to provide enough light to walk about or do evening chores. In areas where the flying insects are busy, it is a good practice to have a light located away from the tent or campfire as a more desirable attraction than the campers. Perhaps the most common light is the pressurized lantern. It is economical to operate on unleaded gasoline or prepared fuel at little more than a penny an hour. The fuel is fed slowly, under air pressure, into a mantle that glows with intense brightness. The candlepower is about equivalent to that of a 100-watt bulb. A gasoline lantern will burn 10 to 13 hours on a single filling, but it must be pumped up with air pressure about every hour or two. Two-mantle models give off about 50 per cent more light than the single mantle.

Some disadvantages apply to all good things. A mantle

lantern must be handled with care to prevent damage to the fragile mesh bags. It is also possible to develop generator trouble with the finely metéred flow of gas required. Always carry a spare for the time your generator goes bad. A valuable but inexpensive addition to these lights is the flint-loaded lighters that can be fitted on as an integral part of the lantern. It is far more dependable and safer than the match or twig most campers resort to for lighting. Carry a small funnel for filling lanterns and stoves and never, never light either one in a tent.

Propane or LP lamps provide a more brilliant light than gasoline and are almost trouble-free. They are, however, much more expensive to burn and should be only used if you are using the same fuel for your stove. It is enough trouble to worry about one type of fuel when you pack.

Electric lanterns and flashlights are available in all sizes, shapes, and intensities. The standard flashlight using two D-cells is very handy for locating objects, nighttime emergencies, and general fun for the kids. Always pack a couple for general use. The larger lamps with sealed beam and using the boxlike six-volt long-life batteries are fine for all types of lighting. One model has a lantern-type head that throws a diffused light much like the gasoline lantern except that it is not as effective. Don't overlook a box of candles in your list of supplies. They often come in handy when all else fails. Small, folding candle lanterns improve the quality of the light given off, and there are no moving parts to wear out. For obvious reasons, never take candles into your tent.

It must be remembered that all types of heat produced by the burning of fuel require oxygen, oxygen that must come from the surrounding air. For this reason, a word of caution is offered here regarding the use of camp stoves, lanterns, etc., within tightly closed areas. If you require a small amount of heat such as a lantern provides, or if you use the type heaters that throw out considerable amounts of heat, whether they use wood, gasoline, or other fuel, make certain that you have some form of ventilation for safe living and sleeping. The most popular camp heaters are the catalytic heaters. The larger models are adjustable, and you can dial heats ranging form 3000 to 5000 BTUs in a three-quart model that burns 18 to 20 hours. A single-heat model of 3500 BTUs heats up to 15 hours on two quarts of fuel. All models burn unleaded gasoline or special fuel and should be lit outside before being brought into the tent. Some units have directional radiation and others radiate their heat in a circle. They all burn without any visible flame and are quite efficient.

Wood-burning stoves are available or they can be constructed from five-gallon cans. Kerosene models are also sold, but kerosene is not a desirable fuel from the standpoint of odor. Once it has been spilled, it seems to linger throughout the entire trip. Again, use caution with all types of heaters; be sure that you have proper ventilation. A snowfall can often prevent your tent from breathing, so get out there and brush the snow away.

The hatchet, or the familiar Scout axe as we know it, is perhaps the one indispensable item for camping. It will be used for everything from driving the tent pegs to building an outhouse. At the established camps, it is the only axe you will need. Carry it on your belt if you intend to travel any distance alone. If you are traveling in the wilderness, you will need a woodsman's axe with a two-and-a-half to three-pound head and a 32- to 36-inch handle. Backpackers may compromise on the Hudson's Bay model, which has a two-pound head on a 27-inch handle. A dull axe is a dangerous axe, as it will have a tendency to glance off your mark rather than to cut in. Keep your blade rust-free by wiping it with oil, bacon grease, or butter, and carry a whetstone to dress up the edge. Never stick your hatchet or axe into a tree, and always walk with the blade facing down and outward in the event you trip. Be certain that no overhead branches are near when you begin swinging, and split your logs on another log, not on the ground. A nick from a small pebble can take a lot of work to remove. Unless you take time to learn to use an axe properly or to watch that another untrained person isn't going to use it, leave it home.

Most knives can be used for camping, but a good one will pay for itself in short order. Price will indicate quality, and the blade should not exceed about four inches in length. Pick one that fits your hand nicely. Wood, bone, or leather rings make good handles. A narrow thin blade is best. This will do most any job from cleaning a fish to skinning a moose. As with the axe, keep the blade honed to a fine cutting edge. Whenever you aren't using your knife, keep it in a sheath, near your back, children are intrigued with the shiny object that can cause serious wounds when far from town. When you are using it, cut so that the edge is always held away from you. This may seem elementary, but there are people who do it otherwise and have scars to prove it.

Everybody sooner or later considers the purchase of a bucksaw. It is a handy tool and will cut firewood faster than an axe. However, it is good for little else, and most firewood can be gathered without it. If you must have one, buy a good one made with Swedish steel.

Additional camp tools should include the proper tools for repairing stoves and lanterns, pliers and large and small screw-drivers for slot and Phillips head screws, fine wire for cleaning generators, friction or plastic electrical tape for repairs and

rope lashing, and a few coathangers, the handiest of all camping items. You will find a hundred uses for them.

One of the pleasures of camping is the fact that you can dress with casual abandon of the contemporary styles. Most campers give the appearance that their pants are sitting down even though the camper is standing. Style is not important in choosing your camp clothes, but comfort is. Choose those garments that protect you from the varied elements, offer freedom and comfort, and will wear well in spite of abuse. They should be roomy enough to allow you to work, play, and travel without binding. For most weather conditions, you should choose light-weight materials, adding additional garments as the temperature drops. Warmth is dependent more upon the insulation of the air between garments than the weight of them.

Since you have underwear at home, it will serve you just as well in camp, especially during the summer months. For colder seasons you may want to add a couple pair of insulated underwear. These can be of the fish-net thermal style or the insulated, quilted models. As with all your clothing, it is better to add on as you need more warmth; it is very uncomfortable to be stuck with one heavy outfit that does not allow you to peel off without danger of exposure and chill.

Shirts should include a pair of T-shirts, two light-weight cotton-flannel shirts, and a heavy woolen shirt. Some campers prefer the light-weight wool over the cotton flannel, since wool feels better and warmer than cotton when wet. Jackets should consist of a light-weight jacket of hard-woven cotton for moderate weather, a wind-resistant or insulated jacket for cool periods, and a windproof heavy coat for rugged temperatures.

Trousers should be tightly-woven and brush resistant, light-weight for summer, wool with knitted bottoms to tuck into your shoes for cold nights, and insulated trousers worn under your regular pants for those blustery days. No outdoor trouser should have cuffs to catch on roots and brush or to gather dirt as you go about. Also, choose your garments with a thought to hard finish; a trek through the brush will soon shred a brand-new pair of flannel trousers. Women should dress much the same way as their husbands while in camp.

Socks should be carried in good numbers, and they should be woven of wool. If you find wool uncomfortable against your feet, wear a thin pair of cotton socks underneath the woolies. Heavy wool socks cushion your stride as you hike and feel a lot more comfortable when you get your feet wet, which you will. Wash and dry your socks regularly, even if you don't get the rest of your laundry finished. There is nothing more comfortable than a fresh pair of socks to brighten your day.

One wide belt will be useful for carrying those items you may wish to carry. An axe, knife, canteen, or mess kit tearing at a narrow belt can become very annoying on a long trip.

Perhaps the most important item in your wardrobe will be your shoes. I can think of no more pitiful character than one who must travel while his feet hurt. For the immediate camping area, a comfortable pair of loafers or moccasins with sole and medium heel will serve nicely. Don't fall for those canoe-style, soft-bottom jobs that allow you to sneak up to a campfire without being heard. You're probably not an Indian, and you will shortly realize it when you hear your arches falling. Add to your list a pair of heavier hunting-style, rubber-sole, leather-top, eight-to-ten-inch-high shoes. Buy them a size larger than you squeeze into at home and use an extra pair of socks to fill them. A day of walking will make your feet "grow" to fit them. Keep your walking shoes greased for softness and water repellency. Don't, however, grease them so thickly that they can't breathe or you will be wearing a pair of real sweat jobs. The rubber soles should be cleated for safe travel over rocks and wet grass. Leather may feel better, but it very soon becomes slick with travel and can cause you to fall. Your high shoes should not be one of the heavy styles used by loggers for long wear and foot protection. Heavy shoes will get heavier and a quarter of a pound picked up and laid down all day will add up fast.

Shoelaces should be loosely strung and tied with a square knot to prevent constant stops to retie them. Tuck the loose ends into the sides of your shoes and you will go all day without bending exercises. The loose lacing will allow your feet to be cooled by the pumping action of air as you walk. Your feet will perspire or a puddle will grab your foot, so you will want to dry your shoes. Don't hurry the job, but place the wet gear near the fire at a safe distance to prevent scorching and hardening of the leather. Some campers place a pair of hand warmers in their wet shoes, and they dry out during the night.

You will need a hat, and we suggest that you take a hard look at the ten-gallon cowboy hat. Don't knock it until you've tried it. Its broad brim and high crown will keep you cool in the summer and warm in the winter. Don't ask us how it got to be so smart, but it did. It is a bit on the expensive side, but a look in the mirror will make the money seem insignificant. One disadvantage will present itself. If you must push through low-hanging limbs, it will try to get away from you. Similarly, on very windy days, it will decide to leave home. If the type you choose doesn't have a chin band, build one in with a strap or lace, placing the tiedown inside when you don't require it. This hat will keep the sun out of your eyes, the rain off your nose, and the bugs busy trying to find you underneath. If you are not the cowpoke type, a peaked baseball hat serves well as a sun shade; some of them are fitted with built-in sun glasses that swing down from the peak. For cold weather, choose a peaked hunting cap of wool with fold-out ear flaps. Don't buy any hat made of plastic or you'll sweat the curl out of your locks. A Navy watch cap is versatile and can be rolled up or down as needed. If you don't care how you look, and you probably don't, any old beat-up felt hat is a good choice, and nobody will steal it.

It will rain. The weather man will say it won't, but he'll be sitting in his office while you get wet. If he says it will be fair, prepare for a light rain or drizzle by wearing water-repellent jacket and trousers. If you close up too tightly in a light rain, you will sweat yourself as wet inside as you get outside and be most uncomfortable in the process. A heavy woolen shirt or jacket will soak up a lot of drizzle before you get wet on the inside.

If the weather man calls for cloudy weather, prepare for a heavy rain. The best choice is probably the poncho with an attached hood. You can get a matching pair of trousers and sit out an all-day rain as snug as a bug in an Axminster. Your poncho will also serve as a ground cloth, as a protective covering of valuables when you are not wearing it, and as a means of covering food when the flies are around. Unless you have to do so, refrain from putting on rubber boots. They will make your feet feel as though you've stuck them in a warm bucket of water in pleasant weather, or in a bucket of jellied consommé in the colder climates. If things get too wet too long, resort to spraying your clothing or shoes with one of the waterproofing compounds.

Nothing, let me say again, nothing is more important to a camper than a rope. The first camper had a rope, and the last camper will have a rope. He will use it on Mars, Jupiter, or Venus, but he will find some way to use it. Campers collect rope. They steal clotheslines, cut up parachutes, unwind "laid" or twisted rope to get smaller rope, and braid small rope to get larger rope. You might say that they are rope happy or happy with rope. But they will have rope wherever they go, and for good reason. Rope holds up tents, wet clothing, tarps, canopies, flies, lanterns, food, and in emergency, their britches.

If you don't have a nail, a tree, a hook, a hanger, or a board, use a rope. It comes in many sizes and many breaking strengths, but be sure you take plenty with you on your camping trips. Hemp is cheap but serviceable; the quarter-inch size will hold 100 pounds or more. Nylon and other synthetic fibers are stronger but are more expensive, especially when you realize that you left it back in town. The common clothesline is cheap, but it deteriorates very quickly. If you aren't going to forget to gather it up when you leave, use a good-quality rope and "whip" the ends by wrapping with strong thread, or dipping in waterproof glue. Nylon and other synthetic rope can be whipped by holding the ends in a flame until they melt into a solid mass.

Learn a few knots before you camp. Actually there are not

too many to remember. The square knot, the half hitch, the clove hitch, and the sheepshank will serve most of your needs. Remember that wet rope will tighten and make untying quite difficult. When you tie your knot in wet rope, place a smooth stick in the knot; to untie, simply pull out the stick, and the knot will be loose enough to unravel quite easily.

The first trip for a new camping family is not only exciting but an extremely important one. The novice will learn more on his first outing than he could obtain from poring over any number of books on the subject. He will drink in the aroma of woodsmoke and brewing coffee and learn why everyone must gaze into the embers of a dying campfire. He will sneeze from dust should he unwisely locate too near a campground lane. He will lie awake absorbed in the awe-inspiring spectacle of inky-black shadows dancing on his canvas roof before brilliant moonbeams. He will discover, with dismay, every pebble, rock, and tree root under his tent which seemed insignificant when setting up camp.

There are a multitude of experiences, both good and bad, pleasant and distasteful. which every first-time camper files away in the back of his mind for future use. A whale of a lot of experimenting goes on; it's part of the fun. The time for testing theories, however, is well in advance of the long-awaited vacation. A couple of week-enders under the belt will do wonders for practical planning and will make the extended camping trip far more enjoyable.

The best place to learn how to camp is by making use of designated campgrounds in state or federal parks or private camping areas. The latter is a campground, open to the general public, which is operated by a private citizen rather than a governmental agency. In most cases, campsites are fully developed and all you have to do is set up the tent or level the trailer.

Campsites in state or federal parks usually consist of cleared areas of various sizes and may be grassy or covered with gravel. Within the site will be a picnic table, a fireplace, and a parking spur. You can expect the same from the average private campground, although many provide water and electrical hookups at the site. In all camping areas, tested drinking water will at least be centrally located.

First stop is always the campground office. Many include a wall map of the campground with currently occupied sites plainly marked. Rules and regulations vary between state and federal parks and most private-campground owners enforce special rules for one reason or another. Often, the camper will be told to select a site, then return to check in.

State and federal parks, and some private campgrounds, too, have a tendency to include more campsites than the area will comfortably support. Sites are often jammed too close together and all facilities overtaxed. This is true mostly of parks near highly populated regions and is done simply because there are so many of us. The demand for additional camping space increases every year. It is understandable, then, that some campsites will be far superior to others. Latecomer Louie often takes what's left, and that is frequently a spot in the overflow area.

Let's assume you have arrived ahead of the week-end crowd at a popular park and that a number of seemingly desirable sites are unoccupied. Nearness to sanitary facilities is important when young children are along. At night, when pressurized lanterns turn the area into a fantasy land, all campsites look amazingly similar. On the other hand, a site next to a well-traveled path is not the best of ideas unless you enjoy parades.

Sites are usually constructed along either side of campground lanes. If the road is paved, fine. A dirt road often turns to dust in dry seasons, and vehicles pulling trailers are notorious for raising dust clouds, even when traveling slowly. Locating on the windward side of a road or lane will minimize an unwanted dust bath. Many roads within camping areas are designed for one-way traffic only. If this is the case in your campground, try to select a site with brush or a barrier of some sort to shield the camp from blinding headlights at night.

A tent camper will be more fussy about his site than one who camps on wheels. He is more concerned about the weather and studies the site for water runoff. Try to visualize the effects of a storm. Will rainwater from a higher elevation wash through the site or do tell-tale channels or veins in the ground indicate otherwise? Is the site high enough to eliminate standing water after the storm has passed?

Thought should be given to construction of the site itself. For the tenter, an elevated, graveled space large enough for the tent (no small order for modern models) is usually preferred by seasoned campers. More often than not, such a space will be the driest spot in a soggy campground. Hidden under most graveled areas is a base of crushed stone. Raindrops disappear almost the moment they fall. One disadvantage is the fact that you almost have to stand on tent pegs to keep them from popping out. Longer than normal pegs driven on a sharp angle toward the tent will do the trick.

A grassy site always appeals to the novice camper. Unless the soil is quite porous, even a high spot will hold moisture for a long period if sheltered from the sun. In addition, dew will collect just about every clear evening and wet feet can be expected. A thick carpet of pine needles can be the ultimate in comfort for the tenter—until it rains. When the elements turn sour you might as well be camping on a sponge.

A lakeshore or pond site is a treasured possession for most campers. With it, unfortunately, you will often have your own personal swarm of mosquitoes. The same is true in many cases with low-lying campsites in brushy areas. Camping in such places can be quite pleasant if you remember to keep windows and doors tightly screened and to apply liberal amounts of mosquito repellent to exposed skin.

Common sense warns of camping under a dead tree or one with dead limbs. Most people fail to realize they should also avoid a site within *falling distance* of a suspect tree. Camping under a grove of smaller trees that are surrounded by taller trees minimizes lightning dangers. Recognizing that lightning usually seeks out the tallest object in the *immediate vicinity* should play an important part in campsite selection. Also for safety reasons, avoid any site located below the high-water line of a stream. Flash floods can raise a docile stream ten feet or more in a very short time.

A number of convenience factors will greatly extend the enjoyment of an outing. For instance, a site open to the sun in the morning but shaded during the heat of the day is a distinct advantage. Also, the doorway of the tent or trailer should face the opposite direction from oncoming weather. Then, in the event of hard, driving rain, the door may be left open to allow free circulation of air.

A site that facilitates the use of a dining fly next to or very near the tent or trailer is not appreciated until wet weather arrives. Then, it's worth its weight in lantern mantles. Some campers fasten large plastic sheets from the fly to the ground on the windward side during periods of blowing rain. Also available is a completely screened-in fly which is erected over and around a picnic table. Although designed to keep out insects, it offers more shelter from rain than an open dining fly. However, we feel the use of an additional "room" for dining is more bother than it's worth, and it takes something away from the pleasure of camping.

Many newcomers to the outdoor world fail to realize full enjoyment from a camping trip because of a fear of the elements. At the first sign of a darkening sky, they hastily begin striking camp. More often than not they get caught in a downpour just about the time the shelter is lowered. Wet tent flapping in the breeze, they hightail it down the highway in search of a dry campground and invariably end up at home thoroughly discouraged.

Plan for rain—hope for rain! There is no more soothing sound on earth than that made by rain on canvas, whether it be from a gentle shower or wind-driven torrent. Most sensational of all is a full-fledged, hammer-and-tongs electrical storm. Everyone should at least once feel the very ground shake and vibrate during an earsplitting thunder clap. Sheltered only by canvas, a camper can fully appreciate day or night the awesome but beautiful sight of billions of volts of electricity leaping across the sky. It's an event that makes man seem infinitely small in the world of nature.

A thunderstorm is usually over quickly. If your site is chosen wisely, it should be perfectly safe. If, however, you have any doubts, your automobile will offer splendid protection, providing you do not touch metal. A steady, all-day rain can be discouraging if the camper has nothing to occupy his time. This is where planning for rain pays off. Save for a rainy day a visit to a nearby attraction or a trip to town. Do anything but break camp and head for home. You can be sure the nicest weather of the week will come on the heels of a period of rain.

To a great many people, the ultimate in camping is a choice location in a remote spot where the only sounds are those produced by nature—the rustle of leaves, the chatter of birds, the gentle, mind-soothing gurgle of water rushing down a rock-strewn stream. Camp visitors may be inquisitive deer, squirrels, chipmunks, jays, and almost always a free-loading raccoon or two. Should you try primitive camping, you can be sure of one thing: that delectable aroma of outdoor food, whether it be pan-fried trout or lumberjack franks, can come from one place only—your campsite.

Primitive camping actually takes in a wide range of camping possibilities. The term usually applies to locations in natural settings without formal facilities of any kind. Recently, many parks have added so-called primitive areas where facilities are limited to the barest essentials.

We will here discuss only campsites outside of parks. Such a site might be an end-of-the-road spot near a mountain stream, a tall-timber camp reached by pack horse, a lakeside location, an island camp, or a temporary overnight site used during canoe or float trips, etc. In essence, the site is created by you and may be as humble or as luxurious as you wish. In most cases, excluding horseback and water-excursion trips, the camper who goes to the trouble of building his own site will usually remain in the same location for a week or longer. This could be a couple of the fellows out to rough it, a family on a wilderness vacation, or as in a case we know, an old-fashioned fishing camp.

Nestled under age-old pines and hemlocks next to rip-roaring rainbow waters is a campsite used by the same group of bewhiskered fishermen year after year. The site is located deep in a heavily forested area and far from the nearest civilization. Their camp definitely falls in the primitive class. Yet as far as comfort and convenience go, it smacks of luxury from start to finish.

About a week before the opening of trout season, two men from the 12-member camp arrive on the scene, tidy up the campsite, and erect the huge, army-surplus tent. Inside the shelter a sandbox is constructed, and a small wood-burning stove placed in its center. The smokepipe, which goes through an asbestos ring in the canvas wall, is wired securely inside and out to safeguard against accident.

Throughout the first week, when not chuck hunting, the two men spend much of their time cutting enough firewood to last a considerable length of time. Cutting and splitting sufficient fuel for both a woodstove and an outdoor fireplace is no easy chore. Work is reduced by the use of a "saw tree," a tree with a V-shaped crotch at a convenient height. The timber to be cut is placed through the crotch and severed quickly with a buck saw.

A large canvas dining fly extends at least 12 feet beyond the tent. It's no accident that the fly shelters a black-cherry stump with countless scratches from fish-scaling knives. Several folding tables are located under the fly, as is a healthy supply of stove wood.

The night before opening of trout season the hideaway becomes alive with one of the lyingest, laughingest, jokingest, fish catchingest bunch of rod-benders ever to assemble in one spot. Everything is ready, even the canvas cabana "john" at the end of the short path through the woods. Long into the night the stove glows cherry red while old friends sit around swapping tales and putting finishing touches on gear.

Somewhere between the de luxe fishing camp and the lone woods traveler zipped snugly into a sleeping bag with nothing more than the sky for a roof, lie camping possibilities limited only by individual imagination. Each situation will be different from the last; each will present a new thrill, a new challenge. Fine! But where do you find a sylvan utopia in this day and age? Actually, many thousands of acres are open to primitive camping. There is so much space in the highly populated East, in fact, that a person could camp every spring, summer, and fall weekend for the rest of his life and not begin to see it all.

This, of course, is a distortion of the picture. The vast majority of people swept up in the adventure of primitive camping reach their secluded spot either by vehicle or boat. Still, the number of such locations suitable for camping is amazingly high. To name just a few possibilities, consider state and federal forest lands, reservoir lands under jurisdiction of the U. S. Army Corps of Engineers, tree farms, private woodlots, islands, lake shores, remote regions along rivers, and so on.

In just about every case, permission will be required from the landowner or agency in charge. During fire seasons (before green-up time in spring and the powder-dry period of late fall), fires of any sort on government lands may be restricted to campstoves. If conditions are overly severe, camping may not be permitted at all. It has occurred in the past where even smoking was banned within a certain distance of timberland. This extreme is rare, however, and permission is usually readily granted.

With the wide range of modern shelters available, it would seem the tent would be far outnumbered by trailers or pickup campers at an undeveloped, end-of-the-road site. Such is not the case, and for good reason. Rarely will you be able to back a vehicle up to a primitive site the way you would at a designated campground. Almost inevitably, the best spot to camp will be some distance from the road, and this is as it should be. It does mean many trips on foot carrying gear, but the rewards of such a setup heavily outweigh the disadvantages.

Heading the criterion for selecting a remote site is the availability of drinking water. Never be fooled by the crystal clear appearance of a stream. Even water flowing through the back country may be polluted from one source or another. Lacking state-tested water, a fresh spring is the next best bet. Many people never hesitate to drink from a head pool or source of a spring. Still, it's far safer to use one of many methods of purifying water before consumption. The flat taste of boiled water can be eliminated by simply passing the water back and forth from one container to another. This replaces lost oxygen.

The ideal site itself will be almost impossible to find and many concessions will be made. A well-drained location is a must. As always, check the terrain for signs of water runoff. Try to visualize a cloudburst and determine as best you can what takes place in your immediate area. Low, almost level land along either side of a stream often means the whole section fills with water during a severe storm. As we said before, locate the high-water line of a stream and erect camp well above the maximum reach of flood waters, no matter how unlikely a flood may be.

As far as possible, limit preparation of the site to removal of necessary objects only. According to one woodsman we know, the only sign of a camp after it has been removed should be a depression in the leaves. While this may not be completely realistic, it is a commendable goal at which to aim. It is not necessary to dig a trench around a tent with a sewn-in floor. Experienced campers never place plastic or other waterproof material under the tent in an effort to keep the floor dry. During a heavy rain, water will usually collect between the floor and the ground cover, resulting in anything but a desirable situation.

Humidity is often surprisingly high in timbered areas. A relatively open site with just enough shade for comfort will contribute greatly to a pleasurable outing. Most seasoned campers agree that the problem of flying insects is somewhat lessened on the windward side of a stream. Compounding the problem of selecting a site is the frequency of standing dead timber and dead limbs in wooded areas.

Fireplaces will have to be constructed out of available materials. Never use rocks or stones that have been submerged under water if it can be avoided. Water trapped in porous rocks or ones with minute cracks will often turn to steam when superheated in a fireplace, and the rock could explode like a bomb.

The best place to build a fireplace, when convenient, is atop a gravel base. If no location other than the forest floor exists, be sure to remove all combustible material down to mineral earth within the confines of the fireplace and dry material for a safe distance around the perimeter, usually a radius of five feet. In so doing, remember that many forest plants and seedlings just getting a start in life may be destroyed unless caution is observed.

Refrigeration at an end-of-the-road camp is usually somewhat more of a problem than at a designated campground. If ice is available within a short drive, the standard family cooler or ice chest may be used to good advantage. Should traveling be undesirable, certain steps such as described earlier should be taken to keep perishable items refrigerator cool for a longer-than-normal duration.

Many people have been fooled by purchasing an ice chest far too large for their needs. It is not only a back-breaking chore to carry such a unit any distance, but after a day or so, its contents floating in water look much like the aftermath of a sunken garbage scow. Cooler failure can lead to anything but a happy outing. Particularly in primitive camping, the most expensive chest is not necessarily the best choice.

Here's what happens with a large chest, and we're speaking of those normally known as a picnic cooler. A block of ice placed in such a unit must immediately begin working against each and every molecule of air warmer than ice itself, every molecule of metal, plastic or other material constituting the unit's surfaces, every molecule of food placed inside. This, in itself, is a tremendous task.

To further complicate matters, opening the lid of any cooler creates a certain degree of suction which draws out a portion of cool air, replaces the void with warmer air from outside. On a summer day, this could mean temperatures of 70° to 90°. The already overtaxed ice must work even harder. Worse yet, the lid of a large cooler remains open for a longer period while the camper sorts through a week's supply of food for wanted items.

Reduction of temperature requires an expenditure of energy from the ice. End product of the energy transmission will be found in the bottom of the chest in the form of water, playing hob with items that should remain dry. It is pure folly to allow a build-up of water on the notion it will aid in cooling the chest. This actually robs the unit of one cooling surface and causes remaining ice to melt more quickly.

The answer to extending refrigeration at the primitive camp is really not as complicated as it may seem. Ice will last longer in a small space. Two small, inexpensive chests will perform far more effectively than one large de-luxe job. Prechill coolers in advance of loading. Then pack one with items of the longest keeping qualities (frozen meats, etc.) and when at camp, don't open until necessary. The other unit should contain all items, such as milk or margarine, that are used frequently. Also in this chest are meats, vegetables, and fruits scheduled for use early in the outing.

A good rule to follow is freeze everything possible that goes into a cooler. It will create additional cooling capacity within the chest and will not draw energy from the ice as quickly. Margarine has better keeping qualities than butter; however, a single stick soon turns to syrup at camp. Before the trip, it's wise to cut margarine into cubes about one-inch square, wrap each individually with aluminum foil, and freeze. At camp, take out of the cooler only as many cubes as required for each meal. Campers who leave refrigerated items such as milk on a table during the meal fail to realize the object increases in temperature rapidly. They pay dearly for the act in melted ice when the item is returned to the cooler.

It is essential not to open an ice chest any more than is absolutely necessary, and then only for a minimum of time. The lid should be opened and closed slowly and gently to prevent undo motion of air particles inside the cooler. Take out of the chest anything that may be refrigerated naturally at the campsite. This further reduces the number of cooler openings. It goes without saying that an ice chest stored in the hot trunk of an automobile in transit or unsheltered from the sun at camp is on the road to an early failure.

One important subject not freely discussed in camping journals is that of primitive sanitary facilities. The trench latrine, as adopted by the Boy Scouts of America, provides an effective outdoorsman's toilet. It can be simply screened by brush or, if desired, partially or completely surrounded by an opaque tarp. At any rate, the site should be located as far from the camp as convenient, and strips of white cloth should be tied to tree limbs to aid in finding the route at night.

Here is one simple method to construct the toilet itself. Select two trees eight inches in diameter and approximately four to five feet apart. Between the two trees dig a trench roughly 12 inches wide, 18 inches deep and at least three feet long. Lash two stout poles on either side of the trees to form a seat at convenient height. Place a roll of toilet tissue on a forked stick pushed into the ground and cover with an inverted can to keep the roll dry. Body waste should first be covered with lime, then with a layer of dirt.

Similarly, a disposal site for grease, dishwater, and wash-water should be constructed outside the perimeter of the campsite. Simply tossing out wastewater is not only against sound conservation practices, it also creates breeding grounds for flies and insects. The matter can be handled quickly by digging a hole about 18 inches deep and 12 inches in diameter. Several inches of small stones or creek gravel goes on the bottom and narrow, flat stones line the sides.

Push tightly and compactly into the hole all normally discarded paper which you may have available. You may wish to bring along some old newspapers for the purpose. The idea is to trap solid particles through absorption of the liquid. Cellophane food wrappers will not work. Try to keep a recess in the center of the mass. After the last use before breaking camp, dig out the soggy mess and place in a hot campfire. It will burn in time with stirring. Refill the hole with dirt.

Along the same lines, garbage from each meal should be burned rather than buried. Some journals advocate burying cans and other non-combustible items, providing food odors are first burned off. This, they claim, eliminates the possibility of animals later digging them up and scattering them throughout the woods. This may be true, but it does leave behind a permanent sign of man whether obvious or not. We maintain that if containers can be carried in full, they can be carried out empty.

Other forms of primitive camping will require adaptation

to meet specific requirements. For instance, it is almost impossible to use tent pegs on a sandy beach. If available, logs, large rocks, or long hunks of driftwood may be used to advantage. Tie a series of ropes to the weight, which should be located several feet from the tent, then bury the object in the sand. Other ends of ropes are tied to the tent's peg straps.

Equipment requirements for float trips or horseback jaunts are greatly reduced. Campsites are seldom used for more than one night. Little site preparation is needed. Small tents that take up little space in the boat or saddle pack are preferred. Such a tent will also minimize the effort in selecting a suitable site. Shores of rivers or streams are not the best camping grounds, because of the numbers of insects. Search higher areas above the weed line for best results.

Here again, adequate drinking water is a problem. At the expense of leaving something else behind, take along several containers of water. The best attitude to assume is that no stream in the entire East is safe for drinking without purification. For cooking purposes, a small one-burner stove will eliminate the need to build a new fireplace each night.

Little more satisfaction can come to a man than to realize that back there a day or a week behind, lies the fringe of civilization. He is on his own, meeting any situation head-on. Staff in hand and gear riding high on his back, he is free to point his steps in any direction; even, if he chooses, to search for the sources of horizons. His stride will attune to a living, breathing outdoor world. For a short time he is a guest of nature, and he feels more a man for it.

Largely owing to modern, lightweight equipment, backpacking has soared into a highly-popular family sport. Many designated, well-developed hiking trails have suddenly come into being all throughout the East. Lengths vary from as little as five miles to the giant Appalachian Trail, which winds more than 2000 miles from Mount Katahdin, Maine, to Springer Mountain in Georgia. Regardless of length, travel is always the same—by foot.

Before attempting a backpacking trip for the first time, the novice should examine his physical condition with a critical eye. Conditioning is important, and there is no better exercise than hiking in the woods. Hiking boots should be well broken in and comfortable. Experiment with trail foods at home to learn which you prefer and the portions required. By all means, try a simple overnighter before an extended trip.

There are many styles of backpacks on the market; all have certain advantages and disadvantages. Packs that are nothing more than large open bags carried on the back are not desirable. Some method of distributing cargo—and keeping it in place—is essential. For maximum comfort, heavy items should go at or near the top of the pack to align with the hiker's center of gravity.

Some manufacturers produce packs with three- or four-tiered compartments complete with zippers or snap fasteners. These not only keep items in place, but specific objects, such as rain gear, may be obtained quickly. A good outfit will be well-constructed, and with reasonable care, should last many, many years. Modern pack frames weigh practically nothing and will keep bulky items away from your back.

Leave behind everything that is not absolutely essential. Some seasoned backpackers go so far as to clip off handles of toothbrushes to reduce weight! Remember, everything you take along will be carried on your back. A fully-loaded backpack, even on a pack frame, should not exceed 30 pounds for a man in exceptionally good physical condition. Twenty-six pounds is a far more realistic weight, especially for an extended trip. Women and children should carry far less.

Loaded packs that may feel comfortable at home have a strange habit of feeling completely different outdoors. Stepping over logs and walking over rough terrain will quickly show if your unit is riding in the proper position. Wide, padded shoulder straps help even on short jaunts. Buckles should be designed so that straps will not slip once adjusted. Make sure there are rings or straps to fasten a fly-rod case to the outside of the pack.

A tent is not essential. Many backpackers have camped for

years and never used more than a canvas or plastic lean-to for shelter in case of rain. Modern tents for backpacking, however, are unbelievably light-weight for their size. Several manufacturers are now producing nylon units, large enough for three adults, which include sewn-in floor, screened windows and door, tent fly and about five feet of headroom to boot. These tents roll into a package three or four inches in diameter and about ten inches long. Most will weigh just about six pounds, including telescoping poles.

Trail foods have improved tremendously over the years. Several companies now specialize in such products, and offer so many items that selection becomes difficult. Most are dehydrated, and many can be picked up at your local grocery store. Plastic tubes are available for jellies and other gooey items. Individually wrapped packets of coffee, sugar, and similar items are wise. A long list of trail food manufacturers will be found in any camping journal.

What about drinking water? Stations for refilling canteens should be known in advance if at all possible. Sites with good drinking water will often be marked on maps produced by trail clubs. The canteen itself should be only large enough for drinking purposes. For the most part, water for cooking will be obtained from springs and boiled.

Every hiker venturing far out into strange country, whether trails are marked or not, should have a topographic or "contour" map of the section, and he should know how to read it. Hills, valleys, and streams will be shown, as well as any buildings present when the map was printed. Contour lines, usually of 20-foot elevations, readily tell the steepness of a mountain.

Study the map closely well ahead of a trip. It will reveal possible campsites with fantastic accuracy. Many mountain streams contain nothing but rocks and dust in the dry season. Look at the map for a stream that heads near the top of a ridge. Chances are that it will be dry at the top and maybe even the bottom of the hillside. Many, many times, pure, sparkling water will gush from the earth about two-thirds down the mountainside, flow on the surface for a short distance, then again disappear underground.

A compass must be used to orient a topo map. Even if you should stray from a trail, you'll quickly find your way back. An individual hopelessly lost should be able to determine his position within a mile or so by matching features of the area with that of the map. Many hikers prefer not to use marked trails; instead, they set a compass and map course for cross-country travel. As a result, they often pass through sections seldom seen by man. This is perhaps the most challenging and rewarding activity in the entire realm of camping.

Many campers contend that the reason they enjoy camping so much is that food always tastes better in the out-of-doors. Even a can of beans heated over the old two-burner seems to increase in flavor. You'll never eat anything at home to equal a meal properly prepared over a wood fire.

A good cooking fire must have a place to live, and that is in a fireplace designed for the purpose. Concrete rings, now used in many state and private campgrounds, are anything but effective. It's often necessary to lift one edge off the ground to get air enough for even a warming fire to burn. Similarly, those handsome stone fireplaces with tall chimneys, seen in many campgrounds and picnic areas, are designed more for appearance than service. Heat is drawn straight up the chimney, and you spend more time feeding fuel than stirring the stew.

To learn to cook over a wood fire, the neophyte chef should have everything going for him from the start. In most cases, this will mean taking time to construct a cooking fireplace. The first step is to make sure such construction is permitted. Some parks and private campgrounds prohibit fires except in authorized places. This is mainly to eliminate open fires on the ground, a practice notoriously famous for starting forest fires. Many areas will permit construction of a second fireplace, provided the site is restored upon breaking camp.

Most fireplaces for cooking purposes are roughly U-shaped and constructed from tiers of available stones. Most will have an opening in front just large enough to accommodate a reflector oven. Actual dimensions will depend on the size of grill used. This could be anything from a campstove grill to heavy material used for industrial catwalks. Whatever is used, make sure the object is sturdy and will not warp with heat. While walls of the fireplace may be six inches or so higher, the grill should be 12 to 18 inches from the ground.

A fireplace on the long and narrow side is superior to the large circular type. Openings between rocks should be chinked with smaller stones when possible to increase the reflecting surface for heat. Most important, make sure the whole business is substantial and won't shift under the weight of cooking gear.

Failure of many outdoor meals comes from the camper's lack of knowledge concerning the type of fire required, or worse yet, his inability to start a fire in the first place. A roaring fire does little more than turn meat to cinders. A small, controlled fire with even heat is the answer. This means that the fire must be started ahead of cooking operations. Leather Lungs Larry will spend half an hour on his hands and knees huffing and puffing before producing a flame of any sort. Chances are his next move will be to smother the whole bit with too much kindling. It's not only possible but expected for the chef to use one match and have a robust fire going within a matter of minutes without blowing on the flame.

High flames are neither necessary or desirable for cooking. The fire should be hottest at the rear of the fireplace and against the split log. A small portion of hot coals should be raked toward the front for keeping already cooked items piping hot while other foods are prepared.

An experienced chef can maintain the temperature of a wood fire with amazing accuracy simply by feel. The newcomer may wish to rely on an oven thermometer, although its use may be a bit misleading. It is better to watch foods closely; if cooking is too fast, move the item away from the hottest part of the fireplace. Foods should be turned or stirred far more often than at home.

A pot of coffee hanging from a "dingle stick" lends atmosphere to a camp scene. However, its use is more picturesque than functional. A dingle stick is a sturdy pole, six or seven feet long. It rests in the fork of an upright stick driven into the ground. The lower end of the dingle stick is tied, staked, or weighted to the ground to counterbalance the weight of the pot dangling over the fire. The danger here is that with constant use, the upright stick may work loose in the ground, causing the whole works to collapse, possibly tossing a pot of scalding hot water or coffee into a camper's lap.

No outdoor chef worth his salt would be without a reflector oven, a simple contraption for baking everything from biscuits, pies, and cakes to meatloaf and fish. Nearly every pioneer cabin had a unit standing before the fireplace. It was replaced by the miracle of the day, the cast-iron wood cookstove. Most reflector ovens today have sloping tops and bottoms that create a wide opening in front and come together in the back. A shelf in the middle and short legs in the back complete the unit.

The reflector oven faces the opening of the fireplace. Unless food items are to bake very slowly, hot coals are not required. Instead a brisk fire fed with "squaw wood"—dead limbs that can be broken by hand—burns directly in front of the oven. Heat radiates inside and reflects from top, bottom, and sides. You regulate heat simply by moving the oven closer or farther away from the fire. Properly placed, items will bake evenly without burning. A solid shelf that does not extend completely to the back is best. Wire or grill used as a shelf allows an overdose of heat, and scorching may result.

Chances are that even highly experienced campers may never have seen a reflector oven in use. This is because modern convenience foods are easy to prepare and the use of a baking oven *sounds* complicated. Nearly anyone can use a reflector oven with a high degree of success the first time. Many commercial models are again available, although a few hours in the home workshop will produce a unit just as efficient.

Living in the out-of-doors is far safer than city life ever has been or ever will be. Few situations develop that cannot be taken in stride through adequate planning and common sense. The reason so few accidents occur in the camping field can probably be attributed to the fact that most campers are prepared to cope with nearly any emergency, large or small. Of course, tents have been set afire, outdoorsmen have suffered broken bones, woods travelers have been hopelessly lost for days. For the most part, however, an accident must be fed a diet of careless moments or it just won't have strength to materialize. Few campers are careless.

A first-aid kit should be a regular part of gear on every camping trip. It should be constructed so that the unit closes tightly to keep contents sterile. Here are items included in the typical camper's out-door medicine chest: band aids, both small and large; gauze or bandage material of several widths; adhesive tape; aspirin tablets; burn lotion; antiseptic soap for cuts, burns, and exposure to poison ivy, poison oak, or poison sumac; steptic pencil; iodine and Merthiolate; toothache and earache remedies; a laxative; a snake-bite kit; scissors; tweezers; needle and thread; a razor blade; safety pins; cloth for a tourniquet; and, of course, a first-aid instruction manual.

In addition to standard items, the first-aid kit should contain an extra supply of special medicine or prescriptions if required by a member of the party. When planning a remote trip that will last longer than normal, consult your physician for stocking medical supplies. Backpackers carry first-aid kits tailored down to essentials.

Most campers realize the seriousness of a conflagration and guard against flying sparks from a campfire. At the same time, many campers never give thought to the fact that a pressurized gasoline campstove or lantern could be the cause of a serious fire. First indication of trouble is the presence of black carbon on the bottom of pots and pans or on the inside of a lantern globe. This is the start of generator break-down and should be corrected immediately.

We observed an advanced stage of generator malfunction many years ago. It was not a pleasant sight. A camper at the next site had difficulty adjusting his campstove while preparing a meal. Although the tank was full, flames were orange and sloppy rather than crisp and blue. Pumping up air pressure made little difference. Unnoticed for a short period, flames finally stopped completely. When the camper struck a match, the whole business went up in a flash!

Here's what had happened. The generator had failed completely. Instead of vaporized fuel, liquid gasoline came through the jets and collected on the bottom of the stove. It was impossible to stop the flow of fuel with the "off" knob. Liquid-fed flames poured out onto the picnic table and splashed onto the ground. The blaze was finally extinguished with a dining fly, but not before serious damage had occurred.

A few simple safety rules should always be observed. (1) Repair equipment at the first sign of trouble. (2) Keep handy a square of canvas or other material to smother a fire. (3) A fire extinguisher should be kept in every camper's vehicle. A can of baking soda is quite effective for grease fires, and should always be near the stove.

One situation that seldom turns into an emergency is the presence of wild animals, either at a designated campground or wilderness site. Animals should not be feared. None will attack without provocation under normal circumstances. However, an animal that acts strangely and shows no fear of man whatsoever should be given a wide berth, on the rare chance it might be rabid. Two species that normally have little fear of human beings are skunks and porcupines. Their defense mechanisms deserve a lot of respect.

Fear of an eastern black bear is common but ridiculous. Most people are treated only to a quick glance at a bruin because the animal is extremely shy. Bears have been known to raid garbage cans at night in a quiet campground. Should this occur at or near your campsite, rattling a few pots and pans will send the animal scurrying off into the woods. There have been rare occasions when a bear has become relatively tame and will accept food from people. This should be avoided at all costs. Usually, all goes well until the food runs out. Then the individual may very well feel the pain of two-inch claws raked across his body. The bear is not attacking; it is simply asking for more food in the only way it knows how.

There are only two poisonous snakes in the Northeast, the

copperhead and the rattlesnake. Both want nothing whatsoever to do with man. The only time a snake will strike is when it thinks it is under attack. It reacts defensively, just as you would do under similar circumstances. When walking in snake country, always walk slowly and avoid high grass when possible. Step up on a large log, then step out as far as possible. Always watch where you put your hands.

One of the most deadly emergency situations that a camper may encounter is that of being caught away from suitable shelter at the approach of a thunder storm. Lightning whacks the earth at a speed of 20,000 miles a second and may measure as much as a foot in diameter, containing many millions of volts. You can't dodge it; you can't run away from it. But you can easily arrange to be somewhere else when the stroke occurs.

Approximately 1400 persons are struck by lightning in this country every year. Strange as it may seem, nearly two-thirds of the people clobbered are seriously injured but live to tell the story. At the same time, an untold number of people could have been killed or maimed over the years had they not reacted with good judgment rather than taking the it-can't-happen-to-me attitude. Lightning deserves more than passing respect. Yet the chances of actually being zapped are infinitesimal if you observe just a few simple precautions.

In order to appreciate safety rules, it is first necessary to understand the nature of lightning. Thunderstorms are born when warm, moist air rises from the earth. Static electricity is created during the process. Tremendous energy is generated within the cloud; the upper portion assumes a positive charge, the dense, lower portion a negative charge.

On earth, an energy field forms beneath the thunderhead and takes on a positive charge. The invisible "ground shadow" keeps pace with the moving cloud, bristling with energy as the electrical potential increases high overhead. A "hot" energy field normally searches for a high spot as the cloud's potential reaches the discharge point. It envelops trees, fences—or you, if you happen to be in the wrong place at the moment.

This is where good judgment prevails: forsake any open

space of significant size if a storm is near. Don't be fooled by thinking the storm is a long way off. If you can hear thunder at all, the last stroke probably occurred within 15 miles. Some locally severe storms move slowly, others cover ground at a surprising clip.

Should a menacing storm suddenly appear while you are outdoors and away from suitable shelter, remembering certain highly important points—and acting quickly—could save your life or the lives of unschooled companions. To repeat briefly, lightning normally searches the highest point within the confines of the moving energy field for electrical release. Often, a tree on the side of a hill will be struck rather than the hilltop itself. For that reason, automatically shun *anything* in your immediate vicinity that forms the highest point—a shed in the open, a lone tree of any size, utility poles, etc.

Good protection will be found in a deep valley, under *short* trees in the *interior* of a dense forest, or in a cave, if such a convenience is readily available. Wire fences should be avoided. Rifles, wet fishing rods or a metal golf club over the shoulder could spell disaster. It is better to discard such items if a storm is imminent.

Locally severe thunderstorms often escape detection by central weather stations. Prime season in the East is July and August and usually in late afternoon or evening. Frequency of storms increase from north to south; New Englanders usually experience 20 to 30 thunderstorm days a season while Floridians usually endure 70 to 90.

The age-old phenomenon of lightning belting the earth is so vitally necessary that little plant life would exist without it. Yet since man's earliest days, lightning has been a source of anxiety and bewilderment. Even today, a flash of light in a cloudless night sky is explained by many as "heat" lightning. Actually, it is a normal electrical discharge from a thunderhead so far away we see only the reflection in the atmosphere. With only the rarest of exceptions, there will be plenty of time to take precautionary action. Lightning is awesomely beautiful, but must be viewed from a distance to be appreciated!

As we near the end of this chapter on camping, we realize how broad a brush we have used to paint a picture of camping. In the space allowed, we have merely touched upon the types of camping, some basic equipment, and a few suggestions to make your camping a bit more pleasurable. The memories of past camping trips become priceless, the joys of future trips limitless. To those of you who are experienced campers, it is our hope that we shall meet somewhere along the trail. If you have not camped, we hope that someday soon you will join us. It is not too late, for nature will continue to put on her show.

Each spring she will begin her change of costume. She will wear her blue skies, her purple violets, her red cardinals, her orange berries, her yellow daisies, and her green mountains. She will change her dress every day you seek her company, from the first ray of dawn to the last firefly at night.

She will present the largest orchestra ever assembled. Her treble section will feature the high-pitched notes of insects, tiny birds, and whistling breezes. Mid-range melodies will include such artists as jays, loons, bumblebees, and brooks. Cymbal clashes will be provided by the lightning of a summer storm, and the bass group will provide the rhythm of great horned owls, bullfrogs, waterfalls, and thunder. The melody is never the same; the song never ends.

Rare perfumes will be splashed about at random just for you. You will sense, rather than smell, the dainty scent of the spring arbutus, and later become heady while camped near a flowering locust tree. You will seek the spots populated by wild honeysuckle and leave to others those atomized by genus *Mephitis*, the skunk.

Your taste buds will tingle with the flavor of carefully seasoned birch bark, sassafras, and young wintergreen shoots. You will select from nature's table such delicacies as wild strawberries, mandrake apples, mountain huckleberries, and beefsteak mushrooms. Even a casually prepared cup of coffee prepared in camp will take on the aroma and savor of a vintage wine.

You will become truly alive, free, and sensitive, aware of the many things you touch. You will thrill at the wiggle of a fresh caught trout, the smoothness of a ground mole's fur, the softness of the down from a thistle or milkweed, and the harsh roughness of an old hickory tree. You will learn to walk stealthily and take pride in the fact that you are accepted by the creatures of nature.

But these gifts that are free for the asking are perhaps not the most important reasons for camping. To most seasoned campers, they serve as a backdrop, an accompaniment, an atmosphere to add to the pleasures of enjoying the company of loved ones, of leaving the confusion and problems of everyday life behind, and of having the time and privacy of setting their lives into proper prospective. For, when they must return to the unreality of the business world, campers find that their problems become a bit easier to solve, that life is a bit easier to face, and that their mountains once again become mole hills during the next trip to the outdoors.

Somewhere out there is a single star, all yours, to camp under. A short distance away is a tiny flower that only you will ever see. There will be a rock for you to pick up and toss that no other man has handled. You will swat your own bug, dip your own cup of water from a mountain stream, listen to your own bird song, and pick your own trail. And all of this will be yours, even if you left your wallet back in camp.